Gallica
Volume 24

MARIE DE FRANCE

A CRITICAL COMPANION

Gallica

ISSN 1749–091X

General Editor: Sarah Kay

Gallica aims to provide a forum for the best current work in medieval French studies. Literary studies are particularly welcome and preference is given to works written in English, although publication in French is not excluded.

Proposals or queries should be sent in the first instance to the editor, or to the publisher, at the addresses given below; all submissions receive prompt and informed consideration.

Professor Sarah Kay, Department of French, New York University, 13–19 University Place, 6th floor, New York, NY 10003, USA

The Editorial Director, Gallica, Boydell & Brewer Ltd., PO Box 9, Woodbridge, Suffolk IP12 3DF, UK

Previously published titles in this series are listed at the end of this volume.

MARIE DE FRANCE
A CRITICAL COMPANION

SHARON KINOSHITA and PEGGY McCRACKEN

D. S. BREWER

First published 2012
D. S. Brewer, Cambridge
Paperback edition 2014

ISBN 978 1 84384 301 6 hardback
ISBN 978 1 84384 373 3 paperback

D. S. Brewer is an imprint of Boydell & Brewer Ltd
PO Box 9, Woodbridge, Suffolk IP12 3DF, UK
and of Boydell & Brewer Inc.
668 Mt Hope Avenue, Rochester, NY 14620–2731, USA
website: www.boydellandbrewer.com

A catalogue record for this title is available
from the British Library

The publisher has no responsibility for the continued existence or accuracy of
URLs for external or third-party internet websites referred to in this book,
and does not guarantee that any content on such websites is,
or will remain, accurate or appropriate

This publication is printed on acid-free paper

CONTENTS

PREFACE

This *Companion* is intended for all those interested in the works of Marie de France – students, teachers, and general readers as well as scholars. Our goal has been to provide a multifaceted overview of this influential author, combining a reconsideration of the *Lais* with an introduction to her lesser-known works, the *Ysopë* (*Fables*) and the *Espurgatoire seint Patriz*, and some attention to the more controversially attributed *Vie seinte Audree*. To do this, we set out to rethink standard questions such as those of origins, context, plot, character, structure, and influence through categories (such as authorship and translation) that seemed to us central to the consideration of medieval literature in general, as well as those (such as space/movement and embodiment) that have special resonance for the texts of Marie de France in particular. We hope in this way to have offered an integrated view that takes account both of the unity of Marie's *oeuvre* and of the distinctiveness of the individual texts.

The critical literature on Marie de France is vast, and our understanding of her texts is informed and shaped by our own reading of the rich, learnèd, and thoughtful work of our colleagues and predecessors. The studies mentioned in our text, notes, and "Further Reading" guide are those that have especially influenced our thinking here or that provide particularly focused discussions of the topics under consideration. Glyn S. Burgess's annotated bibliographies (listed in the first section of the "Further Reading" guide) remain an indispensable point of departure for anyone interested in Marie scholarship.

Finally, the collaborative nature of this work has been one of the most formative and pleasurable aspects of this scholarly *aventure*. We first conceived of the idea of thinking collaboratively about Marie de France many years ago, and we thank the editor of Gallica for giving us a forum in which to do so. This project is the result of a constant stream of email exchanges, punctuated by intense working sessions in Ann Arbor, Santa Cruz, and various conference venues. One of us took the lead in the writing of each chapter, and readers acquainted with the authors' previous work will undoubtedly recognize some familiar interests and styles. Nevertheless, each chapter is the product of long discussion and interchange, making the book much different from and, we think, better than what either of us might have written on our own.

NOTE ON EDITIONS

In this *Critical Companion*, we assume that readers are familiar with Marie de France's *Lais* and therefore do not give extensive plot descriptions or summaries except as needed to illustrate or support our analyses. We do not assume such familiarity with Marie's other works and have provided descriptions accordingly.

We use the following editions throughout, and all translations and emphases are our own, unless otherwise indicated:

L'espurgatoire seint Patriz. Ed. and trans. Yolande de Pontfarcy. Louvain and Paris: Peeters, 1995. We have elided the letters between parentheses in Pontfarcy's edition in order to preserve the octosyllables.

Les fables. Ed. and trans. Charles Bruckner. Louvain: Peeters, 1991. In citations of the fables we have elided the brackets that indicate Bruckner's corrections to the text found in the base manuscript, British Library Harley 978.

Lais de Marie de France. Ed. Karl Warnke, trans. Laurence Harf-Lancner. Paris: Librairie Générale Française, 1990. We use the titles for the *Lais* found in our edition: *L'Aüstic, Le Fraisne,* etc.

The Life of Saint Audrey, A Text by Marie de France. Trans. and ed. June Hall McCash and Judith Clark Barban. Jefferson, N.C.: McFarland, 2006.

Introduction:
The World of Marie de France

Who was Marie de France?

The works associated with Marie de France include the *Lais*, a collection of short narratives influenced by Celtic tales and courtly literature, probably written around 1170; a collection of fables known as the *Ysopë*, probably composed between 1189 and 1208 and partly translated from earlier texts; and *L'espurgatoire seint Patriz* (*Saint Patrick's Purgatory*), translated from the Cistercian monk H. de Saltrey's *Tractatus de Purgatorio Sancti Patricii* in around 1190.[1] She may also have composed a *Life of Saint Audrey* (*Vie seinte Audree*), also attributed to a "Marie," but her authorship of this text is still debated.[2]

People have been writing about Marie de France since the thirteenth century, but all we know about her is her name and that she is the author of three, possibly four, narratives. Since the sixteenth century, critics have succumbed to the temptation to elaborate a biography around her name, and although hypotheses continue to appear, we still have no definitive evidence on which to ground any identification of Marie de France with any of the Maries attested as living in late-twelfth-century France and England.[3]

---

[1]   On dates see *Lais de Marie de France*, ed. Karl Warnke, trad. and intro. Laurence Harf-Lancner (Paris: Librairie Générale Française, 1990), pp. 8–10; *Fables*, ed. Charles Bruckner (Louvain: Peeters, 1991), pp. 1–3; *L'espurgatoire seint Patriz*, ed. Yolande de Pontfarcy (Louvain and Paris: Peeters, 1995), pp. 4–10.

[2]   June Hall McCash, "La vie seinte Audree: A Fourth Text by Marie de France?" *Speculum* 77.3 (2002): 744–77.

[3]   For a thorough and witty account of the biographical research on Marie de France, see R. Howard Bloch, *The Anonymous Marie de France* (Chicago: University of Chicago Press, 2003), pp. 1–24. Bloch himself seeks to "resolve the question of Marie's anonymity not through recourse to documents outside of her works, but through close consideration of the evidence contained in all three of her texts" (18). He finds that Marie is "among the

The means by which hypotheses about authorship are formed illustrate the challenge facing modern interpreters of medieval texts. Over the decades, several different historical figures have been posited as candidates for the author Marie.[4] The first stage in such identifications draws primarily on external evidence: locating a Marie in the historical record who was born on the Continent – preferably in Ile-de-France, the region around Paris – but documented as living in England with ties close enough to the Angevin court to presume to offer her *Lais* to the "noble king" Henry II.[5] Attested dates for these historical figures must coincide with various kinds of internal and external evidence: the earliest possible date (*terminus a quo*) at which a given text could have been composed is supplied by any elements that seem to refer to identifiable events or persons, or to reflect a knowledge of other recognizable works. Conversely, references to Marie or allusions to the texts attributed to her in external datable sources determine the latest date (*terminus ad quem*) for a text's composition.[6]

Working within these constraints and given the patchy survival of medieval evidence, such conjectures can at best be plausible rather than provable. They are subject to modification not only as new historical evidence comes to light (as in the discovery of previously unknown documents), but also as changes in literary theory and criticism call attention to different kinds of linguistic, thematic, or historical criteria. Attempts to identify Marie de France and her *oeuvre* must necessarily remain provisional – working hypotheses that are useful to the extent that they enable us to see the texts in a new light, to add to our sense of their literary, historical, or cultural complexity.

Discussion and debate around the attribution of the *Vie seinte Audree* has recently focused attention on a new candidate for the historical Marie de France: Marie Becket, sister of Archbishop Thomas of Canterbury

---

most self-conscious, sophisticated, complicated, obscure, tricky, and disturbing figures of her time – the Joyce of the twelfth century" (19).

[4]   For a concise listing of the various historical candidates who have been identified as Marie, see Jill Mann, *From Aesop to Raynard: Beast Literature in Medieval Britain* (Oxford: Oxford University Press, 2009), Appendix 1, pp. 309–11.

[5]   Marie's association with France ("Marie ai nun, si sui de France") is "confirmed" by philological evidence that surviving manuscripts of her works seem to have been produced by Anglo-Norman scribes working from a Continental French original. Carla Rossi, however, speculates that "de France" is a "posture d'auteur" that indicates an intellectual affiliation rather than a personal origin. *Marie de France et les érudits de Cantorbéry*, Recherches Littéraires Médiévales 1 (Paris: Classiques Garnier, 2009), p. 114.

[6]   The treatment of case endings in Marie's texts points to a date in the late twelfth or early thirteenth century, before certain morphological changes were generalized.

(martyred in 1170), who was named abbess of Barking by King Henry II in 1173 (the same year as her brother's canonization).[7] The daughter of a merchant from Rouen brought up in London, this Marie could plausibly identify herself as coming "from France," speak a Continental rather than an insular dialect of French, yet be familiar with the linguistic and cultural mix characterizing twelfth-century Britain. As the sister of Henry II's friend and chancellor Thomas Becket, she would have been in proximity both to the Angevin court and to the intellectual circles around the archbishop of Canterbury, including John of Salisbury, Peter of Blois, and Walter Map, whose interests included preoccupations identified in the texts attributed to Marie. Her association with Barking – a monastery populated by members of the Anglo-Norman elite and where women translated saints' lives into French – is taken as another support for the identification.

We do not endorse any particular historical identification of Marie de France, and we take her authorship of *La vie seinte Audree* as uncertain. Although June Hall McCash has identified resemblances between this text and Marie's other works, it would also be possible to highlight the dissimilarities. In particular, the *Audree* lacks the feudal vocabulary of the other works, and although some lines sound like echoes of the *Lais*, the language appears more syntactically diluted and less poetically concentrated than in the other texts. The episodic organization of the text is less orderly, and while the *Audree* pulls together a lot of different kinds of material, the other Marie texts have a stronger narrative organization. For these reasons we do not treat *La vie seinte Audree* among Marie's works in this *Companion*, but we also do not exclude the possibility that many of our conclusions may also apply to this work.

Although we know little about the historical identity of Marie de France, we know a lot about the literary and social worlds in which she lived and wrote. Marie was literate and clearly had access to a library. This could mean that she was a nun, but it certainly means that she was from a privileged background. She lived during the reigns of Henry II and Richard Lion Heart in England and Philip Augustus in France. Her knowledge of twelfth-century institutions and social relations suggests that she was familiar with noble courts, and possibly with a royal court. Her *Lais* are dedicated to a noble king (nobles reis, *Lais, Prologue*, l. 43), whom most scholars identify as Henry II, suggesting that if Marie did not live at court, she certainly had access to it. Marie's familiarity with the

---

7   Rossi, *Marie de France et les érudits.*

Tractatus and possibly the Latin *Life of Saint Audrey* suggests that she had access to religious texts and could have lived in a convent.

All of Marie's works were written in the decades before and after the Third Crusade, the period when Notre Dame de Paris was being built and nunneries and great abbeys were being constructed in England. This makes her work more or less contemporary with that of romance writers like Chrétien de Troyes and the somewhat lesser known Gautier d'Arras (who appears to have used her *Eliduc* as the basis for his romance *Ille et Galeron*).[8] She wrote about a generation after Abelard and Heloise exchanged their letters, a generation before the *Roman de la Rose* was begun by Guillaume de Lorris, and two hundred years before Christine de Pizan, the next woman writer from France to gain enduring fame. Her literary predecessors include the romances of antiquity (*romans antiques*), and her works are contemporary with, or slightly later than, the earliest versions of the Tristan story. Marie's closest contemporaries may have been Clemence, Marie, and another anonymous nun from Barking Abbey who translated the lives of Saint Catherine, Saint Audrey, and Saint Edmund, respectively, into French verse (if she is not herself the Marie who translated the *Vie seinte Audree*).

Marie's world

Marie's use of Anglo-Norman French and her offering of the *Lais* to a "noble king" – generally presumed to be Henry II of England (r. 1154–89) – place her work in the orbit of the so-called Angevin or Plantagenet empire, an extended zone where the cultures of northern France, Occitania, and the Celtic world came together. Though not a term Marie's contemporaries would have used, it is a useful designation for that vast collection of territorial states ruled by Henry II and his sons Richard I (r. 1189–99) and John (r. 1199–1216). These included Normandy, England, and Wales, inherited from Henry's grandfather, King Henry I, through his mother, Matilda; Anjou and Maine, inherited from his father, Count Geoffrey;[9] and Aquitaine (with claims to the county of Toulouse) by right of marriage to the celebrated Eleanor. In the second half of the twelfth century,

---

[8] For a discussion of Gautier's use of Marie's *Eliduc*, see Chapter 7.

[9] "Angevin" is the adjectival form for Count Geoffrey's patrimony of Anjou; "Plantagenet" derives from the sprig of broom he reputedly wore in his cap. One of Geoffrey's illegitimate children was Henry's half-sister Marie – the abbess of Shaftesbury sometimes identified with Marie de France. On historians' use of the term Angevin empire, see W. L. Warren, *Henry II* (Berkeley: University of California Press, 1973), pp. 228–30.

Henry's reign provides the historical backdrop against which to consider elements in Marie's writings (especially the *Lais*).[10] Questions of kingship and lord–vassal relations might be situated in a context where the duke of Normandy was a richer and more powerful territorial ruler than his overlord, the king of France, and issues of repudiation and remarriage might be read in the context of a Plantagenet empire created in part by Eleanor of Aquitaine's divorce from Louis VII of France and her quick and unauthorized remarriage (1152) to his main rival, the future Henry II of England.[11] Another possible "noble king" is Henry and Eleanor's eldest surviving son, Henry. Known to history as "the Young King" (*el rei jove*), he was born in 1155 and crowned "associate king" in 1170. From 1173 until his death a decade later, Young Henry (along with his brothers Richard and Geoffrey) rebelled repeatedly against his father. His propensity for tournaments and for *prouesse, courtoisie*, and *joie* – the very qualities ascribed to the *nobles reis* of the *Lais' Prologue* (ll. 43–5) – not only made him a favorite of poets (most famously Bertran de Born) but dovetails well with the *Lais'* principal concerns.[12]

The emergence of the body of work known as the "matter of Britain" – stories composed originally in Old French, drawing from and developing material adapted from insular Celtic history and legend – was very much a product of this cross-channel milieu, creating the conditions of possibility for a writer who identifies herself as being "from France" to devote herself to the translation, into French, of oral tales in Welsh and Breton (the *Lais*), a Latin text describing a theological innovation identified with the cult of an Irish saint (the *Espurgatoire*), and perhaps the hagiographical tale of an Anglo-Saxon queen (the *Vie seinte Audree*). It has also been posited that Marie would have lived in a milieu where she

---

[10] On the Plantagenet courtly milieu, see Martin Aurell, "La cour Plantagenêt (1154–1204): entourage, savoir et civilité," in *La cour Plantagenêt*, ed. Martin Aurell (Poitiers: CESCM, 2000), pp. 9–46.

[11] Some specific conditions resulting from this dynastic confederation would shift in 1202–04 when King Philip Augustus of France, invoking his right of lordship over Normandy and Anjou, branded John a recalcitrant vassal and stripped him of these continental lands. Over time, this political division severing the Anglo-Norman ruling class from its Norman possessions would contribute to the consolidation of a distinctive insular literature in French.

[12] This identification was first proposed by Ezio Levi. See June Hall McCash, "Sidney Painter (1902–1960): The Issue of Patronage for Marie de France," in *The Reception and Transmission of the Works of Marie de France, 1774–1974*, ed. Chantal Maréchal, Mediaeval Studies 23 (Lewiston: Edwin Mellen Press, 2003), pp. 171–203 (at 187–8). Focus on the Young King highlights strained father–son relations (as in *Yonec* and *Milun*) as one of the *Lais'* preoccupations.

could have gathered something of scientific knowledge, translated from the Arabic, and even Arabic literary traditions.[13] Recent postcolonial-inflected readings have called attention to the complexity of borders of all kinds, reminding us that beneath master narratives of conquest, colonialism, and assimilation we are likely to find an array of shifting political, linguistic, and socio-cultural affinities in which relations of power are negotiated in various, sometimes unpredictable, ways.[14]

The large role Celtic traditions played in the formation of vernacular French literature has long been acknowledged, and much scholarly attention has been devoted to identifying indigenous antecedents of specific characters, plot lines, or cultural phenomena. More recently has come the recognition of the various modes and degrees of transculturation through which the inhabitants of places like Brittany (whose counts were vassals of the dukes of Normandy) and Wales (itself part of a larger "Irish Sea" system) long interacted. Such reformulations begin to suggest different cognitive mappings, reinforced by attentive close readings, of the worlds Marie's work both represents and inhabits. This is a geographically expansive world in which Breton knights carry pieces of patterned silk home from Constantinople and a Norman princess routinely corresponds with an aunt practicing herbal medicine in Salerno.

Marie's languages

Angevin Britain, as readers of the *Lais* are well aware, was a multilingual society. First, as in all of western Europe, Latin was the language not only of the Church but of administration, diplomacy, theology, and science. Then there was Anglo-Norman (the language of the post-Conquest, cross-Channel elite), co-existing with Anglo-Saxon (the language of the conquered majority), together with regional languages like Welsh in the west and Danish in the northeast. One way of approaching the situation of post-Conquest Britain is to imagine a kind of linguistic apartheid, with speakers of Old French, Anglo-Saxon, Welsh, and Scandinavian constituting

---

[13] Sahar Amer, *Esope au féminin: Marie de France et la politique de l'interculturalité*, Faux Titre, 169 (Amsterdam and Atlanta: Rodopi, 1999).

[14] See, for example, Michelle R. Warren, *History on the Edge: Excalibur and the Borders of Britain, 1100–1300* (Minnesota: University of Minneapolis Press, 2000); Jeffrey Jerome Cohen, *Hybridity, Identity, and Monstrosity in Medieval Britain: On Difficult Middles* (New York: Palgrave Macmillan, 2008); and *Cultural Diversity in the British Middle Ages: Archipelago, Island, England*, ed. Jeffrey Jerome Cohen (New York: Palgrave Macmillan, 2008).

relatively separate speech communities reflecting "ethnic" and political divisions. More recently, the theoretical interest in hybridity and contact zones has contributed to the realization that boundaries are porous, often connecting as well as separating peoples and cultures; accordingly, critics have begun turning attention to "the complex interplay of indigenous and imported languages [that] defies neat categorization."[15] The idea of a culture as a monoglot entity proceeding in organic linearity through time and within the territories of the modern nation state cannot adequately represent medieval textual production and linguistic and cultural contacts.[16] Multilingualism has become *bon à penser*: the 2007 Oxford Twenty-First Century Approaches volume *Middle English* goes as far as to devote separate chapters to "Multilingualism" and "Multilingualism on the Page."[17] Similarly, recent work in Translation Studies urges us to move beyond the binary opposition between a privileged "original" text and its derivative translation, rethinking the tendency to dismiss translation as a secondary activity in ways especially pertinent, as we explore in Chapter 2, to the analysis of medieval textuality.[18]

A vernacular literature in Old French emerged in the late eleventh or early twelfth century as a literature of transcription and translation. Among the earliest surviving texts are transcriptions of orally circulated and, arguably, orally composed epics (*chansons de geste*) like the *Chanson de Roland* or the *Chanson de Guillaume*. Since Latin was the

---

[15] Kimberlee Campbell, "Speaking the Other: Constructing Frenchness in Medieval England," in *French Global: A New Approach to Literary History*, ed. Susan Suleiman and Christie McDonald (New York: Columbia University Press, 2010), pp. 179–92 (at 181).

[16] Jocelyn Wogan-Browne, General Introduction, "What's in a Name? The 'French' of 'England,'" in *Language and Culture in Medieval Britain: The French of England c. 1100–c. 1500*, ed. Jocelyn Wogan-Browne et al. (York: York Medieval Press, 2009), pp. 1–13 (at 5). Recent and ongoing work in the "French of England" (FOE) project based at Fordham University and the University of York calls attention to the persistence of Anglo-Norman and Anglo-French (the French spoken in England in the fourteenth and fifteenth centuries) as "a major field awaiting exploration," http://www.fordham.edu/frenchofengland/, accessed 11 November 2010. See also Susan Crane, "Anglo-Norman Cultures in England, 1066–1460," in *The Cambridge History of Medieval English Literature*, ed. David Wallace (Cambridge: Cambridge University Press, 1999), pp. 35–60.

[17] See Robert M. Stein, "Multilingualism," pp. 23–37 and Christopher Baswell, "Multilingualism on the Page," pp. 38–50, both in *Middle English*, ed. Paul Strohm, Oxford Twenty-First Century Approaches to Literatures (Oxford: Oxford University Press, 2007).

[18] See, for example, Emily Apter, *The Translation Zone: A New Comparative Literature*, Translation/Transnation (Princeton: Princeton University Press, 2006) and Michelle R. Warren, "Translating in the Zone," *New Medieval Literatures* 9 (2007): 191–8.

medieval West's language of truth, translating texts from Latin into the vernacular in a sense carried its own justification, especially in the case of hagiographic tales such as the *Vie de saint Alexis* and the *Voyage de saint Brendan*. Many of these texts are in Anglo-Norman, indicating the precocious intervention of the Norman kings of England. Different manuscripts of the *Voyage de saint Brendan*, for example, are dedicated to the two wives of Henry I: Matilda of Scotland (d. 1118) and her successor, Adeliza of Louvain. In the middle of the twelfth century, Old French came into its own as a written language in the so-called *matière de Rome* – the wave of translations of Greek and Roman legends from Latin into French. These – the *Romans* ("romances" or vernacular French versions) of *Enéas* (Aeneas), *Troie* (Troy), *Thèbes* (the Oedipus story), and *Alexandre* – made the stories of antiquity available to a secular nobility at best marginally literate in Latin. These examples of *translatio studii* – the east-to-west transfer of learning alluded to in the prologue of Chrétien de Troyes's *Cligés* (c. 1170s) – were contemporary with (and in one case by the same author as) vernacular histories chronicling the exploits of Henry II's Norman ancestors. Linking the classical past to the Norman present was Wace's *Roman de Brut*, a translation of Geoffrey of Monmouth's *Historia Regum Britanniae*, recounting the history of Britain from its founding by the Trojan refugee Brut down through the days of King Arthur.

In fact, "the complex interplay of indigenous and imported languages" we alluded to earlier may have been much more complex than we ever suspected.[19] Noting the correspondence between the literary genres attested in pre-Conquest Anglo-Saxon literature and the post-Conquest Anglo-Norman tradition, Elizabeth Tyler has suggested that the former may have stimulated the emergence of the latter – that the precociousness of the Anglo-Norman literary tradition in relation to that in Old French may have resulted from a kind of trans-cultural modeling bringing together the language of the colonizers with the cultural forms of the colonized. As Tyler puts it, "The Anglo-Saxon legacy to the twelfth century is not solely about the vitality of English…but about English, Latin and French coming into a shared European literary culture, which was, in turn, deeply shaped by the precocity of English as a written vernacular."[20] This recognition of the place of Anglo-Saxon in the emerging British literary system

---

[19] Campbell, "Speaking the Other," p. 181.

[20] Elizabeth M. Tyler, "From Old English to Old French," in *Language and Culture in Medieval Britain*, ed. Wogan-Browne et al., pp. 164–78. See also Ian Short, "Patrons and Polyglots: French Literature in Twelfth-Century England," *Anglo-Norman Studies* 14 (1992): 229–49.

is fundamental to understanding the project of translation Marie describes in the epilogue to her *Ysopë* and in the momentary traces of that language in the prologues to *Bisclavret* and *L'aüstic*. And something of the ongoing multilingualism of Britain is hinted at in the trilingual Harley 978 (the only manuscript to contain all twelve *lais* attributed to Marie), which – in addition to the *Lais* and the *Ysopë* – contains a variety of Latin texts and the mid-thirteenth-century Middle English lyric, "Sumer is icumen in."[21]

Reading Marie de France

This *Companion* reads Marie's works within the cultural, literary, and linguistic contexts of twelfth-century Anglo-Norman England. We assume that the *Lais*, *Ysopë*, and *Espurgatoire* draw from these contexts, dramatize them, and debate their values. For example, multilingualism enables and implies certain geographical, historical, and political relationships and calls attention to the porosity of boundaries. The three (or perhaps four) texts attributed to Marie all identify themselves as translations: the *Lais* from Breton, the *Ysopë* from Anglo-Saxon, and the *Espurgatoire seint Patriz* and the *Vie seinte Audree* from Latin. Marie is centrally located in the multilingual culture we describe above.

Marie describes her translations in terms of making texts available to readers. She claims to preserve oral tales in the *Lais*, and, in her *Espurgatoire*, to make a purgatory narrative accessible to lay people who cannot read Latin. Unlike her contemporary, Chrétien de Troyes, who in *Erec et Enide* explicitly asserted the superiority of his *conjointure* over the disjointed efforts of previous or competing composers, Marie repeatedly evokes the oral *lais* composed and circulated by the anonymous and collective *Bretons* displaced by her (written) *Lais* without ever denigrating their efforts. Rather, she brings them into French as a gift for a king. In other words, with her translations Marie de France describes a network of interests that cross linguistic boundaries, and it may well be that translation is one of Marie's own primary literary interests.

Indeed, for R. Howard Bloch, Marie is "obsessed with translation."[22] For Bloch, the meaning of translation for Marie is revealed in her use of the polysemic verb *traire* (to draw, to pull) and its homophone *trahir* (to betray). He reads Marie's description of drawing a story from Latin into French (de Latin en Romanz *traire*, *Lais*, Prologue, l. 30) in relation to

---

21 Stein, "Multilingualism," pp. 31–2.
22 *The Anonymous Marie de France*, p. 88.

the homophone *trahir* and representations of betrayal in her work, and he argues that:

> Marie is haunted by the betrayal of a certain plenitude in language that occurs whenever one chooses one tongue over another, one title over another, one term within a single language over another, whenever language is submitted to the reductive, partial, necessarily fragmentary nature of any particular expression.[23]

We see Marie's translations somewhat differently, as evidence of her participation in a multilingual world defined by a network of political, economic, and literary interest and characterized by the circulation of ideas in many languages.

The question of how Marie's texts relate to each other has long been somewhat vexed and it relates directly to her identity as an author. The translation project unites all of Marie's works and may be the clearest link among them. Yet because of the terms in which she identifies herself and because of their very difference from each other, her works invite the question of why Marie writes. And the question is interesting partly because she is a woman. The reasons she gives for writing are different in each work, and name relations of obligation or of ingratiation, a desire for fame, or a desire to make a pious text available to those who cannot read Latin (see Chapter 2). But for many readers, Marie de France is intriguing because she is the rare example of a twelfth-century woman author writing in French.

The question of gender has been an obsession of criticism on Marie de France, and Marie's "feminism" has been much debated.[24] Certainly it is possible to identify a critique of arranged marriages in *lais* like *Guigemar*, *Yonec*, and *Milun*, even though such a critique takes the form of sympathy for the unhappily married woman rather than a direct critique of marriage practices among twelfth-century noble families. Gender is not a strong concern in the *Ysopë*, nor is it much in debate in the *Espurgatoire*.[25] We locate the importance of gender not in authorship but in

---

[23] Ibid., p. 89.

[24] Sharon Kinoshita, "Cherchez la femme: Feminist Criticism and Marie de France's *Lai de Lanval*," *Romance Notes* 34.3 (1994): 263–73.

[25] However, see Sahar Amer, "Marie de France Rewrites Genesis: The Image of Woman in Marie de France's *Fables*," *Neophilologus* 81 (1997): 489–99; and Harriet Spiegel, "The Male Animal in the Fables of Marie de France," *Medieval Masculinities*, ed. Clare A. Lees, Thelma Fenster, and Jo Ann MacNamara (Minneapolis: University of Minnesota Press), pp. 111–28.

the articulation of social and institutional structures in Marie's works. In other words, our guiding principle is not the search for authorial intention, but the identification of textual effects that may or may not reflect a gendered perspective on the part of the author. This is not to say that the author Marie de France is merely a "textual effect."[26] Rather, we argue that Marie's position as a subject situated in late-twelfth-century culture is crucial to understanding her treatment of institutions, social relations, and gender. The *Lais* consistently pay attention to the place of women in feudal structures, but not just to admonish or critique. Marie imagines new possibilities in the form of worlds in which women could choose their own lovers, as in *Yonec*, or rescue men, as in *Lanval*. The *Lais* imagine ways in which women can manipulate and exploit feudal social structures, and they imagine the ways in which those structures may be changed through women's desires and even women's agency, if only in a limited way. That such possibilities are imagined more fully in the *Lais* than in the other texts may be due to a perception that the possibilities for gendered authority are different in explicitly feudal social structures and in stories where love, chivalry, and marriage politics are intertwined. Marie also makes a claim for her own authority in vernacular clerical culture, aligning herself with philosophers (*li philesophe*, l. 17) in the *Prologue* to the *Lais*.[27]

One biographical explanation for the variety of Marie's literary production sees Marie de France as a secular woman who gradually became more concerned with spiritual matters, perhaps taking religious vows late in life, perhaps after a marriage, like Guildalüec in *Eliduc*. According to this hypothesis, Marie's works would follow her life in becoming increasingly less secular and more religious. We have no proof of any such life trajectory for Marie, and reading her literary works for evidence about her life can lead only to the conclusion, as we noted above, that she was educated, she must have had access to a library, and she was familiar with noble society.

Despite their quite different subjects and genres, the *Lais*, the *Ysopë*, and the *Espurgatoire* share certain stylistic and linguistic features, and they share certain themes.[28] Recent studies have identified a unity among

---

26 Bernard Cerquiglini, *Eloge de la variante* (Paris: Seuil, 1989), p. 52.

27 The old woman in Salerno is an analogous figure of authority in Marie's *Les dous amanz*. See Peggy McCracken, "Women and Medicine in Old French Narrative," *Exemplaria* 5.2 (1993): 239–62.

28 Bloch's *The Anonymous Marie de France* is by far the most complete study of the unity of Marie's works.

Marie's works in their shared concern for memory, and in their consistent preoccupation with language and its effects.[29] We will insist less on cohesive unity among the works than on the multivocal responses they offer to questions and to problems posed in their narratives. That is, we move deliberately away from a notion of author as unifying Marie's texts and we approach them as united by a persistent but multifaceted interest in social relations. While the *Lais*, the *Ysopë*, and the *Espurgatoire seint Patriz* may focus on matters chivalric, moral, and spiritual, respectively, all to some degree reflect a preoccupation with the structures of what we will refer to throughout this book as "feudal society." We use this concept with the knowledge that many historians take exception to the term "feudal," preferring to dispense with it entirely.[30] It retains greater currency, however, among French historians of the Middle Ages who are able to distinguish lexically (as Anglophone historians cannot) between *féodalité* (fief-holding) and *féodalisme*.[31] We use the term here to refer to the practice of fief-holding and the ideological values this practice implies. In the literary texts of Marie and her contemporaries, the relationship between lord and vassal functions as a kind of structuring principle of society and is represented in institutions like chivalry, marriage, knighthood, and kingship.

Among the twelfth-century nobility, lord–vassal relations were the glue holding feudal society together. Constituted by the rite of homage (*hommage*) whereby one noble became the "man" (*homme*) or vassal of another, such relations were hierarchical but reciprocal – based on and reinforced by the real and symbolic obligations each owed the other. Thus in return for protection and a fief (the land providing a means of subsistence) given by his lord, the vassal promised forty days of military service (*auxilium*) each year and "counsel" (*consilium*) – the "obligation" to advise his lord that in practical terms amounted to the right to demand

[29] Logan Whalen, *Marie de France and the Poetics of Memory* (Washington, D.C.: Catholic University of America Press, 2008); Bloch, *The Anonymous Marie de France*.

[30] The key text here is Susan Reynolds, *Fiefs and Vassals: The Medieval Evidence Reinterpreted* (Oxford: Oxford University Press, 1994).

[31] For a summary of the debate, see Constance Brittain Bouchard, *Strong of Body, Brave and Noble: Chivalry and Society in Medieval France* (Ithaca: Cornell University Press, 1998), pp. 35–8; and "Féodalisms/Féodalité," in Pierre Bonnassie, *Les cinquante mots clefs de l'histoire médiévale* (Toulouse: Privat, 1981), pp. 82–6. For the continued use of "feudal" in a French context, see, for example, the works of Theodore Evergates: *Feudal Society in the Bailliage of Troyes under the Counts of Champagne, 1152–1284* (Baltimore: Johns Hopkins University Press, 1975) and *Feudal Society in Medieval France: Documents from the County of Champagne* (Philadelphia: University of Pennsylvania Press, 1993).

that the lord behave properly and the obligation to appear at court when summoned (notably at the plenary courts timed for major feast days such as Easter, Pentecost, Ascension, Assumption, and Christmas). Nothing better indicates the power of this paradigm than the way it was generalized to express a range of social relations. The intense, one-to-one bond linking lord and vassal is the direct model for the bond between the lady and her courtly lover: he pledges her his loyalty and service in hopes of winning – or, by the logic of reciprocity governing feudal relations, compelling – her love in return. This is also, of course, a standard model for the Christian's devotion to God: the gestural language of homage, kneeling before the lord with palms together – "hands joined" (*mains jointes*), as the medieval texts put it – is indistinguishable from the attitude of prayer. (In fact, perhaps contrary to modern expectation, the religious use of this model seems to have been derived from feudal precedents, rather than vice versa.[32])

Paying attention to the omnipresence of terms such as lord, vassal, counsel, and their equivalents in Marie's texts reveals (as we will explore in Chapter 3) the extent to which not only the *Lais*, but also the *Ysopë* and the *Espurgatoire seint Patriz*, are structured by the mentality and values of feudal society. Personal bonds and reciprocal obligations structure the larger social world into which Marie inserts her texts. Her works (like many of the objects that circulate in the *lais*) are objects that mediate social relations; as gifts to kings and counts, they constitute Marie's own fame and provoke the slander of those who envy her. All of Marie's works are also about establishing or entering into social relations. Each of them, in different ways, speaks to a tension between a christianizing morality and feudal morality. In fact, Marie's works translate all values into a vocabulary of feudal relations. This is striking in the *Ysopë*, where hierarchies among animals are defined in terms of lords and homage, and where antique morals or Christian moralization in previous fable traditions are translated into Marie's interpretive structure in terms of feudal hierarchies. Such translation is also evident in the *Lais*, where the rewriting of Breton tales into a context permeated by feudal ideology causes the Breton to lose much of its otherworldiness. Lanval's departure with his lady into Avalon is represented as a departure from Arthur's court more than an escape into a faerie Otherworld. *Bisclavret* begins by citing an old distinction between men and werewolves, but the feudal homage of the wolf to the king displaces the separation between the human and the

---

32 Bouchard, *Strong of Body*, pp. 44–5.

otherworldly animal with a familiar lord–vassal relationship that makes the wolf a faithful subject of the king. In fact, in the *Lais* words associated with wonder (le merveille, merveiller) refer surprisingly seldom to the elements we are most likely to identify as otherworldly Celtic marvels, such as the talking, antlered white doe of *Guigemar*. "Marvelous" beings or events are taken largely for granted, located within a larger geography in which Celtic lands cohabit with international circuits of chivalry that can take a single knight from South Wales as far as Norway or Gotland in his quest for reputation and honor, as in Marie's *Milun*.

Organization of this book

Rather than approaching Marie's works in separate chapters, we find that by looking at them together under common questions we find both coherence and debate. That is, sometimes Marie's works speak together in continuous ways, and sometimes they do not. We do not attempt to offer a single, unified view of Marie de France and her works. Rather, we find that the themes and their implications operate on multiple levels, in the text, among the texts, and in the relationship of the author to the text.

Since most readers come to Marie first, if not exclusively, through a study of the *Lais*, we pay them the most attention. Each chapter takes a general category (literary history, history, plot, characters, narrative technique, posterity) and examines it in light of an important theme in order to explore the various ways in which Marie's works intersect with literary and historical contexts, and with each other. In Chapter 2 we explore the literary context in which Marie's works were composed and circulated. We examine representations of circulation, transmission, and interpretation in her narratives to suggest the ways in which the works themselves thematize literary composition, but also to show the ways in which her works are situated within a network of textual traditions and productions in late-twelfth-century England. In Chapter 3 we turn to the social and historical contexts of Marie's works in order to show the extent to which a feudal vocabulary structures Marie's narratives. Feudal values are consistently debated in Marie's works, sometimes to be affirmed and sometimes to be subverted, but always as a system within which characters make sense of their social world. Chapter 4 explores Marie's construction of plot through an attention to movement between, among, and through places in her narratives. Movement is related to change and opportunity, but also to alienation and social unease in her works, and it offers a useful rubric through which to think about the ways in which Marie organizes plot. In Chapter 5 we turn to an examination of characters through a focus on embodiment. Since Marie's works, like other twelfth-century narratives, do not valorize complex psychological motivations in the representation of protagonists, embodiment is a lens through which to examine the construction of character in the *Lais*, the *Ysopë*, and the *Espurgatoire*. Chapter 6 explores Marie's narrative techniques through an examination of variation in her works. Marie uses similar motifs and plot developments to different ends in different works, and attention to the similarities and differences among the elements of plot and style further suggests the play of coherence and dissonance that characterizes her *oeuvre*. Finally, in Chapter 7 we conclude with an examination of the posterity of Marie's narratives. We include here a short description of the manuscripts of Marie's works, all copied well after her lifetime, and a consideration of the ways in which Marie was remembered by her contemporaries and by the later authors who rewrote or borrowed from her works.

Communication, Transmission, and Interpretation: Literary History

"Marie de France" is our name for an author figure who claims to have been born "in France" but composed the texts attributed to her in England, drawing on oral traditions in Celtic and written traditions in Anglo-Saxon and Latin. In contrast to the works of Chrétien de Troyes, who describes his sources more allusively – "a book from the library of my lord Saint Peter in Beauvais" (*Cligés*, l. 21) or "the book of the story of the grail, given him by the count [Philip of Flanders]" (*Le conte du graal*, ll. 64–5) – Marie's sources have been more precisely identified: directly, in the case of the *Espurgatoire saint Patriz*, and indirectly, in the case of the *Ysopë* and the *Lais*. Moreover, Marie persistently calls attention to her own work of linguistic transformation: where Chrétien emphasizes the value-added of his composition – the "mout bele conjuncture" of *Erec et Enide* (l. 14) or the "painne et…antancïon" (l. 29) added to the "[m]atiere et san" (l. 26) supplied by the countess of Champagne in the *Chevalier de la charrete* – Marie explicitly points to the work of "pulling" narratives over from Celtic, Anglo-Saxon, or Latin, respectively, into written *romanz* or *franceis*.[1]

What does the culture in which Marie produced her translations look like? Robert M. Stein gives this helpful overview of the sociolinguistic complexity of England in the wake of the Norman Conquest:

> Celtic speakers were a twice-conquered minority. Danish was still in circulation in the north and east. The great mass of the population was English speaking and probably never learned more than the most rudimentary French. The royal court was francophone. A thin, but very significant, portion of the upper echelons of the aristocracy was similarly francophone. This group, in proximity to royal power and needing to interact in many spheres with the English-speaking population, devel-

---

[1]   Chrétien de Troyes, *Romans*, Classiques modernes (Paris: Livre de Poche, 1994). On *traire*, see Chapter 1, pp. 9–10.

oped as a truly bilingual elite. This group was fluid and changed over time; many of its members arrived from the Continent in various waves of immigration, especially after the marriage of Henry II to Eleanor of Aquitaine further united the Angevin and English elites; many of its members were born in England to descendants of conquerors who had settled, intermarried with native elites and – although still French speaking – had developed a sense of themselves as English....Language choice is throughout the period determined more by the relation of language to power than by any other reason including ancestry or a strong sense of ethnic or national identity.[2]

The multilingualism outlined here is of another order than that found in the Iberian peninsula, where language was, at least in principle, coordinated with religious difference.[3] The complexity and fluidity of Angevin Britain reflected an ongoing process of political and cultural change that would eventually produce a new hybrid language, Middle English. In Stein's description, several features speak to our understanding of Marie and her literary production. The "various waves of immigration" of Continental French-speakers suggest how a woman "from France" could have ended up writing in Britain. The emergence of "a truly bilingual elite" accounts for the nod (however authentically or not) to Anglo-Saxon – as a literary language in the *Ysopë*, or as a courtly spoken one in the *"nihtegale"* (l. 6) of *L'aüstic*. And the association of French with the court, the "upper echelons of the aristocracy," and royal power contextualizes the absolutely determining role that royal or comital patronage played in Marie's textual production. This political, linguistic, and cultural complexity also makes intelligible the multiplicity of perspectives contained both *within* the *Lais* and the *Ysopë* and *across* Marie's *oeuvre* overall. As Stein says of what he calls "polyglot literature": in this "fluid, multilingual social space no single text ever stays comfortably in its generic place or maintains a fixed

2   Robert M. Stein, "Multilingualism," in *Middle English*, ed. Paul Strohm, Oxford Twenty-First Century Approaches to Literature (Oxford: Oxford University Press, 2007), pp. 23–37 (at 24–5).

3   In fact, in Islamic Spain, Arabic frequently functioned as a shared language between Muslims, Jews, and Christians. See David Wasserstein, "The Language Situation in al-Andalus," in *The Formation of al-Andalus*, 2 vols., ed. Maribel Fierro and Julio Samsó (Aldershot, UK: Ashgate, 1998), 2: 3–18. For recent studies of the distinctive multilingual "literary system" of medieval Iberia, see David A. Wacks, *Framing Iberia: Maqamat and Frametale Narratives in Medieval Spain* (Leiden: Brill, 2007); and Jerrilynn Dodds, María Rosa Menocal, and Abigail Krasner Balbale, *The Arts of Intimacy: Christians, Jews, and Muslims in the Making of Castilian Culture* (New Haven: Yale University Press, 2008).

political alignment."[4] Or, as Carla Rossi has proposed, Marie's work fits the exigencies of "the new ruling class of England: a Breton, Norman, and Saxon mix, composed of counts, barons, knights, clerics, treasurers and itinerant judges of the Plantagenêt court, depository of a heterogeneous culture for which new common roots were needed."[5]

This multilingual complexity demands that we take seriously something we all know but seldom stop to consider: how fundamentally medieval literary culture was a culture of translation. As we noted in our Introduction, Old French literature emerges in the late eleventh or early twelfth century as a literature of transcription and translation. At its origin the term *romanz*, eventually yielding the French *roman* and the English word romance, designated not a genre but a language – the Romance vernacular, set explicitly, and at times polemically, over and against Latin, western Europe's language of official thought and communication. Most importantly, unlike modern translators, the writers who set out to "romance" Latin texts like Geoffrey of Monmouth's *Historia Regum Britanniae* or Vergil's *Aeneid* were not preoccupied by issues of fidelity. Rather, the "original" served as the basis of a thoroughgoing adaptation, elaboration, and expansion. The adaptation in question might be temporal, resulting in the well-known "anachronism" of medieval treatments of classical material; cultural, with an eye to local histories, geographies, or literary traditions; or socio-ideological. Thus the French translation of Galbert of Bruges's account of the assassination of Count Charles of Flanders renders the Latin *fortissimus vir*, which "assimilates Charles to Republican Roman canons of virtue," as *un prince bon e vaillant*, which "places him directly into the chivalric world, an aristocratic scale of values" that the text otherwise calls into question.[6]

"The translated text," as Michelle R. Warren writes, "has long occupied a relatively low status within academic culture, due to its seemingly derivative and secondary nature." Understanding a literary tradition in which translation is ubiquitous, therefore, requires "a decentred aesthetic order, one that would set aside the very notion that 'originals' are worth more th[an] translations, 'originality' more than repetition, 'uniqueness' more than similarity. This involves placing texts in relation to each other via strategic alliances that depend less on genre and language than on

---

4 Stein, "Multilingualism," p. 35.

5 Carla Rossi, *Marie de France et les érudits de Cantorbéry*, Recherches Littéraires Médiévales 1 (Paris: Editions Classiques Garnier, 2009), p. 15.

6 Stein, "Multilingualism," p. 33.

culture."[7] If Marie de France's repeated insistence on her own work of translation renders the cult of authorship that has arisen around her name somewhat ironic, it also means that no body of texts is better situated than hers to help decenter our understanding of medieval literary culture. Nothing better indicates the prestige attached to translation than the credit Marie claims for it, her description of the envy her reputation has provoked, and her wariness at the prospect that someone else might try to take credit for her work: if she names herself in the epilogue to the *Ysopë*, it is because "any number of clerks might claim my work for themselves" (Put cel estre que clerc plusur / prendreient sur eus mun labur, ll. 5–6). For Marie, as her prologue and epilogue remind us, even the eponymous Aesop is not an author but a translator (prologue, ll. 17–20 and epilogue 13–15).

Transmission and translation in the *Lais*

A marvel of complexity, Marie's fifty-six-line *Prologue* offers a highly overdetermined explanation of how she came to compose the *Lais*. Beginning with questions of morality and vice, the relationship of the past and present, of Latin and the vernacular, of textuality and orality, and of forgetting and memory, it closes by dedicating the collection to a "noble king," usually presumed to be Henry II of England (r. 1154–89). Of the four reasons she gives for undertaking the *Lais*, three pertain directly to the authorial subject; only the fourth – to assure that the *lais* do not lapse into obscurity – speaks to the value or qualities of the material itself. Marie writes first of all to fulfill the obligation imposed by her God-given intelligence:

> S/he to whom God has given the gift of reason and the eloquence to speak well should not keep silent or hide away but should willingly show him or herself.

> Qui Deus a duné esciënce
> e de parler bone eloquence,
> ne s'en deit taisir ne celer,
> ainz se deit voluntiers mustrer. (*Lais*, *Prologue*, ll. 1–4)

    [7] Michelle R. Warren, "Translation," in *Middle English*, ed. Paul Strohm, Oxford Twenty-First Century Approaches (Oxford: Oxford University Press, 2007), p. 51.

A similar justification occurs in a Latin text composed several decades earlier, probably also in England, for King Henry I (r. 1100–1135), the grandfather of the "noble king" (nobles reis, l. 43) Henry II of the *Lais*:

> [B]ecause God has designed to clothe me in his many-sided wisdom, although I am a sinner, in order that the light given to me should not be hid under a bushel, and at the prompting of the same holy spirit, I have been moved to write this book.[8]

The similarities between this passage and Marie's *Prologue* allow us more easily to recognize the specificity of her vision – minimizing the religious aspect even of her invocation of God, or rather, treating God's gift as a gift (don) that, by the logic of the counter-gift (guerdon), demands a suitable response (as we will explore in Chapter 3). The author of these lines was Petrus Alfonsi, an Iberian Jew who converted to Christianity under the sponsorship of the Aragonese king Alfonso I. He subsequently traveled to England, where he may have served as court physician to Henry I, and where he probably composed his *Disciplina Clericalis* – a collection of tales in Latin, drawn from the Judeo-Arabic tradition.[9] However normative its composition in Latin may seem, his work, located at the intersection between the Norman and Iberian literary systems, introduces a further Semitic–Mediterranean element to the multicultural complexity of twelfth-century Britain.[10] Petrus continues:

> [T]he infirmity of man's physical nature...makes it necessary to break up instruction into small sections so that boredom does not set in. Also I have been mindful of the fact that in order to facilitate remembrance of what has been learnt, the pill must be softened and sweetened by various means, because man is by nature forgetful and has need of

---

[8] *The* Disciplina Clericalis *of Petrus Alfonsi*, ed. and trans. (into German) Eberhard Hermes; trans. (into English) P. R. Quarrie (Berkeley: University of California Press, 1977), p. 103. Subsequent references are noted parenthetically in the text.

[9] According to his own writings, Petrus (Moses Sefardi) converted to Christianity in 1106 in Huesca, with Alfonso the Battler as his godfather. See John Tolan, *Petrus Alfonsi and His Medieval Readers* (Gainesville: University Press of Florida, 1993). On the northern provenance of the *Disciplina Clericalis*, see Suzanne Conklin Akbari, "Between Diaspora and Conquest: Norman Assimilation in Petrus Alfonsi's *Disciplina Clericalis* and Marie de France's *Fables*," in *Cultural Diversity in the British Middle Ages: Archipelago, Island, England*, ed. Jeffrey Jerome Cohen (New York: Palgrave Macmillan, 2008), p. 22.

[10] For Christian–Jewish interactions in northern France, see Kirsten Fudeman, *Vernacular Voices: Language and Identity in Medieval French Jewish Communities* (Philadelphia: University of Pennsylvania Press, 2010).

many tricks which will remind him again of those things he has forgotten. (*Disciplina Clericalis*, p. 104)

In Petrus's (wholly conventional) view, whatever literary art or pleasure he brings to his writing is a palliative for human weakness – for the propensity to boredom and forgetfulness. How different his contemporary reader is from the one conjured by Marie:

> It was common practice among the ancients, as Priscian tells us, to speak very obscurely in the books they wrote in those days so that those who came after them and were obliged to learn what was in the books could comment on the text, adding their reason. The philosophers knew and understood that the more time passed, the more subtle people's reasoning would be, and the better they would be able to prevent the content from being lost.

> Custume fu as anciĕns,
> ceo testimoine Preciĕns,
> es livres que jadis faiseient
> assez oscurement diseient
> pur cels ki a venir esteient
> e ki aprendre les deveient,
> que peüssent gloser la letre
> e de lur sen le surplus metre.
> Li philesophe le saveient,
> par els meïsmes l'entendeient,
> cum plus trespassereit li tens,
> plus serreient sutil de sens
> e plus se savreient guarder
> de ceo qu'i ert, a trespasser. (*Lais*, *Prologue*, ll. 9–22)

Few lines in medieval French literature have occasioned as much discussion as these. Besides being beautifully woven together by the alliterative play of [s]s and [l]s, Marie's claim that ancient philosophers wrote with willful obscurity to insure that her modern contemporaries "be able to gloss the text and put in the surplus of their understanding" (peüssent gloser la letre / et de lur sen le surplus metre, ll. 15–16) vaunts the faculty of human reason, and specifically that of her modern contemporaries. Far from needing "softened and sweetened" works to combat boredom and forgetfulness, Marie's contemporaries thrive on challenging texts that demand the investment of one's full intelligence and attention.

Marie's second reason for undertaking her project is to guard against vice:

Whoever wants to protect him or herself from vice should study and begin a serious piece of work. This is the way to best keep [vice] away and deliver oneself from great grief. Therefore I began to think about translating some good story from Latin into Romance.

Ki de vice se vuelt defendre,
estudiër deit e entendre
e grevose oevre comencier;
par ceo s'en puet plus esloignier
e de grant dolur delivrer.
Pur ceo començai a penser
d'alkune bone estoire faire
e de Latin en Romanz traire. (*Lais, Prologue*, ll. 23–30)

Besides galvanizing her attention in such a way as to preclude falling into vice, translating a "good story" into Romance from Latin, the language of theology, high culture, and administration, is a project that carries its own justification. For Marie, however, the intrinsic worthiness of the project is overridden by her third motivation, to garner praise and renown for her work: "but this would hardly have redounded to my glory: so many others have set out to do the same" (mais ne me fust guaires de pris: / itant s'en sunt altre entremis, ll. 31–2). Driven by the desire to distinguish herself from "so many others," she hits upon a revolutionary new project:

I thought of the *lais* I had heard. I knew for certain that those who first began them from adventures they heard and who sent them out composed them *for remembrance*. I have heard several of them told and I don't want to forget them. I've made rhyming tales out of them, spending many late nights at it.

Des lais pensai qu'oïz aveie.
Ne dutai pas, bien le saveie,
que *pur remembrance* les firent
des aventures qu'il oïrent
cil ki primes les comencierent
e ki avant les enveierent.
Plusurs en ai oïz conter,
nes vueil laissier ne obliër.
Rime en ai e fait ditié,
soventes feiz en ai veillié. (*Lais, Prologue*, ll. 33–42)

At the center of her project, then, is *remembrance*. Typically, her lines are construed to mean that those who first composed these *lais* did so in order that they, the adventures, be remembered.[11] This is all the more significant since *remembrance* is identified as a key preoccupation of Marie's and plays a large part in arguments attributing the *Vie seinte Audree* to her authorship.[12] It is also conceivable, however, to read the lines to mean that those who first composed the *lais* did so in order that they, the singers, be remembered. And though the usual translation seems immediately confirmed by the following lines – Marie does not want the *lais* she has heard to be abandoned and forgotten – the second possibility dovetails seamlessly with the prologue to *Guigemar*, the first of the twelve *lais* in Harley 978:

> It grieves anyone working with good material if it is not done well. Hear, lords, what Marie says – she who is not forgotten in her time. People should praise whoever has earned a good reputation. But whenever you find in a country a man or woman of great worth, those envious of his or her reputation often slander him or her. They want to lower his or her esteem. Thus they begin acting like a bad, cowardly, treacherous dog that turns on people and bites them. I don't want to give up on account of that: if jabberers and slanderers try to turn it against me, it's their right to speak ill.

> Ki de bone matire traite,
> mult li peise, se bien n'est faite.
> Oëz, seignur, que dit Marie,
> ki en sun tens pas ne s'oblie.
> Celui deivent la genz löer,
> ki en bien fait de sei parler.
> Mais quant il a en un païs
> hume ne femme de grant pris,
> cil ki de sun bien unt envie
> sovent en diënt vileinie.
> Sun pris li vuelent abaissier:
> pur ceo comencent le mestier
> del malvais chien coart, felun,

---

[11] They "composed them in order to preserve adventures they had heard" (*The Lais of Marie de France*, trans. Robert W. Hanning and Joan M. Ferrante [New York: Dutton, 1978], p. 29); "to perpetuate the memory of adventures they had heard" (*The Lais of Marie de France*, trans. Glyn S. Burgess and Keith Busby [London: Penguin, 1986], p. 41); "[ils] avaient voulu perpétuer le souvenir des aventures qu'ils avaient entendues" (Harf-Lancner, *Les lais*, p. 25).

[12] See Logan Whalen, *Marie de France and the Poetics of Memory* (Washington, D.C.: Catholic University of America Press, 2008).

> ki mort la gent par traïsun.
> Nel vueil mie pur ceo laissier,
> se jangleür u losengier
> le me vuelent a mal turner;
> ceo est lur dreiz de mesparler. (*Guigemar*, ll. 1–18)

Appealing to the noble "lords" (seignur) who constitute her target audience, Marie explicitly claims not to be forgotten (ne s'oblie, l. 4) by her contemporaries and implicitly identifies herself as a "woman…of great worth" (femme de grant pris, l. 8) who has excited envy rather than the praise such worth warrants.[13] The word *pris* in line 8 echoes line 31 of the *Lais' Prologue* and anticipates its repetition throughout *Guigemar*, thereby aligning the recognition Marie seeks for her literary work with that earned by an internationally renowned chivalric champion.[14]

For Marie, the key to *pris* and *remembrance* is the turn away from Latin to Breton. Rejecting hagiographical tales like the lives of Saint Brendan or Saint Audrey, classical material like the *Aeneid* or the story of Troy, wisdom literature such as Petrus Alfonsi's *Disciplina Clericalis* or the fables of the *Romulus Nilanti*, she opts instead for the tales circulating not just orally but in song.[15] As we learn in the epilogue to the first *lai* in Harley 978:

> The *lai* of *Guigemar*, which is performed on the harp and
> rotte, was composed from this tale you've heard.[16] The music
> is pleasant to listen to.
>
> De cest cunte qu'oï avez
> fu Guigemar li lais trovez,
> que hum fait en harpe e en rote;
> bone en est a oïr la note. (*Guigemar*, ll. 883–6)

---

[13] The author's aspiration to be remembered likewise anchors the prologue of *Erec et Enide*, where Chrétien de Troyes boasts that his story "will be remembered as long as Christianity endures" (iert en memoire / Tant con durra crestïentez, ll. 24–5).

[14] For *pris*, see *Guigemar*, ll. 51, 69, 728.

[15] Within the *Lais* themselves, Celtic references sometimes seem pointedly to displace the classical: in *Lanval*, the fairy mistress's tent is so rich that neither Queen Semiramis nor Emperor Octavian could afford a single panel (ll. 82–6), while the lady herself exceeds Venus, Dido, and Lavinia in beauty (ll. 584–6).

[16] The rotte is a stringed instrument. The name originally refers to a Germanic lyre. In the Welsh context, it likely refers to the *crwth*, a plucked lyre that came to be played as a harp. Oxford Music Online/Grove Music Online (accessed 4 December 2010), http:// www.oxfordmusiconline.com.oca.ucsc.edu/subscriber/article/grove/music/52977?q=rotte&hbutton_search.x=25&hbutton_search.y=8&hbutton_search=search&source=omo_t237&source=omo_gmo&source=omo_t114&search=quick&pos=7&_start=1#firsthit.

As elsewhere in the *Lais*, Marie evokes the anonymous and collective "Bretons" whose songs she has set out to gather (assembler, *Prologue*, l. 47) and rhyme in the *Romanz* vernacular. Her project shows the degree of legitimacy and prestige Old French had acquired over the course of the twelfth century. If the justification for "romancing" high-cultural Latin texts was self-evident, here the narrator emerges as an anthropologist *avant la lettre* – collecting oral material in a non-hegemonic tongue to be translated into and transcribed in the language that will assure its circulation at the court of the "noble king" (*Prologue*, l. 43) and among the "lords" (*Guigemar*, l. 3) who constitute Marie's patrons and target audience. Deploying her God-given gifts of "escïence" and "eloquence" (*Prologue*, ll. 1–2) in novel ways, the narrator transforms (into French) and preserves (in writing) the evanescent eloquence of Celtic oral traditions.

At the same time, the *Prologue* to the *Lais* hints at the complexity of the twelfth-century British literary system. The translation into *Romanz* (l. 30) out of the Latin of the "ancients" has a moral and pedagogical function: to get readers to exercise their God-given faculties in order to decode the original text, overcoming the double obstacle of the obscurities willfully designed by the original authors in addition to those occasioned by the passage of time. In comparison, the translation from Breton, though likewise aimed at neutralizing the effects of history, is presented as an effort of conservation. The contrast, then, is between the threat of the present incomprehension of a not otherwise forgotten but potentially unreadable past, and that of the future eradication of an active but endangered present. The *Prologue* thus stages the complex interplay of three historical moments (past, present, and future), in three languages (Latin, French, and Breton), and two modalities (writing and orality), with Marie positioned right at their center.

The cultural complexity of Marie's project stands out in comparison with a text like the anonymous *lai Tyolet*, set in a remote Arthurian past when England was called "Brittany" (Bretaingne, l. 2) and when knights – bolder, braver, and in every way more intense than they are today – relentlessly sought, and found, adventures.[17]

> [These adventures] were recounted at court just as they had been found/composed. The wise clerks of the time had them all written down. They were put into Latin and written on parchment, because there would still come a time when people

---

[17] Compare evocations of the Arthurian past in the prologue to Chrétien de Troyes's *Yvain*, when lovers were more loyal, etc.

would listen to them with pleasure. Now they are told and retold, and translated from Latin into Romance. The Bretons made numerous *lais* from them, just as our ancestors tell us.

A la cort erent racontees,
si conme eles erent trovees;
Li preude clerc qui donc estoient
totes escrire les fesoient;
mises estoient en latin
e en escrit em parchemin,
por ce qu'encor tel tens seroit
que l'en volentiers les orroit.
Or son dites e recontees,
de latin en romanz trovees;
Bretons en firent lais plusors,
si con dïent nos ancessors. (*Tyolet*, ll. 25–36)[18]

Depicting an Arthurian court always already permeated by Latin, the *Tyolet* prologue seems to cast even Breton oral culture as a secondary derivative of clerical textuality. All memory and transmission passes through Latin, pressing the anthropological immediacy of Marie's work of collection, transcription, and translation into a more conventional mold.

In the *Lais*, by contrast, Marie does much more than deliberately eschew the ink-and-parchment world of "preude clerc" transcribing everything into Latin. In her work, *romanz* is not simply the target language but a frame for acknowledging the multiplicity of living languages, explicitly evoked in the prologue to *L'aüstic*:

[The *lai*], I think, is called "the *Aüstic*"; that's what they call it in their land. That's "russignol" in French and "nihtegale" in pure English.

L'Aüstic a nun, ceo m'est vis,
si l'apelent en lur païs;
ceo est russignol en Franceis
e *nihtegale* en dreit Engleis. (*L'aüstic*, ll. 3–6)

Leaving the title word in Breton simultaneously calls attention to and defamiliarizes the object so named – in keeping, perhaps, with the alienability of the "love" that (only momentarily) binds the two protago-

---

[18] Prudence Mary O'Hara Tobin, *Les lais anonymes des 12e et 13e siècles: édition critique de quelques lais bretons*, Publications romanes et françaises 143 (Geneva: Droz, 1976).

nists. A reduced multilingualism appears in the epilogue of *Chievrefueil*: "Very briefly, I'll tell you what it's called: the English call it 'Gotelef;' the French call it 'Honeysuckle'" (Asez briefment le numerai: / "Gotelef" l'apelent Engleis, / "Chievrefueil" le nument Franceis, ll. 114–16). While the combination of English and French places us squarely in Norman England, the omission of a native Celtic translation is striking, particularly since the *lai*'s composition is attributed to a protagonist "born in South Wales" (En Suhtwales…nez, l. 16), meeting secretly in Cornwall with the Irish-born queen. Still, French serves here as the anchor of a multilingual insular "literary system." This emphasis on linguistic exchange and transformation perhaps accounts for the fact that, unlike Chrétien, who condemns those professional storytellers who "habitually mangle and corrupt" (Depecier et corrompre suelent, *Erec et Enide*, l. 21) their material, Marie never disparages those whose tales she appropriates and rewrites. The English "literary system," it seems, is characterized by a regular contact producing a shared knowledge encouraging both the imitation and translation of preexisting forms and motifs and the emergence and circulation of new ones.[19]

The literary process that began with God's gift of talent to Marie culminates in her presentation of the *Lais* themselves to the king:

> In your honor, noble king – you who are so brave and courtly, toward whom all joy inclines, and in whose heart all good things take root – I undertook to assemble some *lais*, retelling them in rhyme. In my heart, I thought and said, lord, that I would present them to you. If it pleases you to accept them, it would bring me great joy: I would be happy for it ever after. Don't think me overbearing if I dare make you this present. Now hear the beginning!

> En l'onur de vus, nobles reis,
> ki tant estes pruz e curteis,
> a qui tute joie s'encline,
> e en qui quer tuz biens racine,
> m'entremis des lais assembler,
> par rime faire e reconter.

---

[19] Thus Jill Mann situates Marie's work in a "distinctive British tradition with its own lines of affiliation" in which (for example) the Middle English *Owl and the Nightingale* draws on both the *Fables* and the *lai* of *L'aüstic*. Jill Mann, *From Aesop to Raynard: Beast Literature in Medieval Britain* (Oxford: Oxford University Press, 2009), p. 1. See also Susan Crane, *Insular Romance: Politics, Faith, and Culture in Anglo-Norman and Middle English Literature* (Berkeley: University of California Press, 1986).

> En mun quer pensoe e diseie,
> sire, ques vos presentereie.
> Se vos les plaist a receveir,
> mult me ferez grant joie aveir;
> a tuz jurs mais en serrai liee.
> Ne me tenez a surquidiee,
> se vos os faire icest present.
> Ore oëz le comencement! (*Lais, Prologue*, ll. 43–56)

Despite her demurral – "Don't think me overbearing!" – Marie's gesture is bold and dramatic. Undertaking on her own initiative an original project intentionally designed to set her apart from the crowd and to win her *pris*, she seeks after the fact to reach the most powerful of patrons.

Modes of transmission

What modern readers perceive as the "writerly" or self-conscious aspect of Marie's work derives from the frequency with which the *Lais* themselves evoke acts of composition or transmission. Twice, however, Marie goes farther, attributing the original composition of the *lai* to an "internal" author: a third-person protagonist who memorializes his or her first-hand "adventure" in narrative form.[20] In *Chievrefueil* (the briefest of the twelve *lais* at 118 lines), the subject matter is defined from the beginning not merely as the lovers' tryst but as the process by which the story itself came to be composed:

> I am quite pleased and eager to tell you *how, of whom, and about what* the *lai* called "Chievrefueil" was composed. Many people recited it to me and I [also] found it in writing.
>
> Asez me plest e bien le vueil
> del lai qu'um nume Chievrefueil
> que la verité vus en cunt
> *coment fu fez, de quei e dunt.*
> Plusur le m'unt cunté e dit
> e jeo l'ai trové en escrit. (*Chievrefueil*, ll. 1–6)

The *lai* records the charming and deceptively simple story of Tristan's forest encounter with the (unnamed) Iseut:

---

[20] Compare the way Guigemar acts as an internal narrator in recounting his "adventure" (aventure, 313) to the lady who wakes him on the magical ship.

On account of the joy he derived from seeing his sweetheart, on account of what he had written [on the stick?], Tristan, who was a good harper, made a new *lai* of it in order to remember the words, just as the queen had commanded him to do.

Pur la joie qu'il ot eüe
de s'amie qu'il ot veüe
e pur ceo qu'il aveit escrit,
si cum la reïne l'ot dit,
pur les paroles remembrer,
Tristram ki bien saveit harper,
en aveit fet un nuvel lai. (*Chievrefueil*, ll. 107–13)

The syntax here seems ambiguous: are the words Tristan seeks to remember those he carved on the hazel branch or those spoken by the queen during their brief rendezvous? In either case, the *lai* is cast as a mnemonic for or commemoration of messages originally exchanged in secret. The explicit mention of Tristan's talent reminds us of the musical nature of the *lais* (already evoked in the epilogue to *Guigemar*); meanwhile, since Marie has already noted in the *lai*'s prologue that "many people told it to me *and* I found it in writing" (Plusur le m'unt cunté et dit / e jeo l'ai trové en escrit, ll. 5–6), *Chievrefueil* serves as a point of convergence of a multilayered process of transmission, translation, transcription, and (perhaps) versification.

The complexities of internal authorship assume a different form in *Chaitivel*, the *lai* that comes with a double title: "It is called 'Chaitivel.' There are also many people who call it 'The Four Sorrows'" ("Le Chaitivel" l'apelë hum, / e si i a plusurs de cels / ki l'apelent "les Quatre Doels," ll. 6–8).[21] A similar slippage occurs in the final *lai* of Harley 978, whose original name, we are told, was *Eliduc* (l. 23), "but the name is now changed, for the adventure the *lai* recounts befell the ladies" (mes ore est li nuns remuëz, / kar des dames est avenu / l'aventure dunt li lais fu, ll. 24–6), Guildeluëc and Guilliadun. However, where in *Eliduc* the name change remains a metatextual question, in *Chaitivel* the two surviving characters themselves dispute the title of the *lai* spun of their adventures:

"Because I loved you so, I want my pain to be remembered. I'll make a *lai* about the four of you and will call it Four Pains."

---

[21] In Chapter 6, we examine this *lai* as a programmatic exploration of the problematics of non-differentiation.

When the knight heard this, he quickly replied: "Lady, make the new *lai*, and call it The Wretched One."

"Pur ceo que tant vus ai amez,
vueil que mis doels seit remembrez.
De vus quatre ferai un lai
e Quatre Doels le numerai."
Li chevaliers li respundi
hastivement, quant il l'oï:
"Dame, faites le lai novel,
si l'apelez Le Chaitivel!" (*Chaitivel*, ll. 201–8)

Like *Eliduc*, this *lai* poses the alternation between male and female, individual and multiple protagonists. Insisting that his ongoing suffering trumps her punctual loss, the knight, who has lost all, wins the lady to his point of view: "In faith," she said, "that's fine with me. Let's call it 'The Wretched One'" ("Par fei," fet ele, "ceo m'est bel. / Or l'apelum 'Le Chaitivel,'" ll. 229–30). Nevertheless, the epilogue shows that the consensus reached by the protagonists is not quite authoritative:

> Thus was the *lai* begun, completed, and published. Those who diffused it – some of them – call it "Four Sorrows." Each of the names is appropriate, for the content calls for it; mostly, it's called "The Wretched One." Here's where it ends: there's *no more*. I haven't heard *any more* and don't know *any more* about it, nor will I tell you *any more*.

Issi fu li lais comenciez
e puis parfaiz e anunciez.
Icil kil porterent avant,
"Quatre Doels" l'apelent alquant.
Chescuns des nuns bien i afiert,
kar la matire le requiert;
Le Chaitivel a nun en us.
Ici finist, il n'i a *plus*:
plus n'en oï ne *plus* n'en sai
ne *plus* ne vus en cunterai. (*Chaitivel*, ll. 231–40)

From the '*completely* done' (*par*faiz) of line 232 to the four-part repetition of "ne...plus" in the last three lines of the poem, Marie's unaccustomed insistence on the finality of the tale reinforces its thematization of sterility. Rather than emphasizing the chain of transmission (as in her other epilogues), she locates the *lai*'s legacy – its claim to *remembrance* – in its proliferation of titles and points of view.

Alongside internal authorship, the texts likewise thematize communication through their focus on material objects. The objects that fill the *Lais* function as reified bits of stories, relationships, or material histories. They are nodes of interconnection between past and present, points of suture between feudal society and the fairy Otherworld.[22] *Chievrefueil* – along with *L'aüstic* the only *lai* not to bear the name of one (or more) of its protagonists – stages multiple acts of communication, shaped by the dialectics of writing and orality, of secrecy and circulation, that turn around the titular object. On learning that the queen will soon pass by on her way to the Pentecost court at Tintagel, the exiled Tristan carves his name into the branch of a hazel tree, knowing that the queen will recognize it as a sign of his presence, since they had used similar means in the past. "The gist of the inscription" (la sume de l'escrit, l. 61), we are told, is that he has long awaited the chance to see her; that he couldn't live without her; that they were like the hazel and the honeysuckle which, once entwined, would die if separated, culminating in the beautiful couplet: "Fair friend, so it is with us: neither you without me nor I without you!" (Bele amie, si est de nus: ne vus senz mei ne jeo senz vus!, ll. 77–8).

L'aüstic is presented as the culmination of a long process of displacement and transformation. The bird that gives the *lai* its name enters the story as a pretext: the excuse the lady invents on the spot when her husband angrily asks why she gets up so often in the middle of the night:

> "Lord," the lady replied, "whoever has not heard the nightingale sing has no joy in this world. That's why you see me standing here. From here I hear it sing so sweetly at night that it brings me great pleasure. It delights me so and I so desire it that I can't sleep a wink."

> "Sire," la dame li respunt,
> "il nen a joie en icest mund,
> ki nen ot l'aüstic chanter;
> pur ceo me vois ici ester.
> Tant dulcement l'i oi la nuit
> que mult me semble grant deduit;
> tant me delite e tant le vueil
> que jeo ne puis dormir de l'ueil." (*L'aüstic*, ll. 83–90)

---

[22] In Chapter 3 we examine some of the uses of objects as correlatives of identity and lineage. Compare the eponymous objects in Chrétien de Troyes's *Le chevalier de la Charrete* and *Le conte du graal* – objects that trouble or withhold meaning as much as they communicate it.

The rest of the tale, in essence, explains how this *pre*-text becomes the *text* we are reading. The process begins when the lady's husband takes her words literally, snaring the hapless nightingale and, instead of (for example) presenting it to her in a cage, spitefully wrings its neck and throws it (geta, l. 117) at her – echoing the way she and her lover used to throw (geter, l. 44) tokens back and forth to each other – staining her shift with its blood. Sorrowfully gathering up the broken corpse, the lady transforms it into a signifier to communicate to her lover the reason for her absence:

> She wrapped the bird in a piece of samite, writing everything in gold embroidery. She called a serving boy and, entrusting her message to him, sent him to her friend. He went to the knight; delivering his lady's greeting, he recited her entire message and gave him the nightingale.

> En une piece de samit,
> a or brusdé a tut escrit,
> a l'oiselet envolupé.
> Un suen vaslet a apelé.
> Sun message li a chargié,
> a sun ami l'a enveié.
> Cil est al chevalier venuz.
> De sa dame li dist saluz,
> tut sun message li cunta
> e l'aüstic li presenta. (*L'aüstic*, ll. 135–44)

As in *Milun*, the body of the bird is a necessary but not a sufficient signi-fier: redoubled, in *Milun*, by the letters concealed in the swan's plumage, and here trebled by the written words embroidered on the silken cloth and the spoken words delivered by its bearer.[23] Making no further effort to contact the lady, her lover seals the dead nightingale in a custom-made jewel-encrusted gold casket, transforming the bird opportunistically seized upon as the justification of a lovers' rendezvous into a relic com-memorating their now "entombed" relationship. But this is not the end of the transformational chain:

---

[23] Alternatively, E. Jane Burns conjectures that "samit a or brusdé *e tut escrit*" could refer to a reused piece of Islamic silk with Arabic lettering. See her *Sea of Silk: A Textile Geography of Women's Work in Medieval French Literature* (Philadelphia: University of Pennsylvania Press, 2009), p. 51.

> The adventure was told: it couldn't be hidden for long. The
> Bretons made a *lai* of it; it is called the *Aüstic*.

> Cele aventure fu cuntee,
> ne pot estre lunges celee.
> Un lai en firent li Bretun
> e l'Aüstic l'apelë hum. (*L'aüstic*, ll. 157–60)

Like *Bisclavret*, *L'aüstic* preserves a native Breton word as its title. But
where *Bisclavret* (as we shall see) turns around the relation between
generic and proper names, *L'aüstic* contrasts the stability of the signifier
with the multiple transformations of the signified. Beginning as a mere
pretext for the lovers' clandestine meetings, the nightingale is converted
into the symbol of the husband's revenge, then enveloped by multiple
layers of material and verbal covers: the samite wrap, the embroidered
explanation, the messenger's account, the specially commissioned re-
ceptacle, the Breton *lai*, and, finally, Marie's French translation. In a
sense, the mutability of the *aüstic* resembles that of the word *lai* itself,
which in different contexts has been taken to refer (among other things)
to a melody or song, oral sources like those from which Marie claims
to derive inspiration, and vernacular tales such as Marie's *Lais*.[24] The
prologue, text, and epilogue of *L'aüstic* together hint at this metacriti-
cal complexity – the foreign word *aüstic* (like the dead bird to which it
refers) encased as a kind of talismanic remnant in a new *romanz* setting
that bears the same name.

Given the intensity of this attention to the dynamics of transmission
and translation throughout the tales, it is somewhat surprising that the
Lais lack an epilogue. As we see below, the *Ysopë*, the *Espurgatoire seint
Patriz*, and the *Vie seinte Audree* all end with striking epilogues which
have played a large role in the construction of Marie de France as an
author. The concluding lines of the collection as it is preserved in Harley
978 remain those of *Eliduc*, which, echoing other *lais*, describe how "the
ancient Bretons…composed the *lai* to remember, since it should not be
forgotten" (li anciën Bretun… / firent le lai pur remembrer, / qu'um nel
deüst pas obliër, ll. 1182–4). It is left to the reader to assess how well
Marie has acquitted the obligation imposed on her by her God-given
talent, and to wonder at the success of her appeal to the "noble king."

---

[24] For an exhaustive discussion of this point, see Richard Baum, *Recherches sur les
oeuvres attribuées à Marie de France*, Annales Universitatis Saraviensis, Philosophische
Fakultät 9 (Heidelberg: Carl Winter Universitätsverlag, 1968), pp. 29–41.

Ysopë

Of all the texts attributed to Marie de France, none raises questions of authorship and originality more intensely than her *Ysopë*, commonly known as the *Fables*. Anchored by the proper name of a legendary figure who may never have existed, the Aesopic tradition, from antiquity to the present, is the history of its multiple transformations: from Greek into Latin and from Latin into the many vernaculars of medieval Europe, from prose to verse and back again.[25] Of the 102 fables in Marie's collection, the first 40 derive from the eleventh-century *Romulus Nilanti*, representing the English branch of the Latin prose *Romulus* – itself a ninth-century reworking (perhaps from the cathedral school of Reims) of Phaedrus, the more learnèd and difficult of the two main Latin branches of Aesopic material transmitted to the medieval West.[26] Nor was Marie the only twelfth-century writer interested in the Aesopic tradition: roughly contemporary with her Old French *Ysopë*, a certain "Walter of England" composed a Latin *Romulus* destined to become the dominant version of the late Middle Ages, attested in over 200 surviving manuscripts.[27] Meanwhile, the theologian and natural philosopher Alexander of Neckam, foster brother of Richard Lion Heart, produced *two* collections: the *Novus Aesopus* (rendering forty-two of *Romulus*'s prose fables in verse) and the *Novus Avianus* (translating the Greek verse of Babrius into Latin). As Seth Lerer writes, Aesop "always existed to be translated … language change and textual transmission are what fables are about" – and never more so than in the late twelfth and early thirteenth centuries.[28] In this long history of its repeated transformations, Marie's stands out as the first attested translation into a western vernacular tongue.[29]

Given this material's highly conventional nature, it is somewhat ironic that the name by which Marie is known today is derived from her "signature" in this most protean of texts:

---

[25] Mann, *From Aesop to Raynard*, p. 2. For a summary of the tradition, see ibid., pp. 2–8.

[26] The other was Avianus, from the late-antique figure who translated Babrius's Greek versification into Latin couplets. Seth Lerer, *Children's Literature: A Reader's History, from Aesop to Harry Potter* (Chicago: University of Chicago Press, 2008), pp. 41–3. The *Romulus Nilanti* may also have inspired the fables represented in the borders of the Bayeux Tapestry. Mann, *From Aesop to Raynard*, p. 9.

[27] Mann, *From Aesop to Raynard*, pp. 11–12.

[28] Lerer, *Children's Literature*, p. 36.

[29] Mann, *From Aesop to Raynard*, p. 9.

> At the end of this text that I've translated and told in Romance, I will name myself in order to be remembered: my name is Marie and I am from France. Many clerics might try to take my work as their own; I don't want anyone to claim it. Whoever lets himself be forgotten is crazy.

> Al finement de cest escrit
> que en romanz ai treité e dit,
> me numerai pur remembrance:
> Marie ai nun, si sui de France.
> Put cel estre que clerc plusur
> prendereient sur eus mun labur,
> ne voil que nul sur li le die;
> cil fet que fol ki sei ublie. (*Ysopë*, epilogue, 1–8)

In the late Middle Ages, as Keith Busby has shown, Marie's name was in fact more closely linked to the *Ysopë* than to the *Lais*, as if "the genre became largely divorced from the name of its most celebrated practitioner in less than a century after her death."[30] Modern critics, too, have fastened on the *Ysopë* as exemplary of Marie's distinctive style and voice:

> A writer of remarkable range and facility, Marie produced a set of poems that get at the heart of the Aesopic idiom. In her verses, beasts speak in the powerful colloquialisms of the vernacular. Morals appear not with the heavy hand of the schoolteacher but the wit of the courtier. Throughout, there emerges an authorial identity whose self-awareness stands on par with that of Babrius and Phaedrus, authors who had imagined themselves working not just with but also against the authority of Aesop.[31]

As we shall see in the next chapter, Marie's renditions of Aesopic material – in keeping with medieval practices of translation and adaptation – are distinctive in their strong emphasis on feudal relations and other fea-

---

[30] Harley 978 contains "the only copy of *Guigemar* to have an ungarbled version" of the prologue in which Marie names herself. Elsewhere, the *lais* we today take as Marie's appear amidst anonymous *lais bretons* and other short narratives without authorial attribution. Keith Busby, *Codex and Context; Reading Old French Verse Narrative in Manuscript*, 2 vols. (Amsterdam and New York: Rodopi, 2002), vol. 1, pp. 472–3. For a consideration of "generic consciousness" of the *lai* in manuscript context, see Keith Busby, "The Manuscripts of Marie de France," in *A Companion to Marie de France*, ed. Logan E. Whalen (Leiden: Brill, 2011), pp. 310–11.

[31] Lerer, *Children's Literature*, p. 46. He therefore focuses attention on the fable of "the wolf at school" (pp. 47–8).

tures directly related to her presumed place in, or familiarity with, courtly society.

In its proliferation across languages and cultures, the Aesopic material functions as a "text network," Daniel Selden's term for the premodern mode of textuality produced by translation and variation. Stretching from antiquity through the invention of the printing press, the text network was "arguably the most common type of diffusional patterning" in a vast geocultural zone spanning much of Eurasia. Works now as well known as the Alexander Romance and as obscure as the *Life of Ahiqar* circulated, "both within and across languages,…in a bewildering number of differing exemplars, many of which…possessed equal claims to authority," with each variant constituting "less a neutral translation of its *Vorlage*, than an appropriation apposite to ethnically divergent contexts, which brought matters of local dominance, assertion, and resistance unequivocally to the fore."[32] Text networks "explicitly thematize their own dissemination, which suggests that their cross-cultural transmission is less an arbitrary matter dependent upon taste, than structurally encoded in the works themselves."[33] In this light, we can better understand Petrus Alfonsi, author of the *Disciplina Clericalis*, as:

> one of a long string of writers who culled proverbs and fables from various sources, rewrote them in his own words, and forged them into a new and original text. The confusing proliferation of these sources, in their various versions, makes it impossible to point to direct sources for Alfonsi's work. This confusion (or richness) of sources shows that medieval writers and scribes – Muslims, Jewish, and Christian – valued these aphorisms and tales. It also shows a willingness to adapt this material to the needs and circumstances of the various societies through which these stories passed. These writers were not classicists interested in faithful textual transmission; they were storytellers, teachers, and moralizers, and their goal was to make their material accessible and entertaining for their readers and listeners.[34]

As one node in a wide-ranging text network, Marie's *Ysopë* is an early example of the wave of vernacular "wisdom literature" translations making their way into Latin Europe, usually via Latin, from the second half of the

---

[32] Daniel Selden, "Text Networks," *Ancient Narrative* 8 (2009): 1–23 (at 3–4).

[33] Ibid., 13. Compare the *fabliaux*'s thematization and displacement of questions of their own origins. See R. Howard Bloch, *The Scandal of the Fabliaux* (Chicago: University of Chicago Press, 1986), pp. 1–21.

[34] Tolan, *Petrus Alfonsi*, p. 91.

twelfth century. Originally of eastern (Indian) or Middle Eastern (Biblical, Persian, or Arabic) provenance, texts such as *The Seven Sages of Rome* and *Barlaam and Josaphat* circulated in variants that proliferated across linguistic, cultural, and religious lines in ways that wreak havoc with any attempts to assign them to discrete literary traditions.[35] The "literary complex" of the legend of *Barlaam and Josaphat*, for example,

> spread into nearly all the countries of Christendom and is extant in over sixty versions in the main languages of Europe, the Christian East and Africa. The Greek version of the legend was translated into the major Slavonic languages, into Armenian and Christian Arabic; and this latter version gave rise to an Ethiopic translation. All the Western European versions derived from the several Latin translations, the first of which was made from the Greek in 1048. Thus, the legend appeared in French, German, Spanish, English, Italian, Dutch and Scandinavian versions, and even, at the beginning of the eighteenth century, returned to the East in a Philippine dialect. It was also included in Vincent de Beauvais's thirteenth-century *Speculum historiale*, and in the *Legenda aurea* of Jacobus de Voragine in the same century.[36]

The second half of the twelfth century saw the translation of the frame tale collection *The Seven Sages of Rome* into vernacular French – a node in the diffusion of this material throughout Latin Europe:

> Translations and *remaniements* of the *Sept Sages* number in the hundreds, and they appear over a period of 800 years in nearly every European language – rendered from French, or French derivatives, into Latin, Middle English, Middle Scots, Celtic, Italian, Spanish, Dutch, German, Danish, Icelandic, Norwegian, Swedish, Polish, Russian, Armenian, and so on.[37]

[35] On the Asian, especially Mesopotamian antecedents of the Aesopic material, normally taken as a quintessential part of the Greco-Roman tradition, see Haim Schwarzbaum, *The Mishle Shu'alim (Fox Fables) of Rabbi Berechiah ha-Nakdan: A Study in Comparative Folklore and Fable Lore* (Kiron, Israel: Institute for Jewish and Arab Folklore Research, 1979), pp. xix–xx.

[36] Philip Almond, "The Buddha of Christendom: A Review of the Legend of Barlaam and Josaphat," *Religious Studies* 23:3 (1987): 391–406 (at 391). *Barlaam et Josaphat* survives in BNF fr. 1553, the well-known late-thirteenth-century Picard "miscellany" whose fifty-two pieces include the "K" redaction of the *Sept Sages de Rome* and several *lais* (not of Marie de France). See *Le Roman des Sept Sages de Rome. A Critical Edition of the Two Verse Redactions of a Twelfth-Century Romance*, ed. Mary B. Speer, Edward C. Armstrong Monographs on Medieval Literature 4 (Lexington: French Forum, 1989), p. 18; and Busby, *Codex and Context*, vol. 1, p. 472.

[37] Though not extant, the "archetype" version long posited by critics has been dated to c. 1155–90, slightly earlier than or exactly contemporary with the *oeuvre* of Marie de

The ongoing appeal of such material in the later Middle Ages is attested in an inventory of vernacular volumes that the French queen Jeanne d'Evreux purchased from the estate of her sister-in-law, Clémence of Hungary, after the latter's death in 1328. Among the texts specially selected by the queen were a *Barlaam and Josaphat* and "a book containing the *Romance of the Seven Sages* and Aesopic fables."[38]

In the first- or second-century *Life of Aesop* (itself likely reflecting a long preceding oral tradition), Aesop appears as a hideously ugly slave, graced by the gods with "skill in the invention, weaving, and making of Greek fables." After a series of picaresque adventures spent in the service of a pompous philosopher, his skills at storytelling and divining take him to the courts of Kings Croesus of Lydia and Lycurgus of Babylon, and finally to Delphi.[39] In the medieval tradition, on the other hand, the ruler to whom the *Ysopë* is attached is Romulus, the last Roman emperor deposed by Odoacer in 476.[40]

> Romulus, who was emperor, wrote to his son, commanding him and showing him through exemplary tales how he should be on guard so that no man could deceive him.

> Romulus, ki fu emperere,
> a sun fiz escrit, si manda
> e par essample li mustra
> cum il se deust cuntreguaiter
> que hum nel peust enginner. (*Ysopë*, prologue, 12–16)

In what might otherwise be cast as a quintessentially pedagogical scene

---

France. Speer, *Le Roman des Sept Sages*, p. 18 (with further discussion of dating on pp. 67–71).

[38] Joan Holladay, "Fourteenth-Century French Queens as Collectors and Readers of Books: Jeanne d'Evreux and Her Contemporaries," *Journal of Medieval History* 32 (2006): 69–100 (at 85–6).

[39] Leslie Kurke, "Plato, Aesop, and the Beginnings of Mimetic Prose," *Representations* 94 (2006): 6–52 (at 12–13). In Plato's *Phaedo*, Socrates, in prison and awaiting execution, recounts how he had turned to versifying the fables of Aesop (14). Kurke analyzes these references to Socrates' interest in Aesop as a simultaneous acknowledgment and disavowal of the complex relation between the "low" fable tradition and the ambiguous emergence of the Platonic dialogue as mimetic prose.

[40] Historically, this makes the question of the efficacy of his advice to his son something of an inside joke. *Romulus*, as we saw above, was one of the titles under which Aesopic material circulated in the Latin Middle Ages. For Mann, Marie's allusion to Romulus is part of her broader interest in establishing an "aristocratic pedigree" for her work. Mann, *From Aesop to Reynard*, p. 55.

(as in the *Seven Sages of Rome*), the eponymous Aesop is assigned an unlooked-for role:

> To his master, who knew him very well, Aesop wrote some fables he had composed, *translating them from Greek into Latin*. Everyone marveled that he should put his mind to such a task; but there are no fables so foolish that don't contain some philosophy in the concluding morals, where the stories' full essence is found.

> Esopes escrist a sun mestre
> que bien cunust lui e sun estre,
> unes fables ke ot trovees,
> *de griu en latin translatees.*
> Merveille en eurent li plusur
> qu'il mist sun sen en tel labur;
> mes n'i ad fable de folie
> u il n'en ait philosophie
> es essamples ki sunt aprés,
> u des cuntes est tut li fes. (*Ysopë*, prologue, 17–26)

Here the legendary Greek fabulist – his servile status remembered in his relationship to his imperial "master" – is transformed into the original *translator* of the fables from Greek into Latin. As in her other works, Marie explicitly thematizes questions of transmission and translation. The "sen" that Aesop brings to his task, moreover, echoes the "sen" that, in the *Prologue* to the *Lais* (l. 16), the moderns are pictured as investing in their interpretation of classical texts. But the suggestion that the philosophy to be gained in the process must first be extracted from the "folie" of the fables, rather than from the obscurity of the ancients, takes us far from the world of the *Lais*.

In retrospect, something of this recalibration is hinted at in the opening passage of the prologue:

> Those who are educated should focus their attention on good books, writings, exempla, and stories that the philosophers composed, wrote, and conserved. For morality's sake, they wrote down the good proverbs they heard so that those who put their effort into good could benefit. This is what the ancient fathers did.

> Cil ki seivent de lettrerure
> devreient bien mettre lur cure
> es bons livres e es escriz

> e as essamples e as diz
> ke li philosophe troverent
> e escristrent e remembrerent:
> par moralité escriveient
> les bons pruverbes qu'il oieient
> que cil amender se peüssent
> ki lur entente en bien eüssent;
> ceo firent li ancïen pere. (*Ysopë*, prologue, ll. 1–12)

As in the *Lais*, Marie opens with something like the obligations that fall on the learnèd, this time devoid of the religious framework suggested by the talent given by God. In contrast to the "ancients" and "philosophers" of the *Lais*, moreover, those described here write, not obscurely in antici-pation of the intellectual prowess of those to come, but openly – the better to further their education. In this context, it is easy at first to assume that this education is primarily moral; the quick cut to Emperor Romulus and his son, however, highlights the eminently *practical* wisdom needed "to guard against" (cuntreguaiter) a sordid world of schemers and deceivers.

Moving from ancient to modern scenes of patronage, the subse-quent lines introduce another significant difference. In the *Lais*, Marie had responded to God's gift of talent by choosing her own project and presenting the results to the "noble king." This time, in contrast, the choice was not her own:

> I, who had to versify them, would not at all have thought of recounting much of what is found here. Nevertheless, I was summoned by he who is the flower of chivalry, learning, and courtesy; since such a man was doing the asking, there was no way I wanted to avoid putting work and effort into it; never mind who might think me base for responding to his request.

> A mei, ki dei la rime faire,
> n'avenist nïent a retraire
> plusurs paroles que i sunt;
> mes nepuruc cil me sumunt,
> ki flurs est de chevalerie,
> d'enseignement, de curteisie;
> e quant tel hume me ad requise,
> ne voil lesser en nule guise
> que n'i mette travail e peine,
> ki que m'en tienge pur vileine,
> de fere mut pur sa preere. (*Ysopë*, prologue, ll. 27–37)

Curiously, Marie characterizes her work as "rhyming" (la rime faire, l. 27), rather than translating, the fables that "Aesop" had rendered from Greek into Latin. Of course there is something slightly paradoxical in translating into the vernacular a text whose widespread diffusion in the Middle Ages was the result of its popularity as a schooltext for learning Latin.[41] Focusing on the work of versification rather than translation perhaps hints at the elevation of material about which Marie herself visibly harbors reservations. The flattering insistence on her patron's courtly accomplishments cannot quite efface the hint of coercion implied in the choice of the verb "dei" or conceal the fact that this time, what she has invested in the project is "travail e peine" rather than, as in the *Lais*, the value-added (surplus) of her "sen" (*Lais, Prologue*, l. 16).[42]

The project of romancing the *Romulus* corpus would seem to suggest that Marie is returning to the exercise she had explicitly eschewed in the *Lais*: translating a text from Latin into Old French. Not until the text's epilogue do we belatedly learn that this is not in fact the case:

> This book is called Esope because he translated it and wrote it down, turning it from Greek into Latin. King Alfred, who loved it, then translated it *into English*, and I versified it in French as fittingly as I could.

> Esopë apel'um cest livre,
> qu'il translata e fist escrire,
> del griu en latin le turna;
> li reis Alvrez, que mut l'ama,
> le translata puis *en engleis*,
> e jeo l'ai rimee en franceis,
> si cum jeo poi plus proprement. (*Ysopë*, epilogue, ll. 13–19)

No evidence of an Anglo-Saxon *Aesop* survives. Still, the multilingual Britain described in Chapter 1 suggests that the scepticism that has met Marie's claim on the grounds that "it is hard to imagine a twelfth-century French-speaker being able to understand Old English" is ripe for reconsideration.[43] Whether or not we lend credence to Marie's assertion, she sketches an itinerary – from Greek to Latin to Anglo-Saxon to French – whose unanticipated rerouting of the *matière de Rome* into a kind of

---

[41] Mann, *From Aesop to Reynard*, pp. 6–7.

[42] We are reminded of Chrétien de Troyes in the prologue of *Le chevalier de la charrete*, contributing his "painne et...antancïon" (l. 29) to the "san" (meaning, l. 26) imposed on him by his patron, the countess of Champagne.

[43] Mann, *From Aesop to Reynard*, p. 10.

matter of Britain evokes the proliferating nodes of the text network over the straight lines of *translatio studii*, as articulated in the prologue to Chrétien de Troyes's *Cligés*.[44] Nor is Marie's *Ysopë* the end of the story: reversing the usual directionality of Latin-to-Romance transmission, her vernacular version subsequently served as a partial source for the Latin prose translation known as the *Romulus LBG*, as well as the late-twelfth- or early-thirteenth-century Hebrew collection *Fox Fables* (*Meslai Shu'alim*) by Rabbi Berechiah ben Natronai ha-Nakdan.[45]

Also in the epilogue, Marie finally names the paragon of chivalry who had charged her with the unwanted commission:

> It was for love of Count William, the most valiant in any realm, that I undertook to write this book, translating it from English into Romance.

> Par amur le cunte Willame,[46]
> le plus vaillant de nul realme,
> m'entremis de cest livre feire
> e de l'engleis en romanz treire. (*Ysopë*, epilogue, ll. 9–12)

In these four lines, Marie reveals a literary system in which it was possible to imagine the transmission of a work originally in the Greco-Roman

[44] Chrétien de Troyes, *Cligés*, ed. and trans. Charles Méla and Olivier Collet (Paris: Librairie Générale Française, 1994), ll. 30–9.

[45] Mann, *From Aesop to Reynard*, pp. 10–11. Born in France, Berechiah has been tentatively identified with a "Benedictus le Poncteur" (a literal translation of "Berechiah ha-Nakdan") mentioned in a late-twelfth-century document from Oxford – placing him, like Marie, in an Anglo-Norman context. Berechiah ha-Nakdan, *Fables of a Jewish Aesop*, trans. Moses Hadas (New York: Columbia University Press, 1967), p. xvi. Though some "correspondences of detail," including a misreading of "cerfs" (deer) for "serfs" in Fable 41, suggest that Marie was Berechiah ben Natronai's immediate source, Schwarzbaum emphasizes their common descent from the *Romulus* tradition (*Mishle Shu'alim*, p. xxxii). On the misreading, see Marie de France, *Fables*, p. 272n. Recently, Michael Chernick has suggested that Berechiah ben Natronai ha-Nakdan may also have authored a tale of "King Solomon's Daughter," which combines narrative elements recognizable from *Guigemar*, *Yonec*, *Les dous amanz*, and *Bisclavret*. Michael Chernick, "Marie de France in the Synagogue," *Exemplaria* 19:1 (2007): 183–205.

[46] The identity of Count William, like that of Marie herself, has been the object of much conjecture. Candidates have included Henry II's illegitimate son William Longsword and the celebrated knight William Marshal; see June Hall McCash, "Sidney Painter (1902–1960): The Issue of Patronage for Marie de France," in *The Reception and Transmission of the Works of Marie de France, 1774–1974*, ed. Chantal Maréchal, Mediaeval Studies 23 (Lewiston: Edwin Mellen Press, 2003), pp. 178–84. Carla Rossi proposes William de Mandeville, earl of Essex – the candidate originally proposed by Sidney Painter. See Rossi, *Marie de France et les érudits de Cantorbéry*, p. 188.

wisdom literature tradition from *Anglo-Saxon* to French – all this at the instigation of a noble, chivalrous, and courtly patron, bypassing Latin and the clergy entirely. What we may be glimpsing here is something like "the new ruling class of England: a Breton, Norman, and Saxon mix, composed of counts, barons, knights, clerics, treasurers and itinerant judges of the Plantagenêt court, depository of a heterogeneous culture for which new common roots were needed."[47] In fact, for all the conventional piety with which Marie concludes her epilogue – "Now I pray God Almighty that I may undertake the kind of task that will allow me to dedicate my soul to him" (Ore pri a Deu omnipotent / kë a tel ovre puisse entendre / që a lui pusse m'alme rendre (*Ysopë*, epilogue, ll. 20–2) – what distinguishes the *Fables*, as we see in the next chapter, is their thoroughgoing adherence to the mentalities of feudal society.

Espurgatoire seint Patriz

In the *Espurgatoire seint Patriz*, Marie de France finally does what she had explicitly rejected before: translate a text from Latin into French – namely, the *Tractatus de Purgatorio Sancti Patricii* by the Cistercian monk H. de Saltrey:

> *In the name of God* – may He be with us and send us his grace – I want to write down in Romance, as the book tells us, for the sake of memory and remembrance, the place where one enters the pains of Purgatory, *that God showed Saint Patrick.*

> *Al nun de Deu* – qui od nus seit
> e qui sa grace nus enveit –
> voil en romanz mettre en escrit,
> si cum li livres le nus dit,
> en remembrance e en memoire,
> des peines de l'Espurgatoire
> *k'a Seint Patriz volt Deus mustrer*
> le liu ou l'om i deit entrer. (*Espurgatoire*, ll. 1–9)

God is present here both at the beginning and ending of this opening passage, not as the initiator of a personal exchange in which a gift of talent must be requited, but as the prime mover who revealed the mouth of Purgatory to Saint Patrick and in whose name Marie sets out to tell

---

[47] Rossi, *Marie de France et les érudits de Cantorbéry*, p. 15.

about it. Gone are references to "the philosophers" and "the ancients."
For Marie, the Latin text is inseparable from the spiritual subject matter
that seems to displace the worldly concerns evident in her previous two
translations. Reading biographically, one would be tempted to construct a
narrative of conversion – of a turn *to* religion and *away* from the concerns
of the secular world. The story of precisely how Marie came to translate
this text is, however, more ambiguous:

> A worthy man asked me to do it a while ago. That's why I've
> now undertaken to set myself to this task: to respect and honor
> him. So if he wants and is willing – may he always keep me in
> his good graces – I'll relate what I've heard about it.

> Uns prosdom m'ad peça requise;
> pur ço m'en sui ore entremise,
> de mettre mei en cel labur,
> pur reverence e pur s'onur.
> E si lui plest e il le voille
> – k'en ses bienfaiz tuz jurs m'acoille –
> dirai ço ke j'en ai oï.[48] (*Espurgatoire*, ll. 9–15)

In contrast to her enthusiasm in composing the *Lais* "in honor" of the
noble king, or even the *Ysopë* "for love" of the courtly Count William,
the initiative here lies wholly with the patron who commissioned the work
that has in turn led her (back) to God:

> Never would I have undertaken [this task] nor set out to study
> it if you, who are so sweet and dear to my heart, had not asked
> me. I haven't heard or read much about it. What I have heard
> has increased my love of God and my desire to serve God, my
> Creator. This is why I would like to open this text and make
> it known.

> ja de ço ne m'entremesisse
> n'en estudie ne me mesisse
> si ne fust pur vostre priere
> k'en mun quer est duce e chïere.
> Poi en ai oï e veü;
> par ço ke j'en ai entendu,
> ai jo vers Deu greignur amur
> de Deu servir, mun Creatur.

---

[48] This wording suggests *oral* transmission, as if Purgatory had previously been
explained to her or that discussion of it were in the air.

> Par quei jo vodrai aovrir
> ceste escripture e descovrir. (*Espurgatoire*, ll. 21–30)

Against the grain of biographical explanations of her choice of project, Marie represents her "greater love" for God as the result, not the cause, of the externally imposed task of translation.

If the alleged Anglo-Saxon provenance of the *Ysopë* called attention to the British literary system, the *Espurgatoire* extends that system into the wider world of the Irish Sea. One of the earliest texts in Anglo-Norman, the early twelfth-century *Voyage de saint Brendan* (a vernacular translation of the Latin *Navigatio Brendani*), was probably commissioned by the English queen Matilda of Scotland (the first wife of King Henry I "Beauclerc" and maternal grandmother of Henry II). Patron to an "international group of poets and composers," Matilda came from a family keenly interested in literary transmission.[49] Her father, Malcolm III Canmore of Scotland, kept a multilingual court and was himself conversant in Gaelic, English, and French; her mother, the Anglo-Saxon princess Margaret, was an "avid collector of manuscripts" who assembled what would become the royal library of Scotland.[50] Two of Matilda's brothers were also patrons of the arts. Alexander (together with his queen, Sibyl) commissioned a "truly cosmopolitan" poem on the missionary saint Columba: "a monk with an English name [Simeon] at a church [Iona] within the Norwegian kingdom wrote verses commemorating an Irish saint for a Scottish king under the direction of an Orkney/Manx bishop [William "the Old" of the Orkneys]."[51] David (r. 1124–53) – the favorite uncle of Henry II – was a childhood friend of Ailred of Rievaulx; his court became "a meeting ground for Gaelic, Old English, and French literary interests." Among the visitors to his court was the future saint Malachy (mentioned in l. 2074 of the *Espurgatoire*), the "sometime bishop" of the Irish see of Armagh, whose death (1148) and canonization provide the *terminus a quo* for Marie's source text, H. de Saltrey's *Tractatus de Purgatorio Sancti Patricii*. Malachy visited Scotland c. 1140 while returning to Ireland from Rome (where he was made papal legate for Ireland), via Clairvaux (where

---

[49] Benjamin Hudson, *Irish Sea Studies 900–1200* (Dublin: Four Courts Press, 2006), p. 204.

[50] Ibid., p. 202. One "miracle" from a biography by Margaret's confessor, commissioned by her daughter, Matilda, relates that a gospel book lost while the queen was crossing a river was later retrieved, undamaged, on the far shore. Perhaps not incidentally, similar incidents are told of Saints Columba and Cuthbert – saints of interest to Matilda's brothers Alexander and David, respectively. Ibid., p. 202.

[51] Ibid., p. 206.

he got to know Saint Bernard, who subsequently wrote his biography).
Stopping in at King David's court at Carlisle, Malachy (according to his
Vita) cured the king's sick son and engaged in discussions on the Irish
origins of Saint Cuthbert.[52] In the mid twelfth century, the Scottish court
was an important point of contact between British and Continental intellectual circuits on the one hand and "a Gaelic-speaking cultural area that
extended from southwest Ireland to northwest Scotland" on the other.[53]

Questions of translation are written into the *Espurgatoire* itself.[54] When
Abbot Gervais sends the monk Gilbert to Leinster to claim land the king
of Ireland had promised the Cistercians for the new monastery of Balt-
inglass:

> The monk said he didn't know how he would live there. He
> hadn't learned and didn't speak the language of that country.
> The king said: "Never fear. I'll introduce you to a worthy man
> and good translator." Then he summoned the knight Owein,
> asking him to go with [Gilbert] and instruct him.

> Li moines dist k'il ne saveit
> coment il i arestereit:
> il ne saveit ne n'out apris
> le language de cel païs.
> Li reis lui dist: "N'en doutez mie,
> jo vus metrai en compaignie
> un prodom e bon latimer."
> Don apela le chevaler
> Owein, si lui preia e dist
> k'od lui alast, si l'apresist. (*Espurgatoire*, ll. 1951–60)

The partnership lasts for two and a half years, during which (as Gilbert
reports) Owein "lived piously and most honestly" (seintement / viveit e
mult honestement, ll. 1985–6) – his exemplary behavior simultaneously
illustrating the profound effects of his adventure in Saint Patrick's Purga-

---

[52] Ibid., pp. 213–14 and ibid., pp. 207–8. R. Howard Bloch emphasizes the role
played by Malachy and the Cistercian order in general in "The Conquest of Ireland and the
Colonization of the Afterlife." See *The Anonymous Marie de France* (Chicago: University
of Chicago Press, 2003), pp. 281–3. Carlisle, in the oft-contested borderlands between
England and Scotland, is the site of Arthur's court in *Lanval* (Kardoeil, l. 5).

[53] Hudson, *Irish Sea Studies*, p. 198. On the economic and political networks within
and beyond the Irish Sea, see our further discussion of Hudson's *Irish Sea Studies* in
Chapter 3.

[54] For an extended analysis of the link between linguistic translation and the mediating
function of Purgatory itself, see Bloch, *The Anonymous Marie de France*, pp. 229–40.

tory and guaranteeing his account of the experience. (The adverbs "hon-estement" and "seintement" are repeated in ll. 1993–4, confirming that Owein continued to live in exemplary fashion after Gilbert's departure.)

But the multiple nodes in the chain of transmission – Owein via Gilbert to H. de Saltrey to Marie – call for multiple acts of authentification:

> Gilbert told these events to the author, who recounted them to us, just as Owein and the monk I mentioned had told him – events I have here told and written down for you. Afterwards I spoke to two ordained abbots from Ireland[55] and asked them if all this could be true.

> Gileberz conta icel fait
> a l'autor, k'il nus ad retrait,
> si cum Oweins li out conté
> e li moignes dunt j'ai parlé,
> ço que jo vus ai ici dit
> e tut mustré par mun escrit.
> E puis parlai j'a dous abbez
> d'Irlande, erent bons ordenez,
> si lur demandai de cel estre
> si ço poeit veritez estre. (*Espurgatoire*, ll. 2057–66)

The "autor" mentioned in line 2058 is H. de Saltrey, author of the Latin source that "I" (jo, l. 61), Marie, has transmitted in *her* text ([s]*un* escrit, l. 62). The "I" who subsequently interviewed the two Irish abbots, however, is not Marie but H. – her French "j[o]" translating his "Ego autem" from the long version of the *Tractatus*. In her critical edition, Yolande de Pont-farcy forestalls confusion by providing subheadings separating "Epilogue I" (ll. 2057–62) from the "Testimony of the Irish abbots" (ll. 2063 ff.), even though nothing in the text itself "indicates … that the first person" of line 2063 "refers to the monk of Saltrey."[56] The brief testimony of the two abbots (reported in indirect discourse) is followed by the testimony of a bishop (nephew of Saint Malachy's companion) and chaplain – both recounted in the first person and containing additional first-person ac-

---

[55] The reassurance that these abbots were properly ordained speaks to the reformist Church's campaigns against Celtic institutions such as lay abbots. See *L'espurgatoire seint Patriz*, p. 257n.

[56] Marie omits the hedging shown by H. de Saltrey, who repeatedly insists on his literal fidelity to the story related by Gilbert "as I understood it," then adds, "if anyone were to blame me, they should know that it's on your orders that I wrote this." *L'espurgatoire*, p. 257n.

counts *en abyme* (ll. 2071–296). Just when the text seems in danger of spinning out an endless chain of authenticating reports, Marie punctuates it with her final epilogue:

> I, Marie, have set the book of *Purgatory* in memory in the vernacular, so that it be understandable to and suitable for lay people.

> Jo, Marie, ai mis, en memoire,
> le livre de l'Espurgatoire
> en romanz, k'il seit entendables
> a laie genz e convenables. (*Espurgatoire*, ll. 2297–300)

In context, "I, Marie" is not (only) an assertion of authorial self-consciousness but a move to distinguish "I, Marie" from the "I, H. de Saltrey" of l. 2063. The key theme of memory is evoked, but secondarily to the primary task of translation: with the circulation of the *Tractatus*, Owein's story is in no danger of falling into oblivion; in that form, however, it remains inaccessible to the very audience it is meant to serve. Thus Marie labors to render "understandable" (entendables) not that which has been written obscurely, but that which has been written in Latin. As Owein was a "Latimer" (l. 1957), she is a "Romancer." And when she writes, "Now let us pray to God that by His grace, we be cleansed of our sins. Amen" (Or preiom Deu ke par sa grace / de nos pechiez mundes nus face. Amen, ll. 2301–2), it is with the knowledge that, thanks to her translation, the laity will know that, in the creation of Purgatory, God has provided the means to do exactly that.

Courtly Love and Feudal Society:
Historical Context

Vernacular literature, writes the historian Georges Duby, was one of the forms "forged to assert the independence of a culture, that of warriors, which was arrogant and, in its enjoyment of life, was resolutely opposed to the culture of the priests."[1] Against a view of medieval society as a seamless whole – a view that assumes the consonance between religious and secular society and thus predisposes us to expect learnèd culture to influence the vernacular culture of its day – Duby invites us to consider concerns like marriage and adultery, chivalry, honor, and good lordship, specific to the secular nobility and especially liable to run afoul of ecclesiastical regulation.[2] In this chapter we turn to Marie de France's engagement with twelfth-century historical institutions as she imagines feudal relations in all their variations and permutations. Her representations range from the critical to the ideal, shaping not only the world of knights, ladies, and kings but also the animal world and life in the hereafter.

The *Lais*

The world of the *Lais* is resolutely secular. Even tales with the most strikingly otherworldly elements are set in feudal principalities or kingdoms wracked by wars or playing host to contests of chivalric honor, where erotic love is frequently expressed through a vocabulary of fief-holding. Guigemar first appears as the son of a vassal of the king of Lesser Brittany in those ancient times when Hoël "ruled the land" (tint...la terre,

---

[1]   Georges Duby, "On Courtly Love," in *Love and Marriage in the Middle Ages*, trans. Jane Dunnett (Chicago: University of Chicago Press, 1994), pp. 56–63 (at 57). See also Peter Haidu, "Repetition: Modern Reflections on Medieval Aesthetics," *Modern Language Notes* 92.5 (1977): 875–87.

[2]   Thus for Peter Haidu, the twelfth-century *roman* "reinvents itself ... *against* the textual models occupying the literary terrain of its day." Haidu, "Au début du roman, l'ironie," *Poétique* 36 (1978): 443–66 (at 444), emphasis added.

Guigemar, l. 27). When it comes time to "make his reputation" (sun pris querre, l. 51), he travels to Flanders, where "there were always conflicts and wars" (out tuz jurs estrif e guerre, l. 52), then to Lorraine, Burgundy, Anjou, and Gascony, where he proves himself a knight without peer. When the wounded hero first meets his lady aboard the enchanted ship, her first assumption is that he has been "exiled on account of war" (eissilliez pur guerre, l. 310). As for Lanval's fairy mistress, her magical world is situated at the margin of an Arthurian kingdom threatened by invasion:

> Arthur, the brave and courtly king, was staying in Carlisle on account of the Scots and Picts who were ravaging the country. They invaded the land of Logres, very often laying it waste.

> A Kardoeil surjurnot li reis,
> Artur, li pruz e li curteis,
> pur les Escoz e pur les Pis
> ki destrueient le païs;
> en la terre de Loegre entroënt
> e mult suvent le damajoënt. (*Lanval*, ll. 5–10)

After bestowing her favors on Lanval, his secret lady cautions him never to reveal her existence, or he will never "have seizin over [her] body" (de mun cors saisine aveir, *Lanval*, l. 150) again.

The corollary to the *Lais'* secular orientation is their aggressive marginalization of the "culture of the priests." In the romances of Chrétien de Troyes, the hermits inhabiting the margins of human society are at least honest and pious. The *Lais*, in contrast, portray religious figures in highly ambivalent ways. In *Guigemar*, the unhappy *mal-mariée* is guarded by "an old hoary priest [who] had lost his lower members" (Uns vielz prestre blans e floriz…les plus bas membres out perduz, ll. 255, 257), as if any other kind of priest were not to be trusted. Several *lais* represent the clergy as compliant with or sympathetic to the desires of the feudal nobility, in contravention of contemporary Church law. In *Le Fraisne*, the archbishop of Dol agrees to undo the marriage he has just performed between Gurun and Codre so that Gurun may marry Fraisne instead, despite the active campaign waged by the twelfth-century Church against aristocratic practices of divorce or repudiation.[3] In *Yonec*, it is the abbot of Caerleon who reveals that the former king of the land had been killed on account of his love for a lady of Caerwent and who (after Yonec takes venge-

---

[3]   Sharon Kinoshita, "Two For the Price of One: Courtly Love and Serial Polygamy in the *Lais* of Marie de France," *Arthuriana* 8.2 (1998): 33–55.

ance on his stepfather) presumably countenances the lady's burial "in the sarcophagus ... next to the body of her lover" (el sarcu ... delez le cors de sun ami, ll. 554–5). In *Chaitivel*, the lady makes a "large offering" (grant offrendre, l. 170) to the "very rich abbey" (mult riche abeïe, l. 169) in which her three dead suitors have been laid to rest, in contravention of the twelfth-century condemnation of tournaments and the ban refusing burial in sacred ground to any knights killed in one. In *Eliduc*, the convent proves an expedient way for the protagonist to separate from his first wife in order to marry his second.[4] Most shocking of all is the unnamed mother of *Le Fraisne*, who would rather face the moral consequences of murdering her child than to be shamed by her neighbors: "I would rather make amends to God than to shame and dishonor myself" (Mielz le vueil vers Deu amender / que mei hunir ne vergunder, ll. 93–4).

At the heart of feudal society was the bond between lord and vassal. Technically, this bond was constituted by the ceremony of homage: the vassal pledged his fidelity (comprising the obligations of *auxilium* and *consilium*) to his overlord – usually, though not invariably, in exchange for a fief. (It is this emphasis on "fief-holding" that gives us our modern term *féodalité*.) Ideally, the feudal bond expresses a deep, honor-bound sense of loyalty, commitment, and obligation. Chivalric literature frequently emphasizes the intensity of this connection; to be the vassal of a great lord is the greatest privilege to which a knight can aspire. In the *Chanson de Roland*, the apparent opposition between Roland, described as "brave" (*preux*), and Olivier, who is "wise" (*sage*, l. 1093), is resolved in the assertion that "both are exemplary vassals" (ambedui sunt de grant vassalage, l. 1094) – their complementary strengths corresponding to the two feudal obligations of *auxilium* and *consilium*, respectively. The *Lais*, on the other hand, complicate or problematize this relationship in various ways. *Le Fraisne* distinguishes between Gurun's "fief-holding knights" (chevalier fiefé, l. 324), who through the force of *consilium* oblige him to give up the titular heroine to marry Coldre, and his "household knights" ([l]i chevalier de la maisun, l. 365), who, together with the squires and servants, are greatly distressed at the impending departure of Gurun's concubine and their *de facto* mistress: "they expressed extraordinary grief

---

[4] On the condemnation of tournamenting, see Constance Brittain Bouchard, *Strong of Body, Brave and Noble: Chivalry and Society in Medieval France* (Ithaca: Cornell University Press, 1998), p. 125. On the controversy of whether a marriage was dissolved when one of the partners entered religious orders, see Kinoshita, "Two For the Price of One," 48–9.

at the prospect of losing her" (merveillus duel pur li faiseient / de ceo que perdre la deveient, *Le Fraisne*, ll. 367–8).

The logic of reciprocity structuring lord–vassal relations is formalized in the institution of the "countergift" (*guerdon*) – the "gift in return" automatically expected in exchange for a gift bestowed, a favor granted, or a service rendered. In medieval literature, the *guerdon* – more than a reward or even a moral obligation – seems to imply an almost ontological principle that any act inevitably, inexorably calls forth another. It functions as a plot device in the romances of Chrétien de Troyes, when Lunete takes it upon herself to assist Yvain as the *guerredon* (*Le Chevalier au Lion*, l. 1013) for the civility he alone had shown her at the Arthurian court, or when the anonymous lady who had previously done Lancelot a service appears near the conclusion of the *Chevalier de la charrete* to demand Méléagant's head in return. In the *Lais* of Marie de France, the *guerdon* explicitly occurs only twice: in *Guigemar*, when Meriaduc summons the protagonist to his tournament *par gueredun* (l. 749) – an episode we shall examine below; and in *Le Fraisne*, where the heroine's mother promises a *bon gueredun* (l. 120) to the handmaid who suggests disposing of her unwanted infant in a monastery instead of killing it: "She was very happy and promised she would have a *fine reward* if she rendered her this service" (Grant joie en out; si li promist, / se cel servise li faiseit, / *bon gueredun* de li avreit, ll. 118–20).

How does courtly love figure into this matrix of feudal values?[5] At first glance, nothing seems more subversive to the vassal's profession of devotion to his lord than his adulterous passion for the lord's wife. Georges Duby, however, has famously characterized courtly love as "an educational game" between men, an apprenticeship in moderation whose rules "*reinforce* the rules of the ethics of vassalage."[6] In this perspective, courtly love does not so much challenge the hierarchical relationship between lord and vassal as graft itself onto it. The lover's profession of obedience and devotion simply substitutes the lady in the place normally reserved for her husband, maintaining or even intensifying the central values of homage. The coordination of the two registers, feudal and courtly-erotic, is facilitated by their shared vocabulary of love, expressed by the verb *aimer* and its derivatives. The deployment of the

---

[5] As is well known, the term "courtly love" (amour courtois) was a nineteenth-century invention, first introduced by Gaston Paris in his discussion of the *Chevalier de la charrete* in *Romania* 12 (1883): 459–534.

[6] Duby, "On Courtly Love," p. 63, emphasis added.

feudal vocabulary of love is familiar to us from epic texts: in the *Chanson de Roland*, Ganelon's assertion, "I do not love you at all" (Jo ne vus aim nïent, l. 306) is less the emotional outburst of an irascible stepfather than a performative declaration signaling the rupture of any feudal or familial bonds between them; conversely, Bramimonde's declaration, "I love you very much, lord" (Jo vus aim mult, sire, l. 635) is not a profession of affection but her endorsement of the political alliance Ganelon has just concluded with her husband. Something of the semantic breadth of medieval expressions of love also appears in the word *druërie* (translated "love-friendship" in several of the passages cited in this chapter). Though loosely the equivalent of "love," in context it often suggests the contractual overtones of a favor bestowed or the public acknowledgment of a token given.

In the *Lais*, however, the relationship between vassalic and marital or erotic love is never as straightforward as Duby's model suggests. The quintessential courtly triangle of lord–lady–vassal/lover occurs only once in the *Lais*: in *Chievrefueil* – an episodic outtake from the larger legend of Tristan and Iseut. Elsewhere, Marie gives us a cast of adulterous lovers who are outsiders (*Guigemar*, *Yonec*), with no connection to their lady's husband, and unmarried maids (*Les dous amanz*, *Milun*) who choose lovers in defiance of paternal strictures. At least four of the *lais* (*Equitan*, *Bisclavret*, *Lanval*, and *Eliduc*) may be read as experimentational variants of the interrelation between feudal and courtly love. Together, the tales read like a kaleidoscopic collection of variations on the junctures and disjunctures between these two fundamental fields of affective relations in feudal society.

Like Chrétien de Troyes's *Le chevalier de la charrete*, *Lanval* sets the conventional triangle of lord–lady–vassal at the Arthurian court. Marie's variation, however, presents a feudal system out of balance: the king is a negligent lord and his queen is an overzealous lady, first in her lust, then in her vindictiveness. As the *lai* opens, Lanval is left out of Arthur's generous distribution of "wives and lands" (femmes e terres, l. 17) to the other knights of the Round Table, despite having "served the king so much" (tant aveit le rei servi, l. 40). Despondent over his plight, Lanval wanders off into the forest where he happens on the beautiful lady who will become his secret mistress. Her wealth is limitless, epitomized in a tent so rich that neither Queen Semiramis nor the emperor Octavian could have afforded even its right flap – a comparison that casually evokes, only immediately to dismiss, both exotic eastern and Roman imperial splendor. Their initial encounter stages medieval literature's two ways of falling in love: from afar, presumably by hearsay, and face-to-face, ignited by the sudden glimpse of a beauty that serves as shorthand for a conventional bundle of desirable feudal and courtly qualities:[7]

> "Lanval," she said, "fair friend, on account of you I came from my land; I have come seeking you from afar…because I love you more than anything." He looked at her and saw she was beautiful; love stings him with the spark that lights up his heart, setting it on fire.

> "Lanval," fet ele, "bels amis,
> pur vus vinc jeo fors de ma terre;
> de luinz vus sui venue querre …
> kar jo vus aim sur tute rien."
> Il l'esguarda, si la vit bele;
> amurs le puint de l'estencele,
> ki sun quer alume e esprent. (*Lanval*, ll. 110–12, 116–19)

Mutually smitten, the two conclude a pact of reciprocal devotion:

> "I will do what you command. For you I will abandon everyone. I don't want ever to be separated from you: this is what I most desire." When the maiden heard him say how much he could love her, she granted him her love and her heart.

> "Jeo ferai voz comandemenz;
> pur vus guerpirai tutes genz.
> Ja mes ne quier de vus partir:
> ceo est la riens que plus desir."
> Quant la pucele oï parler
> celui ki tant la pout amer,
> s'amur e sun cuer li otreie. (*Lanval*, ll. 127–33)

These are not the only things she bestows on him: "Then she gave him another gift: never would he want for anything than he would have as much as he desired" (Un dun li a duné aprés: / ja cele rien ne vuldra mes / que il nen ait a sun talent, ll. 135–7). The only condition is that he never speak of her or their love.

This condition only makes sense in light of what happens next. For

---

[7]   Gurun, in *Le Fraisne*, likewise falls in love with the titular heroine without having seen her: "He heard about the girl and began to love her" (De la pucele oï parler; / si la cumença a amer, ll. 257–8). On this expansive understanding of "beauty," see Zrinka Stahuljak et al., *Thinking Through Chrétien de Troyes*, Gallica (Cambridge: Brewer, 2010), pp. 114–15.

all her obvious Celtic antecedents, Lanval's lady is no otherworldly fairy seeking to lure him away from his world; on the contrary, despite his willingness to stay with her forever, she soon insists on his return to the real world of the court: "'Friend,' she said, 'Get up! You can't stay here any longer. Go away; I'll stay here'" ("Amis," fet ele, "levez sus! / Vus n'i poëz demurer plus. / Alez vus en; jeo remeindrai," ll. 159–61). Newly equipped with the fruits of her generosity, Lanval not only escapes the penury to which Arthur's stinginess had previously condemned him but himself becomes a font of feudal largesse. Setting himself up in town rather than at court, Lanval (re)distributes gifts on a lavish scale – giving out everything except the "wives and lands" (femmes e terres, l. 17) that remain the prerogatives of the king:

> In town, there wasn't a knight in need of lodging whom he didn't send for and richly aid. Lanval gave out expensive gifts, Lanval ransomed captives, Lanval clothed the jongleurs, Lanval gave out great honors, Lanval spent generously, Lanval gave out gold and silver: there was neither stranger nor friend to whom he hadn't given something.

> N'ot en la vile chevalier
> ki de surjur ait grant mestier,
> que il ne face a lui venir
> e richement e bien servir.
> Lanval donout les riches duns,
> Lanval aquitout les prisuns,
> Lanval vesteit les jugleürs,
> Lanval feiseit les granz honurs,
> Lanval despendeit largement,
> Lanval donout or e argent:
> n'i ot estrange ne privé
> a qui Lanval n'eüst doné. (*Lanval*, ll. 205–16)

Only after he has displayed such outsized generosity – poetically under-scored by anaphora – does Lanval win a place among Arthur's knights. One day, while picnicking in an orchard at the foot of the queen's tower, Gauvain says:

> By God, lords, we have been acting poorly toward our companion Lanval in not inviting him with us; he is so generous and courtly, and his father is such a rich king.

> Par Deu, seignur, nus faimes mal
> de nostre cumpaignun Lanval,

> ki tant est larges e curteis
> e sis pere est si riches reis,
> que nus ne l'avum amené. (*Lanval*, ll. 231–5)

Where Lanval had previously languished alone and friendless, his new visibility – he "is so *generous* and courteous" (tant est *larges* e curteis, l. 233) – wins him a place in Gauvain and Yvain's inner circle. Once there, he quickly comes to the attention of the queen; addressing him in terms not unlike those used by his secret mistress, she offers him the "love" and solicitude withheld by the king:

> Lanval, I've greatly honored, cherished, and loved you. You may have all my love: tell me what you want! I grant you my *love-friendship*; you should be very happy with me!

> Lanval, mult vus ai honuré
> e mult cheri e mult amé.
> Tute m'amur poëz aveir:
> kar me dites vostre voleir!
> Ma *druërie* vus otrei;
> mult devez ester liez de mei! (*Lanval*, ll. 265–70)

For Lanval, however, amorous devotion to the lady, far from reinforcing the ethics of vassalage, enters into direct competition with it:

> "Lady," he said, "leave me alone! I am not interested in loving you. I have long served the king and don't want to violate my fidelity. Never, for you or your love, will I wrong my lord."

> "Dame," fet il, "laissiez m'ester!
> Je n'ai cure de vus amer.
> Lungement ai servi le rei,
> ne li vueil pas mentir ma fei.
> Ja pur vus ne pur vostre amur
> ne mesferai a mun seignur!" (271–6)

Stung when she accuses him of not liking women but comely boys,[8]

---

[8] As William Burgwinkle perspicaciously observes, "According to the literary logic of [the year] 1160 accusations of sodomy invariably mean that the marked man will be proven not guilty of having performed such acts." For Lanval as for Enéas, "[t]he acquittal serves as a performative speech act marking only their full integration into maculinist chivalric discourse and a sign that they will henceforth be seen only within the terms of that discourse. Any transgressions against that discourse will henceforth be invisible."

Lanval unleashes a retort that reaffirms his heterosexuality at the cost of compromising him both with his mistress and with the king:

> I love and am the friend of a lady who is more worthy than any I know; … any one of her servants – the humblest girl – is superior to you, your majesty, in body, face, beauty, manners, and goodness.

> … jo aim e si sui amis
> cele ki deit aveir le pris
> sur tutes celes que jeo sai …
> une de celes ki la sert,
> tute la plus povre meschine,
> valt mielz de vus, dame reïne,
> de cors de vis e de bealté,
> d'enseignement e de bunté. (*Lanval*, ll. 295–7, 300–4)

The first part of his declaration violates the condition of silence imposed on him by his lady; the second, as he soon learns, pulls down on him the full weight of Arthur's disfavor.

Given the drama of the queen's subsequent false accusations, it is easy to overlook the fact that what stirs the king's ire is not Lanval's presumed attempt to seduce his wife but his temerity in suggesting that any woman is more beautiful than the queen:

> The king said angrily: "Vassal, you have greatly wronged me! You launched into a base speech – shaming and vilifying me and slandering the queen. Your boast is madness! Your friend is far *too* noble if her maid is more beautiful and worthy than the queen!"

> Li reis li dist par maltalant:
> "Vassal, vus m'avez mult mesfait!
> Trop començastes vilein plait
> de mei hunir e avillier
> e la reïne laidengier.
> Vantez vus estes de folie!
> Trop par est noble vostre amie,
> quant plus est bele sa meschine
> e plus vaillanz que la reïne." (*Lanval*, ll. 364–72)

William E. Burgwinkle, *Sodomy, Masculinity, and Law in Medieval Literature: France and England, 1050–1230* (Cambridge: Cambridge University Press, 2004), pp. 151–2.

For a household vassal to set his sights on the lord's wife is only natural. What is truly scandalous is the suggestion that she is not the most beautiful and desirable woman imaginable. Why? Because of the point we made earlier: that beauty functions here – as in other examples of courtly literature – as the visible signifier of a cluster of noble qualities (wealth, power, and birth; chivalric virtues, such as courage, loyalty, and, for men, skill in arms) and courtly accomplishments (such as politeness and refinement of speech). Correspondingly, depreciating the queen's beauty is not just to insult her personal physical appearance; it is to question her possession of the attributes naturally marking those at the summit of feudal society. And to disparage the queen (referred to throughout this *lai* by her title rather than by her proper name) is, by extension, to disparage the king. If courting the lady is an apprenticeship in feudal subordination, then impugning her beauty amounts to a symbolic rebellion against one's lord.

In the ensuing scene, the magical romance of the lone knight and his fairy mistress gives way to a kind of feudal procedural: Arthur convenes his vassals (Tuz ses humes a enveiez, l. 384), who counsel that Lanval is entitled to his day in court, provided he can find pledges (ll. 392, 399) to guarantee his appearance. Lacking "relatives or friends" ("parent ne ami," l. 401), Lanval appeals to Gauvain, who, with his "companions" (l. 403), agrees to stand surety for the accused. What they are pledging is no joke: "The king says to them: 'I release him to you, guaranteed by whatever lands and fiefs each of you holds from me'" (Li reis lur dit: "E jol vus les / sur quan que vus tenez de mei, / terres e fieus, chescuns par sei," ll. 404–6). On the appointed day, "the guarantors turned Lanval over" (li plege unt Lanval rendu, l. 420) to the court. The barons summoned to render judgment soberly deliberate the fate "of the free/noble man from another land who had gotten so entangled in local affairs" (del franc hume d'altre païs / ki entre els ert si entrepris, ll. 431–2):

> Several of them want to ruin him because their lord willed it. The duke of Cornwall said: "There will be no fault as far as we are concerned. For, whoever likes it or not, the law must prevail. The king has accused his vassal, whom I've heard you call Lanval. He accuses him of betrayal and charges him with calumny for boasting of a love that angered our lady. It is the king alone who is charging him. By my faith, the truth of it is, he shouldn't have spoken out, if only because one should always honor one's lord. He will bind himself by oath, and the king will deliver him over to us. If he can get his witness and

his friend came forward and what he said of her were true, the queen would be vexed. He would then be pardoned for not having spoken in order to vilify her. And if he can't have his witness, we need to tell him this: that he'll lose his position serving the king, who will have to dismiss him."

Encumbrer le vuelent plusur
pur la volenté lur seignur.
Ceo dist li dus de Cornuaille:
"Ja endreit nus n'i avra faille;
kar ki qu'en plurt ne ki qu'en chant,
le dreit estuet aler avant.
Li reis parla vers sun vassal,
que jo vus oi numer Lanval;
de felunie le reta
e d'un mesdit l'achaisuna,
d'une amur dunt il se vanta,
e madame s'en curuça.
Nuls ne l'apele fors le rei:
par cele fei que jeo vus dei,
ki bien en vuelt dire le veir,
ja n'i deüst respuns aveir,
se pur ceo nun qu'a sun seignur
deit um par tut porter honur.
Un sairement l'en guagera,
e li reis le nus pardurra.
E s'il puet aveir sun guarant
e s'amie venist avant
e ceo fust veirs que il en dist,
dunt la reïne se marrist,
de ceo avra il bien merci,
quant pur vilté nel dist de li.
E s'il ne puet guarant aveir,
ceo li devum faire saveir:
tut sun servise pert del rei,
e sil deit cungeer de sei." (*Lanval*, ll. 433–62)

The legalism of the proceedings – peppered with terms such as *dreit, felunie, mesdie* – is palpable. Throughout most of the *lai*, the protagonist has most frequently been referred to as a "knight" (chevaliers, ll. 39, 77, 107, 262, etc.). Here, picking up on lines 3–4 of the prologue, the end rhyme "Lanval" and "vassal" (ll. 439–40) makes the stakes of the trial clear: Lanval is being tried for the way his encounter with the queen reflects on his relationship to the king. (Arthur had angrily interpellated him as "vassal" [l. 365] when first summoning him to answer the queen's accusation.) Thus when Lanval's lady appears (against all his expectations) to vindicate his words, she addresses[9] the king in language appropriate to the circumstances:

> "Arthur," she said, "hear me, and these barons I see here [as well]. I loved a vassal of yours: this is the one! I mean Lanval!"

> "Artur," fet ele, "entent a mei,
> e cist barun que jeo ci vei!
> Jeo ai amé un tuen vassal.
> Veez le ci! Ceo est Lanval!" (*Lanval*, ll. 631–4)

Her appearance, in both senses of the term, accomplishes two things. First, Lanval is immediately acquitted in a show of due process: with the king having accorded in advance that "whatever decision they would legally render" (Ceo qu'il en jugerunt par dreit, l. 643) would be binding, the barons of the court unanimously judge Lanval to have spoken the truth about his lady's beauty. More subtly, it highlights the king's negligence towards the knight here pointedly described as his vassal: having received neither a wife nor a fief in the earlier distribution, Lanval has acquired great wealth and a lady whose surpassing beauty make her both an idealized object of desire and an alternative suzerain.

When Lanval jumps on his lady's palfrey as she rides out of court, the transformation is more than a happily-ever-after ending:

> He went off with her to Avalon, as the Bretons tell us, to a very beautiful island; that's where the young man was *taken*.

> Od li s'en vait en Avalun,
> ceo nus recuntent li Bretun,
> en un isle qui mult est beals;
> la fu *raviz* li dameiseals. (*Lanval*, ll. 659–62)

Previously called either a knight or a vassal, Lanval is suddenly reduced to the status of a "young man" or "squire" (dameiseals) as if, in mounting the lady's palfrey instead of his own warhorse (destrier, l. 41), he had relinquished all claim to *cheval-erie*.[9] This impression is reinforced by the past participle "ravished" (raviz), signifing that socially complex practice

---

[9] Guigemar is likewise referred to as "dancel" (l. 37) and "vadlez" (l. 43) at the outset of the *lai* bearing his name; later, he is called "dameisels" (ll. 84, 368) and "chevalier" (ll. 280, 295, 302, 377, 395, etc.).

(of which *women* are typically the object) of rape and abduction.[10] And in fact, Lanval disappears from the face of the earth: "After that, no one heard anything else about him, nor can I tell you any more of him" (Nuls n'en oï puis plus parler, / ne jeo n'en sai avant cunter, ll. 663–4). Opting out of the feudal system altogether, he achieves (presumably) personal bliss at the cost of social erasure.[11]

Both *Equitan* and *Bisclavret* stage a variation of the feudal triangle: not a hapless vassal caught between his king and queen, but the relationship between an unmarried king and his married vassal. Instead of emphasizing the congruence between feudal and amorous love, *Equitan* takes their incompatibility as its point of departure. From the moment the eponymous king falls in love with his vassal's wife, erotic passion and feudal responsibility are cast as distinct and mutually exclusive:

> If I love her, I'm doing wrong; she's the wife of my seneschal.
> I owe him the same faith and love that I want him to give me.

> E se jo l'aim, jeo ferai mal:
> ceo est la femme al seneschal.
> Garder li dei amur e fei,
> si cum jeo vueil qu'il face a mei. (*Equitan*, ll. 75–8)

The relationship between the king and his seneschal may be unequal, but it is reciprocal and mutually binding: to merit and maintain his vassal's allegiance, Equitan must conduct himself as a good feudal lord.

For a king, however, the danger inherent in an illicit affair is uncoupled from the threat of direct political reprisal. Where the amorous vassal playing the dangerous game of courting his overlord's wife must temper his ardor with circumspection and moderation, Equitan experiences no such constraints. From his vantage point atop the feudal hierarchy, he yields to the seduction of courtly discourse, casting aside all feudal scruple:

> What a waste of a beautiful woman if she did not love and take a lover! What would happen to her *courtoisie* if she didn't love out of *love-friendship*? There isn't a man in the world that wouldn't be much better for it.

---

[10] See Kathryn Gravdal, *Ravishing Maidens: Writing Rape in Medieval French Literature and Law* (Philadelphia: University of Pennsylvania Press, 1991).

[11] See Sharon Kinoshita, "'Cherchez la femme': Feminist Criticism and Marie de France's *Lai de Lanval*," *Romance Notes* 34.3 (1994): 263–73.

> Si bele dame tant mar fust,
> S'ele n'amast e dru n'eüst!
> Que devendreit sa curteisie,
> s'ele n'amast de *druërie*?
> Suz ciel n'a hume, s'el l'amast,
> ki durement n'en amendast. (*Equitan*, ll. 83–8)

In the quick transition between his original compunction at the thought of pursuing his vassal's wife to this justificatory rhetoric of mutual self-improvement, Equitan has rationalized away all political responsibilities and concerns, plunging headlong into the alternate reality of courtesy and love.

The lady, in contrast, inhabits a social world devoid of such courtly banter. Like Laudine in Chrétien de Troyes's *Yvain*, she is surprised by this discourse of love: "My lord," she says, "I must have some time to think; this is so new to me, I have no idea what to say" (Sire ... / de ceo m'estuet aveir respit. / A ceste primiere feiee / n'en sui jeo mie cunseilliee, ll. 121–4).[12] For the wife of the king's seneschal, what Equitan proposes is no game: the discrepancy in their power and status is not a mere detail that can be pretended away:[13]

> You're a king of high nobility, and I'm not at all of such fortune that you should single me out for *love-friendship*. If you get what you want from me, I have no doubt about it: you'll soon get tired of me, and I'll be far worse off than before.

> Vus estes reis de grant noblesce;
> ne sui mie de tel richesce
> qu'a mei vus deiez arester
> de *druërie* de n'amer.
> S'aviëz fait vostre talent,
> jeo sai de veir, n'en dut nïent,
> tost m'avriëz entrelaissiee,
> j'en sereie mut empeiriee. (*Equitan*, ll. 125–32)

---

[12] On Laudine's incredulity at Yvain's protestations of courtly love, see Stahuljak et al., *Thinking Through Chrétien de Troyes*, pp. 131–2.

[13] Had she read her Andreas Capellanus, she could have borrowed from the script of the woman of simple nobility importuned by a man of higher nobility (Book I, Part IV, Dialogue 7) and protested that his extravagant praise of her detracted from the courtesy he ought to show other women "more worthy of the honor," making him seem less worthy; similarly, any special favor she might show him would be "to the disadvantage of others who have as much desire to serve [her] as [he has], or perhaps even more" (Andreas Capellanus, *The Art of Courtly Love*, trans. John Jay Parry [1941; rpt. New York, 1969], pp. 95–6).

She, in fact, has her own ideology of love, based not on the submission of one partner to the other but on parity:

> If I should love you and satisfy your desire, *love-friendship* wouldn't be equally shared between us. Because you're a powerful king and my husband is your vassal, I'm sure you believe your rank entitles you to my love. Love is unworthy if it is not equal.

> Se issi fust que vus amasse
> e vostre requeste otreiasse,
> ne sereit pas uël partie
> entre nus duus *la druërie*.
> Pur ceo que estes reis puissanz
> e mis sire est de vus tenanz,
> quideriëz a mun espeir
> le dangier de l'amur aveir.
> Amur n'est pruz, se n'est egals. (*Equitan*, ll. 133–41)

The conventional tropes of courtly love, she seems to understand, invert but preserve the inequalities that put her at the king's mercy. The love she proposes instead is truly subversive – outside and unstructured by feudal hierarchies of power.

For the king, however, the appeal of courtly love is precisely the thrill of the submission demanded of the courtly lover. The lady's tiresome insistence on equality threatens to spoil the excitement of the game. By rejecting her reservations as "uncourtly" (mie fin curteis, l. 155) and accusing her of "bourgeois trading" (bargaigne de burgeis, l. 156), he makes light of her distress at the discrepancy in their ranks by reminding her of the shared nobility that distinguishes them both from the non-noble *vilain*. Despite his name, what Equitan seeks is not an exchange between equals, but the delicious novelty of abasement. Cajoling the lady, he begs to be dominated:

> Don't think of me as king but as your vassal and your lover …
> You be the lord and I'll be the servant – you be the proud one and I'll be the supplicant.

> Ne me tenez mie pur rei,
> mes pur vostre hume e vostre ami …
> Vus seiez dame e jeo servanz
> vus orguilluse e jeo preianz. (*Equitan*, ll. 174–5, 179–80)

Titillated by the prospect of humiliation, Equitan takes courtly discourse's metaphorical inversions of hierarchical relations to literal extreme. Finally, worn down by his insistence, seduced by the prospect of holding a king in thrall, or perhaps simply mindful of the consequences of saying no, the lady gives in and becomes Equitan's mistress. The language Marie uses to narrate their affair suggests a kind of secret marriage; it is also lexically marked by a vocabulary of equal as well as reciprocal exchange, as if the lady's ideology of love had prevailed: "They *took each other* by exchanging rings and *promised* themselves to *each other*. They kept their promises and *loved each other* well" (Par lur anels *s'entresaisirent*, / lur fiances *s'entreplevirent*. / Bien les tindrent, mut *s'entramerent*, ll. 185–7).[14]

From the beginning of the *lai*, an odd interchangeability had marked Equitan's relationship to the lady's husband as well, with the king willingly delegating his feudal responsibilities to his vassal in order to devote himself to the hunt: the seneschal "took care of his land for him, governed and administered it" (Tute sa terre li guardout / e meinteneit e justisout, ll. 23–4). Now, the king's trysts with the seneschal's wife draw him farther and farther away from the public functions of kingship:

> When they were to speak together the king informed his followers that he wanted to be bled privately. The doors of his chamber were closed, and no one was so daring, if the king didn't summon him, that he would ever enter there.

> quant ensemble durent parler,
> li reis faiseit dire a sa gent
> que seigniez iert priveement.
> Li us des chambres furent clos;
> ne trovissiez hume si os,
> se li reis pur lui n'enveiast,
> ja une feiz dedenz entrast. (*Equitan*, ll. 192–8)

If the affairs of the kingdom are tended to nonetheless, it is because his vassal has progressively stepped in to fulfill his role: "the seneschal held court and heard pleas and complaints" (Li seneschals la curt teneit, / les plaiz e les clamurs oeit, ll. 201–2). Now, with the seneschal discharging the public functions of kingship while Equitan takes his pleasure with the seneschal's wife, the exchange between lord and vassal seems complete.

The one responsibility that cannot be fulfilled by proxy, however, is the begetting of an heir to continue the royal line. In the twelfth century,

---

[14] The line that resolves the second couplet, however, falls with a thudding finality: "Then died of it in the end" (puis en mururent e finirent, l. 188).

as hereditary succession emerged as a prime factor in political stability, dynastic politics assumed greater and greater importance. Rulers went to great lengths to engender sons to inherit their realms. While their vassals tolerated, and even encouraged, a range of marital practices condemned by the Church, what was intolerable was for the ruler to neglect his responsibility to assure dynastic succession. To this aspect of kingship, Equitan remains oblivious:

> The king loved [the seneschal's wife] for a long time, and had no desire for any other woman; he didn't want to marry and never allowed the subject to be raised. His people held this against him.

> Li reis l'ama mult lungement
> que d'altre femme n'ot talent.
> Il ne voleit nule espuser;
> ja n'en rovast oïr parler.
> Sa genz li tindrent mult a mal. (*Equitan*, ll. 203–7)

The very loyalty that makes Equitan an exemplary lover renders him, in the eyes of his vassals, an irresponsible king.[15] As the feudal politics of lineage intrudes on the king's courtly idyll, the barons' discontent reanimates the lady's fears: "you're going to take a wife, some king's daughter, and you will leave me" (Femme prendrez, fille a un rei, / e si vus partirez de mei, ll. 221–2). He assures her he will do neither. And then, incredibly, Equitan adds:

> Believe me, this is the truth: *If your husband were dead*, I'd make you my lady and my queen; I wouldn't be deterred by any man.

> Saciez de veir e si creez,
> *se vostre sire fust finez*,
> reïne et dame vus fereie;
> ja pur nul hume nel lerreie. (*Equitan*, ll. 231–4)

Transported by his passion, Equitan makes the lady an extravagant proposition: to translate their courtly play into feudal reality. The price of this extraordinary transformation, however, is nothing less than the life of the seneschal, her husband and his vassal.

---

[15] The motif of the lord who discomfits his vassals by refusing to take a wife recurs in *Le Fraisne* (ll. 323–39).

The dénouement of *Equitan* plays out in a logic of just returns as the king and the seneschal's wife fall victim to the very strategem they have devised to dispose of her husband. (At no point does it occur to either of them that the lady might divorce and remarry – an omission contrary to the recourse to serial polygamy imagined at the conclusion of both *Le Fraisne* and *Eliduc*.) Lest we miss the point, Marie – as in no other of the eleven *lais* – conspicuously appends a moral to her tale: "He who seeks to do ill to others has it rebound upon him" ("tels purchace le mal d'altrui / dunt tuz li mals revert sur lui, ll. 315–16).[16] This boomerang effect is familiar to us from *Guigemar*, in which the arrow the protagonist shoots at the white doe "rebounds" (resort ariere, l. 97) and strikes him in the thigh, causing the wound curable only by the woman who will suffer incomparably on account of his love. But where Guigemar's wound is curable, the king and his mistress must die for their actions – an object lesson against indulging personal desires without at least the cover of feudal rectitude (as at the end of *Guigemar*) but also, perhaps, a cautionary tale on the perils of a claustrophobic world without the possibilities of repudiation and remarriage.

In contrast to *Equitan*, *Bisclavret* – another tale of a king, his vassal, and the vassal's wife – gives what is perhaps the *Lais*' most idealized representation of feudal relations. As the *lai* opens, the titular protagonist appears to epitomize the perfect balance between feudal and marital love:

> He was a handsome and good knight who conducted himself in a noble fashion. He was on close terms with his lord and loved by all his neighbors. His wife was very worthy and behaved very seemingly. He loved her and she him.

> Beals chevaliers e bons esteit
> e noblement se cunteneit.
> De sun seignur esteit privez
> e de tuz ses veisins amez.
> Femme ot espuse mult vaillant
> e ki mult faiseit bel semblant.
> Il amot li e ele lui... (*Bisclavret*, ll. 17–23)

But the catch is not long in coming:

> But one thing troubled him/her very much: that during the week she lost him for three entire days, during which she

---

16 This is also the moral of several fables, as we shall see below.

didn't know where he went or what he was doing. Nor did any
of his/her people know anything about it.

> ... mes d'une chose ot grant ennui,
> qu'en la semeine le perdeit
> treis jurs entiers qu'el ne saveit
> que deveneit ne u alout,
> ne nuls des soens nïent n'en sout. (*Bisclavret*, ll. 24–8)

Disguised by the easy flow of Marie's artful octosyllables, a small but
significant shift occurs: in lines 25 through 28, "the lady" has clearly
become the grammatical subject. Line 24, "mes d'une chose ot grant
ennui," serves as the pivot. At first, it seems to refer to the knight, the
grammatical subject of lines 17 through 23 ("but one thing troubled *him*
very much"); in retrospect, however, it becomes obvious that it refers to
his wife: "but one thing" – her husband's repeated absences – "troubled
her very much."[17]

The difference, though admittedly minor, introduces issues of perspective and perception that will loom increasingly large in the development
of the plot. As the tale turns out, the lady is wrong to fear the werewolf, at
least before she betrays him, so the steps she takes to shun him are wrong
and misguided. Yet one could certainly make a case for the lady's reaction. The prologue had pointedly told us that "The werewolf is a savage
beast" (Garulf ... est beste salvage, l. 9) that lives in the forest, devouring
men; surely it is not unreasonable for the lady to flush with fear at the
news and decide never again to lie with a man who regularly morphs into
such a fearsome creature.[18] But when does she begin to feel fear? At first
she seems troubled only by her husband's unexplained weekly absences,
though perhaps her fear that her questions will provoke his anger (jeo
criem tant vostre curut, l. 35) is a tip-off. When she finally does broach
the issue, Marie reports it in direct speech: in this seemingly intimate
and unmediated exchange, the lady's (changing?) emotions are, ironi-

[17] The ambiguity is lost in translation: "Et pourtant la dame avait un souci" (Harf-
Lancner, *Les Lais*, p. 19); "but one thing was very vexing to her" (*The Lais of Marie
de France*, trans. Robert W. Hanning and Joan M. Ferrante [New York: Dutton, 1978],
p. 92); "but one thing caused her great worry" (*The Lais of Marie de France*, trans. Glyn
S. Burgess and Keith Busby [London: Penguin, 1986], p. 68).

[18] See Matilda Tomaryn Bruckner, "Of Men and Beasts in *Bisclavret*," *Romanic
Review* 82.3 (1991): 251–69. In Chapter Five we examine in greater depth the interpretive
dilemma posed by the "garwalf" as a question of species versus the individual as well as
of embodiment.

cally, covered over by the courtliness of their dialogue and the measured alternation of addresses to "Sire" (ll. 32, 43) and "Dame" (ll. 39, 53, etc.).

When the lady sends for the man who eventually becomes her second husband, she is not capitalizing on the opportunity to take a lover; instead, she formally accords him a love she had never before deigned to bestow – "she had never loved him nor pledged him her love" (ele ne l'aveit unc amé / ne de s'amur aseüré, ll. 107–8) – in exchange for his promise to dispose of the werewolf's hidden clothing, locking him into his animal form. The non-reciprocal nature of their affective relationship is confirmed in the lines, "He thus married the lady *whom he had long loved*" (La dame a cil dunc espusee, / *que lungement aveit amee*, ll. 133–4). Yet the narrator's sympathies are never in doubt: Bisclavret is "betrayed" (traïz, l. 125) by his wife's actions and properly "avenged" (vengiez, l. 234) when he bites off her nose. Does the lady love her new husband? The question is dismissed as irrelevant.

The dilemma momentarily posed as a triangle of husband, wife, and lover is soon recast as a triangle between wife, vassal, and king. For where the lady readily forsakes the husband who had never previously given her cause for alarm, the king judges Bisclavret not by what he seems to be but by what he does:

> As soon as he saw the king, he ran to him to beg mercy. Having taken him by the stirrup, he kissed his leg and foot. The king saw this and was very frightened. He summoned all his companions. "Lords," he said, "come here; look at this marvel – the way this beast is rendering obeisance! It has human reason: it's begging mercy! Drive all these dogs back; make sure no one harms it! This beast has understanding and reason. Hurry up! Let's go! I'll confer my peace on this beast and won't hunt any more today."

> Des que il a le rei choisi,
> vers lui curut querre merci.
> Il l'aveit pris par sun estrié,
> la jambe li baise e le pié.
> Li reis le vit, grant poür a;
> ses cumpaignuns tuz apela.
> "Seignur," fet il, "avant venez
> e ceste merveille esguardez,
> cum ceste beste s'umilie!
> *Ele a sen d'ume*, merci crie.
> Chaciez mei tuz cez chiens ariere,
> si guardez que hum ne la fiere!

> *Ceste beste a entente e sen.*
> Espleitiez vus! Alum nus en!
> A la beste durrai ma pes:
> kar jeo ne chacerai hui mes." (*Bisclavret*, ll. 145–60)

In the quick cut between his fear and the observation he makes to his household companions, the king sees what the lady could not: that despite his form, Bisclavret is still governed by social relations, remaining the king's "man" even when his shape is that of a "beast" (beste, ll. 153, 157). Not incidentally, what the king recognizes as "human reason" (sen d'ume, l. 154) is specifically the werewolf's feudal obeisance.[19] In *Lanval*, we are told not to be surprised if the protagonist fails to gain Arthur's favor, for "a *stranger* ... is miserable in a foreign land when he doesn't know where to seek help" (*huem estranges* ... mult est dolenz en altre terre, / quant il ne set u sucurs querre, *Lanval*, ll. 36–8). Yet in *Bisclavret*, even the beast is recognized for the man (vassal) he is – not at home but in the *altre terre* of the king. The homoerotic flavor of their mutual devotion and affection – back at court, Bisclavret "bedded down near the king" (pres del rei s'alout culchier, l. 177) every night – once again sets the king in contrast to Bisclavret's wife, who "hadn't wanted to lie beside him any more" (ne voleit mes lez lui gisir, l. 102).

The naturalization of Bisclavret's presence at the king's court can be traced through the repeated evocations of "marvel" or "wonder" (*merveille*), which in other texts is often a code word for the Celtic tradition.[20] At first, it is the sight of the *garalf* humbling himself like a vassal and following the king loyally about his castle that qualifies as a "merveille" (ll. 152, 168). But soon the entire household grows so accustomed to Bisclavret's civil behavior that when he attacks his wife's new husband at the king's plenary court, "Almost everyone greatly *marveled*, for never had he behaved this way toward any man he saw" (Mult s'esmerveillent li plusur; / kar unkes tel semblant ne fist / vers nul hume que il veïst, ll. 204–6). And when he sets upon his ex-wife and tears off her nose, it is a "wise man" (sages huem, l. 239) of the court who bids the king look deeper into the affair with the self-reflexive observation that "We have seen many marvels occur here in Brittany" (Meinte merveille avum veüe / ki en Bretaigne est avenue, ll. 259–60). But now, the marvel

---

[19] Karl Steel, "How to Make a Human," *Exemplaria* 20.1 (2008): 3–27; Peggy McCracken, "Translation and Animals in Marie de France's *Lais*," *Australian Journal of French Studies* 46.3 (2009): 206–18.

[20] At ll. 16, 97, 204, 218, and 259.

is neither a hidden Otherworld nor a secret lover but quite simply a werewolf who acts like a werewolf.

In *Equitan* it is the king who precipitates the crisis between a vassal and his wife; here, the king rights the wrong a wife had perpetrated against his vassal. Using torture (destreit, l. 255; destresce, ll. 264, 265) to elicit the truth from the wife, the king restores first Bisclavret's clothes – and with them his human form – and then his feudal fortunes:

> The king ran to embrace him. He hugged and kissed him more than a hundred times. As soon as he had the opportunity, he restored all his land; he gave him more than I am telling.

> Li reis le curut enbracier;
> plus de cent feiz l'acole e baise.
> Si tost cum il pot aveir aise,
> tute sa terre li rendi;
> plus li duna que jeo ne di. (*Bisclavret*, ll. 300–4)

Meanwhile, Bisclavret's former wife is exiled along with the man "for whom she had betrayed her lord" (pur qui sun seignur ot traï, l. 308) and to whom she will bear a line of noseless daughters. The *lai* thus ends on a note of feudal plenitude conspicuously devoid of women. If *Equitan* illustrates the disorder unleashed by the combination of heterosexual desire and the forced heteronormativity of the feudal politics of lineage, *Bisclavret* pictures the restoration of harmonious relations between king and vassal as a relation unmediated by women.[21]

In light of this ending, let us circle back to the first *lai* in Harley 978, *Guigemar*. In comparison with the curious conclusion of *Bisclavret*, the resolution of *Guigemar* seems a model *courtly* ending, with the protagonist and his lady happily reunited after a long separation. The only discordant note is the odd delay in the recognition scene, in the anomaly of Guigemar's believing the evidence not of his eyes but only of the belt. A closer look, however, reveals a much more troubled and troubling world in which the lovers' reunion is bought at the cost of a scandalous breach of feudal honor. The *lai* unfolds in three episodes, linked (as we elaborate in Chapter 4) to three different settings. The effect is to cast Guigemar as

---

[21] William Burgwinkle evokes the *lai*'s "omnipresent" homoeroticism: the "terrifying forest turns out to be the royal hunting ground, the playground of the King. The King appears to be unmarried.... Like all good kings, he sleeps among his men ..., and status at court is determined by how close you get to him." For Burgwinkle, *Bisclavret* "opens a fissure in heterosexist discourse" in which homoeroticism "is for once not written over with a heterosexual imperative." *Sodomy, Masculinity, and Law*, pp. 168–9.

the protagonist of tales in three distinct genres: a chivalric adventure, in which he wins renown but is called to account for his neglect of love; the interlude of the *mal-mariée* (closely resembling *Yonec*), set in an enclosed fortification accessible only by magical ship; and the war story pitting Meriaduc against a hostile neighbor. This third act brings the first two explosively together in an apparently seamless "happy ending" that ultimately exposes their incompatibility.

In the *lai*'s concluding episode, the story of the lovers' happy reunion after a two-year separation is interwoven with a drama of warfare and shifting feudal alliances. Guigemar comes to the castle where his lady has taken refuge only when Meriaduc – who "was making war against his neighbor" (guerreiot un suen veisin, l. 693) – proclaims a tournament. Ostensibly this returns us to the first panel of our narrative triptych, which had the protagonist traveling as far as Lorraine, Burgundy, and Gascony in search of adventure. This time, however, Guigemar's appearance is no accident:

> [Meriaduc] summoned many knights – Guigemar the first among them. He sent for him – not only as a friend and companion but on account of a *guerdon* – to come to his assistance and not fail him in this time of need.

> Mult i ot semuns chevaliers;
> Guigemar fu tuz li primiers.
> Il l'i manda par gueredun
> si cum ami e cumpaignun,
> qu'a cel busuin ne li faillist
> e en s'aïe a lui venist. (*Guigemar*, ll. 747–52)

The summons is much more than a narrative ploy to reunite the protagonist and his lady: Guigemar and Meriaduc are not mere acquaintances but "friends and companions" (ami e cumpaignun, l. 750) – a phrase pointing to something like the bond linking Roland and Olivier in the *Chanson de Roland*. What's more, Guigemar is beholden to Meriaduc. Having (it seems) carried on his life of arms despite his grief at losing his lady, Guigemar is called upon to pay up an obligation – here defined as military assistance (*auxilium*) – the *gueredun* owed in repayment of an unspecified debt of honor to his "friend and companion."

In the recognition scene, however, the episode returns to the enchanted world of the *antive cite*, even as our fascination with the fairytale-like expedient of the knot and the belt vies with our (modern) consternation at Guigemar's failure to recognize his lady. Completely forgetting the obligation he had come specifically to discharge, Guigemar turns to Meriaduc and, in a curious combination of direct and indirect discourse:

> asks and begs Meriaduc to give her to me, by his mercy! I will become his liegeman; I will serve him for two or three years with a hundred or more knights.

> Meriadu requier e pri,
> rende la mei, sue merci!
> Sis huem liges en devendrai;
> dous anz u treis le servirai
> od cent chevaliers u od plus. (*Guigemar*, ll. 841–5)

In this syntactically and politically confused speech, Guigemar proposes replacing the horizontal bond between him and his "friend and companion" with a fixed-term vertical contract (anticipating Eliduc's agreement with the king of Exeter) in which he would acknowledge himself to be Meriaduc's liegeman.[22] When Meriaduc refuses – for he, too, loves the lady and wants her for himself – Guigemar immediately "defies" (desfie, l. 855) him. Taking with him not just his own men but *all* the knights who had answered Meriaduc's call, Guigemar offers his services to his enemy:

> That night they came to the castle of [the neighbor] who was at war with Meriaduc. They were given lodging by its lord, who was very happy about Guigemar and his military assistance: he now knew his war was over.

> La nuit sunt al chastel venu,
> ki guerreiout Meriadu.
> Li sire les a herbergiez,
> ki mult en fu joius e liez
> de Guigemar e de s'aïe;
> bien set que sa guerre est finie. (*Guigemar*, ll. 863–8)

The next day, this newly assembled force sets out to attack Meriaduc's "castle" (chastel, l. 873). When their first assault fails, Guigemar turns his attention to "the city" (la vile, l. 875) instead.

> The number of his friends and retainers grew so much that he starved out all those within. He captured and destroyed the castle, slaying the lord inside it.

---

[22] On liege homage, see Bouchard, *Strong of Body, Brave and Noble*, pp. 45–6.

Tant li crurent ami e genz,
que tuz les afama dedenz.
Le chastel a destruit e pris
e le seignur dedenz ocis. (*Guigemar*, ll. 877–80)

Having come to fulfill his *guerdon* to Meriaduc, Guigemar ends up unleashing a war of destruction against his erstwhile "friend and companion." The extreme violence of his siege and conquest of the castle and
what could under other circumstances easily be construed as his *traïsun*
in slaying Meriaduc are occluded, first, by the intense compression of
these events into a mere three lines and, secondly, by the exigencies of the
love story, fulfilled in the narrator's quick cut to the long-deferred happy
ending: "Joyfully, he carried his friend away. Now his troubles are over"
(A grant joie s'amie en meine. / Ore a trespassee sa peine, ll. 881–2).
The perfect composition of this final rhymed couplet covers the aston-
ishingly incongruous juxtaposition of the lovers' joy, on the one hand,
and the castle's smoldering ruins, on the other. All narrative threads are
wrapped up with a rapidity that allows no second thoughts on Guigemar's
course of action to surface. From this two-line happily-ever-after, Marie
immediately jumps to her concluding epilogue: "The *lai* of Guigemar was
composed from this story you have [just] heard" (De cest cunte qu'oï avez
/ fu Guigemar li lais trovez, ll. 883–4). Through its virtuoso manipulation
of episodic construction and generic form, *Guigemar* manages what, in
a kind of daring narrative wager, it poses as the incompatibility between
feudal and amorous love, to the advantage of the latter.

The *Lais* and the feudal politics of lineage

Central to medieval secular society is what we have elsewhere called
the feudal politics of lineage.[23] In the Middle Ages, lineage was the way
nobles defined their place in the world, negotiated their politics, and transmitted their values. *We* may think of Erec as Enide's husband and of Yvain
as the knight of the Lion, but to the characters they meet they are above
all "King Lac's son" and "King Urien's son," respectively. Throughout
the *Lais*, concern for lineage is often the element upsetting the narrative status quo. In *Equitan*, as we have seen, it is the barons' growing
discontent at the king's refusal to marry that piques the lady's fears and

[23] Sharon Kinoshita, "Heldris de Cornuälle's *Roman de Silence* and the Feudal Politics
of Lineage," *PMLA* 110.3 (May): 397–409.

so precipitates the lovers' murderous plans. In *Le Fraisne*, it is similarly
Gurun's vassals who insist that he put aside his concubine in order to take
a proper wife. In *Yonec*, the old advocate of Caerwent, "because he had
a fine patrimony, married in order to have children to be his heirs after
him" (Pur ceo qu'il ot bon heritage, / femme prist pur enfanz aveir, / ki
aprés lui fussent si heir, ll. 18–20). And in *Eliduc* (in a variation on the
theme of the *Les dous Amanz*, which we shall turn to below), the king of
Exeter is at war with his neighbors because:

> He was an old and aged man. He had no male heir of his body.
> He had a marriageable daughter. Because he didn't want to
> give her to his peer, he was making war on him, laying all his
> land to waste.

> Vielz huem e anciëns esteit.
> Charnel heir madle nen aveit;
> une fille ot a mariër.
> Pur ceo qu'il ne la volt doner
> a sun per, cil le guerreiot,
> tute sa terre si guastot. (*Eliduc*, ll. 93–8)

For everyone from kings to barons to simple knights, marriage and pro-
creation were not solely personal matters but political and social obligations. They were the means through which feudal society reproduced
itself in a stable and orderly manner.

It is this centrality of lineage as an organizing principle of feudal
society that gives courtly love its subversive edge. Despite the prevalence
of illicit love as a staple theme of medieval literature, such affairs rarely
result in illegitimate children within this literature. From queens like Iseut
and Guenevere to the unfaithful wives in *Guigemar* and *Equitan*, adulterous women remain childless because, in a society so strongly based
in genealogical politics, the threat of illegitimacy was regarded as "too
serious to be treated lightly in literature."[24] Strikingly, the *Lais* feature
two exceptions: *Yonec*, whose titular protagonist is the son of the anonymous heroine and her lover, the ruler of a near-by occulted kingdom; and
Milun, whose premarital affair with a lady above his station results in a
son whose true parentage is revealed only when he has proven himself a

---

[24] Georges Duby, *The Knight, The Lady, and The Priest: The Making of Modern
Marriage in Medieval France*, trans. Barbara Bray (Chicago: University of Chicago Press,
1994), p. 222. For a different view, see Peggy McCracken, *The Romance of Adultery:
Queenship and Sexual Transgression in Old French Literature* (Philadelphia: University
of Pennsylvania Press, 1998), pp. 119–43.

knight "without peer" (Senz Per, l. 340) (as well as, punningly, "without father"). In each case, a son born of an illicit affair, brought up as the child of the woman's husband, eventually grows up to vindicate his parents' secret love and (re)claim his paternal heritage. If these *lais* dare to imagine what most courtly literature cannot, it may have to do with the fact that both are set in Wales – a distinctive culture on the margins of the Anglo-Norman world in which illegitimate children were more easily tolerated than in the rest of feudal Europe and, significantly, often shared in their biological father's inheritance.[25]

In these *lais* of threatened genealogical interruption, material objects often function as objective correlatives of lineage. This is not surprising: medieval society was a world of objects – the inseparability of the cult of saints from the adoration of their relics being a salient example.[26] In *Guigemar*, the heroine's belt guarantees her identity as the titular protagonist's lover even if all "women look very much alike" (femmes se resemblent asez, l. 779). But the correlation between object and identity is particularly striking in cases involving parents and children. In *Le Fraisne*, the mother who a moment before had been ready to kill her infant daughter to preserve her own honor now makes sure that the foundling is sent into the world in a way befitting her birth:

> They wrapped the noble child in a bit of very good linen and, on top of that, a patterned silk: her lord had brought it from Constantinople, where he had been. Never had such a good one been seen.

> En un chief de mult bon cheinsil
> envolupent l'enfant gentil
> e desus un paile roë;
> sis sire li ot aporté
> de Costentinoble u il fu;
> unques si bon n'orent veü. (*Le Fraisne*, ll. 121–6)

Throughout the *Lais*, as in all medieval literature, silk is the signifier par excellence of nobility, wealth, and desirability. In *Lanval*, two exceedingly comely maids "dressed in purple sendal alone against their naked flesh" (de cendal purpre ... vestues / tut senglement a lur chars nues, ll. 477–8)

---

[25] For an extended reading of these two *lais* in historical context, see Sharon Kinoshita, *Medieval Boundaries: Rethinking Difference in Old French Literature* (Philadelphia: University of Pennsylvania Press, 2006), pp. 105–32.

[26] See Patrick Geary, *Furta Sacra: Thefts of Relics in the Central Middle Ages* (Princeton: Princeton University Press, 1978).

and a second pair "dressed in soft new silk" (dous pailes freis" (l. 515) precede their mistress to court to ensure that rooms curtained "in silk" (de pailes, l. 496) be prepared for her. Fraisne's silk is unusual, however, in the specificity with which its provenance is described. Since other texts typically give no indication of how silks from Alexandria, Constantinople, or Almería come to adorn the courts of France or England, the explanation that Fraisne's father had personally brought this *paile roë* back from Constantinople compels our attention in an ambiguous yet overdetermined way.[27] It marks this otherwise ordinary Breton knight as a world traveler – a crusader, perhaps, or a pilgrim who had traversed the Byzantine capital on the way to or from the Holy Land. Since medieval silks that survive to the present day were, almost without exception, preserved in ecclesiastical treasuries, the fact that the knight had given the *paile* to his wife instead of to an ecclesiastical foundation at once confirms the *Lais'* worldly orientation and gives us a broader glimpse into the workings of twelfth-century secular society.[28] Most of all, the silk is intended to signal the foundling's noble birth – a function reinforced by the second object the lady appends to her child:

> Taking part of one of her laces, she ties a big ring to [the infant's] arm. It contained an ounce of pure gold and was set with a jacinth, and the band bore an inscription around it. Wherever the girl might be found, let everyone know that she was, in truth, nobly born.

> A une piece d'un suen laz
> un gros anel li lie al braz.
> De fin or i aveit une unce;
> el chastun out une jagunce;
> la verge en tur esteit letree.

---

[27] The Old French word *paile* is derived from the Latin *pallium*, designating the mantle worn by archbishops and, by extension, the silk of which they were most often made; *pallia rotata* (> *paile roë*) were decorated with rows of roundels filled with human or animal figures, characteristic of many fine silks manufactured in the Muslim or Byzantine Mediterranean. Sharon Kinoshita, "Almería Silk and the French Feudal Imaginary: Towards a 'Material' History of the Medieval Mediterranean," in *Medieval Fabrications: Dress, Textiles, Clothwork, and Other Cultural Imaginings*, ed. E. Jane Burns (New York: Palgrave Macmillan, 2004), pp. 168, 242 n. 2. A *paile roë* (l. 505) also adorns Muldumarec's tomb in the abbey of Caerleon at the conclusion of *Yonec*.

[28] Compare Erec's donation of a *paile vert* in the Guiot manuscript (BNF fr. 794) of *Erec et Enide*. Kinoshita, "Almería Silk," pp. 165–6. A famous example of an ecclesiastical donation is the so-called "shroud of Saint-Josse," a samite silk from tenth-century Khurasan (eastern Iran) brought to an abbey in the Pas-de-Calais and today housed in the "Islamic Arts" section of the Louvre.

> La u la meschine iert trovee,
> bien sacent tuit veraiement
> qu'ele est nee de bone gent. (*Le Fraisne*, ll. 127–34)

Indeed, thanks to the ring and the "beautiful and costly silk" (le paile ... riche e bel, l. 208), the porter and his daughter who rescue the foundling immediately recognize her as "highborn" (nee de halte gent, l. 210). The *paile* and *anel* are again evoked together (ll. 303, 309) when Fraisne runs away from the abbey with Gurun, taking these links to the past with her:

> The girl took good care of them. She locked them in a chest and had the chest carried with her; she didn't want it left behind or forgotten.

> La meschine bien les guarda;
> en un cofre les enferma.
> Le cofre fist od sei porter,
> nel volt laissier ne ubliër. (*Le Fraisne*, ll. 313–16)

As in *Guigemar*, "material" objects furnish the proof of the deepest human relations. Gurun's new mother-in-law marvels at Fraisne's unimpeachable behavior around the bride who is to displace her, even feeling some regret over her fate. Only upon seeing the silk Fraisne has spread upon Gurun's nuptial bed, however, does recognition begin to dawn:

> She looks at the silk on the bed, for never had she seen such a fine one – excepting only the one she had given away with the daughter she had concealed.

> Le paile esguarde sur le lit,
> que unkes mes si bon ne vit
> fors sul celui qu'ele dona
> od sa fille qu'ele cela. (*Le Fraisne*, ll. 423–6)

The silk – "*your* piece of silk" (*vostre* paile, 484) says the lady to her husband in belatedly confessing her misdeed – is distinctive and instantly recognizable, serving to reconnect Fraisne to her proper rank and lineage. In a world in which beauty, nobility, courtesy, and gentility are each assumed to be co-signifiers of the others, Fraisne is the exception that proves (in the double sense of testing and confirming) the rule. Effortlessly deflecting multiple threats to the feudal politics of lineage – accusations of adultery, child abandonment, the failure of the male line, and concubinage – the *lai* concludes with the titular heroine (and her twin

sister Codre) well placed in socially suitable marriages. In the end, a precious Byzantine *paile roë* sets right all the disturbances unleashed by the
mother's slanderous and ill-tempered accusation.

Les dous amanz presents quite a different scenario, one in which a
mutually advantageous love match is short-circuited precisely by the
single-minded devotion and determination of the courtly lover. The *lai*
is presented as an etiological tale: how a mountain outside Pistres, in
Normandy, came to be named "the two lovers" after the adventure of the
only child of the region's first king. The plot of the father so attached to
his daughter that he refuses to bestow her in marriage of course animates
the "first verse" of Chrétien de Troyes's *Erec et Enide*, where the impov-
erished vavassor's stubborn and unreasonable determination to give his
daughter only to the son of a count or a king is resolved by the timely
arrival of a knight in need of arms and a beautiful lady to defend. But
it also partakes of a more widespread and sinister tale-type in which the
father's over-attachment to his beautiful and motherless daughter is born
of incestuous desire[29] – hinted at here in the king's inability to leave his
daughter alone:

> He was close to her night and day. He was comforted by the
> girl (since he had lost the queen). Many thought ill of it, and
> even his own [retainers] criticized him on account of it.

> pres de li esteit nuit e jur;
> cunfortez fu par la meschine,
> puis que perdue ot la reïne.
> Plusur a mal li aturnerent;
> li suen meïsme l'en blasmerent. (*Les dous amanz*, ll. 30–4)

Whether his subjects suspect an illicit attachment or are simply scandal-
ized at their king's failure to secure his dynastic succession (either by
contracting a politically suitable match for his daughter or by remarrying
to engender a male heir of his own) remains unclear; it is to quell his
people's dissatisfaction that the king hits on the expedient of the physical
challenge: whoever would marry his daughter must carry her to the top
of the nearby mountain without stopping to rest.

---

[29] This is the motif of "the father who wanted to marry his daughter (Aarne–
Thompson–Uther Type 510B), http://www.pitt.edu/~dash/type0510b.html (accessed 17
June 2011). This is the theme of Peau d'Ane, for example in Philippe de Beaumanoir's
La Manekine, trad. C. Marchello-Nizia (Paris: Stock, 1980).

In the meantime, however, the princess has contracted her own elective affinity with the young son of a local count:

> He frequented the king's court, staying there often. He fell in love with the king's daughter and repeatedly asked her to grant him her love and to love him for the sake of love-friendship. Because he was brave and courtly, and because the king much esteemed him, she granted him her love; he humbly thanked her for it. They often spoke together and loyally loved one another – hiding it as best they could so no one would notice.

> En la curt le rei conversot,
> asez sovent i surjurnot;
> la fille le rei aama,
> e meinte feiz l'araisuna
> qu'ele s'amur li otriast
> e par druërie l'amast.
> Pur ceo que pruz fu e curteis
> e que mult le preisot li reis,
> li otria sa druërie,
> e cil humblement l'en mercie.
> Ensemble parlerent sovent
> e s'entramerent leialment,
> e celerent a lur poeir
> qu'um nes peüst aparceveir. (*Les dous amanz*, ll. 61–74)

They are perfectly suited to one another: "noble and handsome" (gent e bel, l. 58), "brave and courtly" (pruz...e curteis, l. 67), the "young man" (damisel, l. 57) is just the sort of consort the Pitrois might wish as their future lord. In fact, the king's own high estimation of the young man's worth (l. 68) plays no mean role in winning him the princess's affection. He humbly requests and she duly grants him her "druërie," even as the *lai*'s repeated evocation of the youth of the "two children" (dui enfant, l. 10) leaves room to doubt the degree of their carnal engagement.[30]

The win–win proposition of the happy lovers whose marriage would secure the royal succession, however, turns into a nightmare scenario because of the king's excessive, quasi-incestuous attachment: "If he asked her father for her, he knew that he loved her so much that he would not want to give [her] to him" (S'a sun pere la demandot, / il saveit bien que tant l'amot / que pas ne li voldreit doner, ll. 87–9). The princess devises the remedy of contacting a relative "very knowledgeable about medi-

---

[30] Further on in the text he is called "vaslez" (l. 127) and "damisels" (ll. 153, 178).

cines" (mult...saive de mescines, l. 107) to procure a potion that will artifically enhance her lover's strength. Though the young man easily and joyfully undertakes the expedition to Salerno and back, when the day of the trial comes he fails to take advantage of the special elixir he has procured, despite his sweetheart's repeated urging: "The girl often begged him: 'Friend, drink your medicine!'" (Sovent li prie la meschine: / "Amis, bevez vostre mescine!" ll. 209–10). The near-homophony of "meschine" and "mescine" is perhaps a tip-off that only with the latter can he hope to win the former. But, laments the narrator, "he had no moderation" (n'ot en lui point de mesure, l. 189), and though he staggers his way up the mountain with his sweetheart in his arms, he collapses and dies at the top – a victim of the same lack of measure that had done in Equitan and the seneschal's wife.

Strikingly, in *Les dous amanz* (in contrast to the grail legend), the sterility of the royal line does nothing to compromise the fertility of the land. On the contrary: when the princess realizes her lover is dead, she throws the phial away in despair, spilling its contents all over the mountain. As a result, "the whole country was considerably improved" (mult en a esté amendez / tuz li païs e la cuntree, ll. 226–7) by the beneficial plants sprung from the herbal mixture. The princess, on the other hand, barely survives her lover but dies when "grief for him touched her heart" (Li duels de lui al quer li tuche, l. 236). The legacy, then, of the father's stubborn attachment to his daughter is a fertile land and a geographical landmark, at the cost of the extinction of the royal lineage whose memory is preserved not by the Normans but by the Bretons.[31]

Transitions

The final *lai* in Harley 978, *Eliduc*, seems excessive on all counts. At 1184 lines, it is by a good margin the longest *lai* in the collection, structured by a logic of reduplication – two lords, two wives, even two titles – that we shall further examine in Chapter 6. It opens with a feudal order in disarray; it concludes over a thousand lines later as the three protagonists, having made their peace with that world, abandon it in order to embrace a life of spiritual meditation. The disorder stems from the simultaneous intensity

---

[31] Since the mountain memorializes the protagonists – "On account of the children's adventure, the mountain is named 'Two Lovers'" (Pur l'aventure des enfanz / a nun li munz des Dous Amanz, ll. 251–2) – neither the prologue nor the epilogue makes further mention of "remembrance."

and instability of love, both feudal and courtly-erotic. The prologue tells us that the titular protagonist and his first wife, Guildeluëc, "loved each other most loyally" (mult s'entramerent leialment, l. 12) but that he subsequently "loved" (ama, l. 15) the maiden Guilliadun. At the outset of the story, Eliduc "loyally" (leialment, l. 32) serves the king of Brittany, the overlord who "greatly loved and cherished him" (mult l'amot e cherisseit, l. 31). The king's love and loyalty, however, do not prevent him from turning against Eliduc as a result of the undue credence he lends to his peers' envious slander. Crossing the Channel to the kingdom of Logres with ten of his knights, Eliduc offers his services to a king who "loved [them] very much and cherished them well" (mult les ama, mult les ot chiers, l. 120). It is this king's daughter whom Eliduc falls in love with and eventually marries, in a briefly recounted happy ending that precedes their final withdrawal from the world. Eliduc's dilemma is a reminder that in the Middle Ages, love is always a social relationship. Caught between his loyalty to two lords and his love for two women, the protagonist's ideal relations with his king, on the one hand, and his wife, on the other, are troubled by excess, changeability, and a logic of repetition.

Prized for his "prowess" (pruësce, l. 35) and entrusted with the rule of the kingdom whenever his master is away, Eliduc:

> was allowed to go hunting in the forest. No forester was so bold as to dare to deny him or ever complain.

> Par les forez poeit chacier;
> n'i ot si hardi forestier
> ki cuntredire li osast
> ne ja une feiz en grusçast. (*Eliduc*, ll. 37–40)

It is no surprise that the special privileges Eliduc enjoys relate to hunting, the noble and even royal pastime par excellence. Guigemar's reversal of fortune takes place not when tournamenting abroad but when hunting in the forest on a visit home. In *Equitan*, the fact that "the king would not give up his hunting" (li reis ne laissast sun chacier, l. 27) for anything but war serves as our first indication of his propensity to neglect his responsibilities; later, hunting provides the pretext for him to meet the seneschal's wife face-to-face for the first time (ll. 48–9) and to set the plot of the seneschal's assassination in motion (ll. 248–9).[32] This literary convention, however, reflects a fraught historical situation. In England, the Forest

---

[32] In *Bisclavret*, it is when the king "went hunting in the forest" (ala chacier a la forest, ll. 136–7) that he meets up with Bisclavret, who has been languishing there a year.

was a zone comprising all sorts of land (including cultivated fields and townships) over which the king exercised special rights; in particular, "beasts of the chase ... could be taken only by the king or by those that had his warrant." Under Henry II, the king's foresters, who administered the justice and fines incurred for the violation of Forest Law, were feared and hated. "For them violence took the place of law, extortion was praiseworthy, justice was an abomination and innocence a crime," wrote the biographer of Saint Hugh of Lincoln. For Walter Map, "they eat the flesh of men in the presence of Leviathan, and drink their blood."[33] For all the tale's nominal Breton setting, the fact that men such as these would not dare to cross Eliduc suggests the extraordinary level of privilege and entitlement a twelfth-century audience would have understood him to enjoy, fully accounting for the envy of his peers.[34]

Despite the love and favor bestowed on Eliduc, the (unspecified) defamation of his peers eventually turns the king against him. In *Lanval*, Marie accounts for the protagonist's predicament by appealing to the experience of her noble audience: "*Lords*, don't be surprised: a stranger, with no support, is sad in foreign lands when he knows not where to seek help" (*Seignur*, ne vus en merveilliez: / huem estranges, descunseilliez / mult est dolenz en altre terre, / quant il ne set u sucurs querre, ll. 35–8). In *Eliduc*, the explanation takes the form of a well-attested "peasant's proverb" (proverbe au vilain):

> As a reproof, the peasant upbraiding his ploughman says that a lord's love isn't a fief. It is a wise and canny man who keeps his lord's loyalty and loves his good neighbors.

> Li vileins dit par repruvier,
> quant tencë a sun charuier,
> qu'amurs de seignur n'est pas fiez.
> Cil est sages e veziëz,
> ki leialté tient sun seignur,
> envers ses bons veisins amur. (*Eliduc*, ll. 61–6)

In a rare breach of the *Lais*' resolutely courtly tone, this peasant's proverb

---

In *Yonec*, the jealous husband feigns going hunting (l. 303) in order to trap his wife with her lover.

[33] W. L. Warren, *Henry II* (Berkeley: University of California Press, 1973), pp. 390–5.

[34] On envy as a widespread theme among the writers associated with the court of Henry II, see R. Howard Bloch, *The Anonymous Marie de France* (Chicago: University of Chicago Press, 2003), pp. 155–9, who also cites Walter Map among his contemporary examples.

(anticipating the world of the *Ysopë*) casts lord–vassal relations less as a reciprocal bond based on honor and fidelity than as a raw competition for power and favor.

Lanval faces disfavor by disappearing into the countryside. Eliduc, in contrast, elects a form of self-exile. Exhorting his own vassals "loyally" (leialment, l. 73) to look after his wife, he crosses the sea to Totnes, where he lucks into a local political scene composed of a patchwork of petty kingdoms rent by conflict: "There were many kings in the land, with strife and war reigning among them" (Plusurs reis i ot en la terre, / entre els ourent estrif e guerre, ll. 89–90). For Eliduc, it is a perfect opportunity: "Having found war there, he didn't want to go any further" (Ne voleit mes avant aler, / quant iluec a guerre trovee, ll. 104–5). His choice of sides, moreover, is dictated not by moral or ethical criteria but by the purest mercenary logic: "He wanted to do all he could to assist whichever king was in the most dire straits and to remain *in his pay*" (Le rei ki plus esteit grevez / e damagiez e encumbrez / voldra aidier a sun poeir / e *en soldees* remaneir, ll. 107–10). While the verb "aidier" evokes the formal obligation of military assistance (*auxilium*) the vassal owed his lord, the mention of *soldees* (giving us our modern word "soldier") – echoing the prologue's mention of the protagonist's going off "in search of wages" (soldees querre, l. 14) – clearly evokes the pragmatic world of knights-for-hire that by the second half of the twelfth century was undermining the material bases of chivalric culture.[35]

Having been both overly favored and (unduly?) victimized by a system ostensibly meant to guarantee the stability of feudal society, Eliduc now remakes himself into a mercenary leader with a difference. Summoning "the poor knights living in the town" (les chevaliers mesaaisiez / ki el burc erent herbergiez, ll. 139–40), he invites them to throw their lot in with his, with the proviso that they will take neither "goods nor coin" (livreisun ne deniers, l. 144) during "the first forty days" (des quarante jurs primiers, l. 143), corresponding to the term of military service (*auxilium*) vassals traditionally owed their lords annually. When "enemies" storm the gates of the city, the newly formed company is immediately given the chance

---

[35] In the time of Henry II and Philip Augustus, these mercenaries included not only *cottereaux* (combatants "of low birth…fighting with weapons considered unworthy of a knight") but also *sergents à cheval*, "fighting on horseback in the style of knights… recruited in all probability from the lowest ranks of the nobility – those too poor to possess a fief owing military service – or from among commoners, including bourgeois from the cities now armed as knights." Gabrielle Spiegel, *Romancing the Past: The Rise of Vernacular Prose Historiography in Thirteenth-Century France* (Berkeley: University of California Press, 1993), p. 20.

to prove itself, spontaneously joined by fourteen knights of the city. Using their local knowledge, they ambush and defeat the enemy in the forest. Eliduc distributes the booty they recover to his men, then delivers the captured prisoners to the king. Rejoicing at Eliduc's feat, "the king loved and cherished him greatly. He kept him a full year [in his service and] made him guardian of his lands" (mult l'ama li reis e cheri. / Un an entier l'a retenu … / de sa terre guardein en fist, ll. 266–7, 270). Through his social and political savvy as much as his skill at arms, Eliduc secures a temporary master to replace the overlord who had spurned him.

Though narrated in wholly conventional terms, the love that springs up between Eliduc and the princess challenges the established order at every turn. Confessing her inconvenient passion to her chamberlain, the maiden laments: "I love the new *mercenary* – the good knight Eliduc" (jeo eim le novel *soldeier*, / Eliduc, le bon chevalier," ll. 339–40).[36] In a literary universe in which passion rarely transgresses the bounds of social hierarchy, the princess worries that she may have overstepped all limits of propriety:

> Alas! How my heart has been taken unawares by a foreigner! I don't know if he is well-born, and if he suddenly goes away, I will be miserable. I've been mad to commit myself in this way.

> Lasse! Cum est mis quers suzpris
> pur un hume d'altre païs!
> Ne sai s'il est de halte gent,
> si s'en ira hastivement,
> jeo remeindrai cume dolente.
> Folement ai mise m'entente. (*Eliduc*, ll. 387–92)

The jeopardy in falling in love with this foreigner is twofold: first, his lineage is unknown, and secondly, since he has no ties to the land, he might abandon her at any moment (tinged with the suggestion that a lover not of *halte gent* would be more likely to leave her). From Eliduc's perspective, on the other hand, their love faces a different double obstacle: "He wanted to remain loyal" (Sa leialté voleit guarder, l. 467), "both to keep faith with his wife and because he was with the king" (tant pur sa femme guarder fei, / tant pur ceo qu'il est od le rei, ll. 475–6) – the

---

[36] The same rhyme, though in reverse order, recurs when the maiden recounts her plight to Eliduc's wife: "I loved a knight – the good mercenary Eliduc" ("Mult ai amé un chevalier, / Eliduc, le bon soldeier," ll. 1073–4). In each instance, Harf-Lancner's modern French translation mitigates the scandal by translating the rhyme words as "chevalier" and "guerrier."

grammatical structure emphasizing the parallel between his marital and feudal obligations. Later, in contemplating the pain of leaving behind the woman he loves, Eliduc articulates in the first person his non-negotiable debts to both king and wife: he needs to return home, for "my lord has written to me to recall me according to my sworn oath, and there's also my wife" (mis sire m'a par brief mandé / e par sairement conjuré / e ma femme de l'altre part, ll. 595–7). Likewise entering into the equation is the term contract he has sworn to Guilliadun's father: "Beauty, by oath, I am truly your father's. If I took you with me, I would belie my faith to him" (Bele, jeo sui par sairement / a vostre pere veirement / se jeo vus en menoe od mei, / jeo li mentireie ma fei, ll. 685–8).

Despite his experience of "lies" (losenge, l. 50) and betrayals and his canny ability to exploit his chivalric skills, Eliduc (the character) continues to believe in an idealized world governed by the feudal values of loyalty and counsel.[37] It is not certain that *Eliduc* (the *lai*) feels the same. Like *Le Fraisne*, it turns on a case of serial polygamy, tolerating the dissolution of marriage for political or personal convenience in defiance of the Church's defense of marriage as an indissoluble bond. In this case, it is the very attenuation of feudal bonds that holds out a promise of a happy love, for in contrast to Eliduc's obligation to his liege lord, the loyalty he owes the king of Exeter is temporary. What had seemed a liability now turns to his advantage: once the term of his contract has expired, Eliduc (having presumably helped his lord to restore order in Brittany) devises an excuse to return to England to spirit away the object of his desire.

Just what Eliduc has in mind is not clear. Before returning to Brittany, he had raised the possibility of marrying Guilliadun, only to dismiss it: "If I were married to my love, *Christianity would not allow it*" ("S'a m'amie esteie espusez, / *nel suferreit crestiëntez*," ll. 601–2). But now, as Guilliadun sneaks off at night to board Eliduc's waiting ship, all thoughts of feudal loyalty, dynastic fortune, and religious prohibition are apparently abandoned. Once the ship is caught in a violent storm on the high seas, however, the discourse of divine vengeance rings out in the voice of one of Eliduc's crew:

> Then one of the sailors loudly cried: "What are we doing? Lord, you have inside with you the one who is causing our deaths. We'll never reach land! *You have a faithful wife but you're bringing another back* in defiance of God and the law,

---

[37] Compare variations on *leialté* (ll. 65, 73, 467 and 944–5) and *cunseil* (ll. 75, 559, 608, 743, 876, 925).

right and faith. Let us throw her into the sea! Then we could
still make it."

Uns des eschipres haltement
s'est escriëz: "Que faimes nus?
Sire, ça enz avez od vus
cele par qui nus perissuns.
Ja mes a terre ne vendruns!
Femme leial espuse avez
e sur celi altre en menez
cuntre Deu e cuntre la lei,
cuntre dreiture e cuntre fei.
Laissiez la nus geter en mer,
si poüm sempres ariver." (*Eliduc*, ll. 830–40)

The sailor's condemnation vividly draws attention to the legal ambiguity
of Eliduc's action. In effect, he is taking a second wife while the first is
still living – like Philip I, the early-twelfth-century French king repeatedly
condemned by the pope for repudiating his first wife, Bertha of Holland,
in order to marry Bertrada de Montfort, wife of his vassal, the count of
Anjou.[38] Though Eliduc himself had previously acknowledged that such
a marriage would be anti-Christian – "nel suferreit crestiëntez" – he now
makes short work of the protesting sailor, clubbing him with an oar and
throwing his body into the sea. In the meantime, however, Guilliadun has
fainted from shock at learning that her lover is already married. Unable to
revive her, Eliduc thinks her dead. By the time the ship reaches port, the
moral ambiguity surrounding their bigamous elopement has been doubly
silenced, by the murder of the dissenting sailor and by the "death" of the
prospective bride.

 Having laid Guilliadun to rest in a local convent and promised to take
monastic vows so that he may pray every day over her tomb, Eliduc is
momentarily reunited with his wife, but, in an inversion of all courtly
convention, "was never cheerful toward her nor spoke a good word to
her" (unkes bel semblant ne fist / ne bone parole ne dist, ll. 961–2).
Seeking the source of his melancholy, Guildeluëc comes upon the "dead"
but still beautiful Guilliadun, revives her with a magical herb and, on
hearing her tale, asks her husband for a piece of his estate so that she
may found an abbey and he may be free to take "her whom he loves so
much" (cele ... qu'il eime tant, l. 1127) in a way that will free him from
the charge of bigamy:

---

[38] Duby, *The Knight, The Lady, and The Priest*, pp. 3–22.

In a grove near the castle, at the hermitage chapel, he built a church and erected a house [of religion]. He endowed it with significant land and wealth: he'll have all he needs. When everything was done, the lady (along with thirty nuns) took the veil and established the rule of her order.

Pres del chastel enz el boscage
a la chapele a l'ermitage,
la a fet faire sun mustier
e ses maisuns edifiër.
Grant terre i met e grant aveir:
bien i avra sun estuveir.
Quant tut a fet bien aturner,
la dame i fet sun chief veler,
trente nuneins ensemble od li;
sa vie e sun ordre establi. (*Eliduc*, ll. 1135–44)

What are we to make of this turn? On the one hand, canon law "required that *both* spouses agree to abandon the marriage vow when one or both desired a life of celibacy."[39] On the other, the details of this foundation narrative – the nunnery's association with a hermit, the specification of its size, and, especially, the social rank of its donors – ring true to conditions in the early and mid twelfth century. In this period of political instability (perhaps reflected in *Eliduc* in the troubles besetting both Brittany and Exeter), new monasteries were often endowed by landed petty lords and knights of modest station rather than the titled aristocrats whose foundations had dominated the previous century. Most interesting for our purposes is the prominent role that women with some knowledge of the world – widows, wives who left or were left by their husbands (like Guildeluëc) or who took vows alongside their husbands (like Guilliadun) – played in female monasticism in this era.[40] While they may be acting in violation of canon law, the resolution devised by Eliduc and Guildeluëc is in perfect consonance with their times.[41]

[39] Penelope D. Johnson, *Equal in Monastic Profession: Religious Women in Medieval France* (Chicago: University of Chicago Press, 1991), pp. 31–2. For an expanded reading of the politics of remarriage in the *Lais*, see Kinoshita, "Two For the Price of One."

[40] On the growth of female monasticism in France and England from the late eleventh century to c. 1170 as one symptom of a "matrimonial crisis" of "too few marriageable men for too many nubile women," see Bruce L. Venarde, *Women's Monasticism and Medieval Society: Nunneries in France and England, 890–1215* (Ithaca: Cornell University Press, 1997), pp. 89–132 (esp. pp. 89–92, 95, 128–9).

[41] Venarde thus cites the *lai* at the outset and conclusion of his chapter on "Social and Economic Contexts in the Eleventh and Twelfth Centuries." See *Women's Monasticism*, pp. 89–91, 131–2.

Still, the happy ending of *Eliduc* can be sustained only through conden-
sation and displacement:

> Eliduc married his sweetheart. The day he married her, the
> celebration was carried out with great honor and ceremony.
> They lived together a long time, bound by a perfect love.
> They gave many alms and did great good, until they devoted
> themselves to God.

> Elidus a s'amie prise;
> a grant honur, od bel servise
> en fu la feste demenee
> le jur qu'il l'aveit espusee.
> Ensemble vesquirent meint jur,
> mult ot entre els parfite amur.
> Granz almosnes e granz biens firent,
> tant que a Deu se cunvertirent. (*Eliduc*, ll. 1145–52)

The remaining twenty-eight lines of the *lai* describe Eliduc's foundation
of a church (or, effectively, a male monastery) to accompany the abbey
he had previously endowed for Guildeluëc:

> He put the wife he so dearly cherished together with his first
> wife.... They prayed God for their friend, ... and he prayed
> for them in turn.

> Ensemble od sa femme premiere
> mist sa femme que tant ot chiere....
> Deu preiouent pur lur ami ...
> e il pur eles repreiot. (*Eliduc*, ll. 1165–73)

The true "happy ending" turns out to be an abandonment of the world and
a turn to spiritual life:

> Each one made a great individual effort to love God in good
> faith, and [all of them] achieved a beautiful end: God's mercy,
> divine truth!

> Mult se pena chescuns pur sei
> de Deu amer par bone fei
> e mult par firent bele fin,
> la merci Deu, le veir devin! (*Eliduc*, ll. 1177–80)

The prologue of *Eliduc* had set its three protagonists in gendered opposition: after whom would the *lai* be named? By its end, the three, having ex-

changed feudal and courtly-conjugal love for divine love, move from their triangulated relations to a common devotion to God, their three stories melded into a single anonymous voice (signaled by the third person plural "firent") that functions as a palinode for the *lai* and, in Harley 978, for the collection as a whole.

The *Fables* and feudal society

Known to modern readers in forms ranging from Aesop's *Fables* to the *Fables* of La Fontaine, the corpus of Marie de France's *Ysopë* might at first glance seem to be the least rooted of all her texts in the intricacies of medieval society. Quite the contrary, the "morals" purveyed by such familiar tales as "The Crow and the Fox" or "The Ant and the Grass-hopper" seem timeless in their simplicity and universal applicability. Yet, as Hans Robert Jauss and (more recently) Jill Mann have persuasively shown, the *Ysopë* is permeated by the ethos of feudal relations, signaled by the prevalence of "specific socio-economic terms such as *seignur, vileins, riche hume, povre hume, baruns, produme, franz hume* … closely intertwined with a system of moral values."[42] Relationships among animals, among men, and between animals and men are defined by their adherence to *lëauté* and *honur*, on the one hand, or their resort to *felunie* and *traïsun*, on the other. In this world as in the *Lais*, "The loss of public esteem is the worst sanction that this society can bring to bear."[43]

In the *Lais*, vertical power relations are tempered by the ideal of the reciprocity of responsibility, however unequal the partners. Thus in *Equitan*, although the king is ultimately undeterred from acting on his desire for his seneschal's wife, he hesitates at least long enough to acknowledge the principle that "I owe him the same faith and love that I want him to give me" (Guarder li dei amur e fei, / si cum jeo vuel k'il face a mei, *Equitan*, ll. 77–8). Lords are less likely to be bad outright than negligent (like Arthur in *Lanval*) or susceptible to bad counsel (like the king of Brittany in *Eliduc*). Elsewhere, lords behave responsibly – like Gurun, who heeds his vassals' demand that he marry and even agrees

---

[42] Hans Robert Jauss, *Untersuchungen zur mittelalterlichen Tierdichtung* (Tübingen: M. Niemeyer, 1959) and Jill Mann, *From Aesop to Reynard: Beast Literature in Medieval Britain* (Oxford: Oxford University Press, 2009), p. 57.

[43] The "unembarrassed proliferation of moral abstractions" such as *felunie* and *traïsun* where the *Romulus Nilantii* uses adjectives is one example of the way Marie's transformation of her sources exceeds the merely linguistic. Mann, *From Aesop to Reynard*, pp. 58, 59.

to their choice of bride (*Le Fraisne*, ll. 338–54) – or ideally – like the king in *Bisclavret* who recognizes the werewolf as his loyal vassal where even the werewolf's wife does not. In the *Lais*, raw power and coercion are wielded, rather, within the family, by authoritarian husbands (*Yonec, L'aüstic, Chievrefueil*) and fathers (*Les dous amanz, Milun*) who impose their will on their hapless wives and daughters.

In the *Fables*, on the other hand, bad lords are the rule, wielding a brute power unattenuated by the bonds of mutual obligation. The powerful routinely victimize the weak to their own advantage. In the second tale of the collection, a wolf accuses a lamb drinking downstream from him of muddying his water, then blames it for an alleged slight committed by its father. When the lamb protests, the wolf seizes and kills it:

> Thus do powerful lords, viscounts, and judges behave towards those in their power: for greed's sake, they invent false reasons to ensnare them. Often they summon them to court. They strip them of flesh and skin, just as the wolf did to the lamb.

> Issi funt li riche seignur,
> li vescunte e li jugeür,
> de ceus qu'il unt en lur justise;
> faus' acheisuns par coveitise
> treovent asez pur eus confundre:
> suvent les funt a pleit somundre,
> la char lur tolent e la pel,
> si cum li lus fist a l'aignel. (2:31–8)

In Fable 50, when a wolf who had given up meat for Lent spies a succulent sheep, he rationalizes away his vow by calling it a salmon rather than a sheep – as if the near homophony of the rhyme words "mutun" (l. 19) and "saumun" (l. 20) effaced the theological infraction.[44] Nor do the powerful heed the conventions of feudal society. In Fable 7, "The Wolf and the Crane," the crane who requests the "great reward" (grant loër," 7:15) he had been promised for extracting a bone stuck in the wolf's throat is told that his "good reward" (bon luër, 7:24) is not having had his head bitten off. "Thus it is," the lesson goes, "with the bad lord" (Autresi est del mal seignur, 7:33):

---

[44] The moral, on the other hand, makes this an example of the way the evil-hearted (humme de mauvais quer, 50:23) are unable to resist gluttony (glutunerie, 50:25) and lechery (lecherie, l. 26).

If the poor man does him a service and then requests his *reward*, he'll get none but his bad will. Because he's in his power, [the poor man] owes him thanks for his life.

... si povres hum li fet honur
e puis demant sun *gueredun*,
ja n'en avera si maugré nun;
pur ceo qu'il seit en sa baillie,
mercïer li deit de sa vie. (7:34–8)

In courtly texts, the *gueredun* is, as we saw above, more than a simple reward: it is a formalization of the principle of reciprocity structuring feudal society. Here it is callously denied by a powerful lord who refuses any social constraint on his superior power.[45] The lesson to Fable 6 exhorts the weak to be wary: "Those with bad lords over them" (qui sur eus unt les maus seignurs, 6:26) should do everything possible to prevent those lords from allying with the wise or the rich, for "the stronger [a lord] is, the worse he behaves toward them" (Cum plus est fort, e pis lur fet, 6:31).

The *Ysopë*'s extensive interrogation of the nature of lordship may be seen in the numerous fables involving the king of beasts, the lion. The baseline, as it were, is set in the double adventure of Fable 11, which places the lion by "custom and law" (custume e leis, 11:1) at the head of a feudal-monarchical hierarchy over all the world's animals, including a bullock (his seneschal) and a wolf (his provost). One day, the lion, bullock, and wolf hunt and kill a stag – their collective effort signaled by the plural verbs "chacerent" and "l'escorcerent" (11:9,10). When it comes to the division of the spoils, however, the lion claims the entire carcass for himself: the first part as king, the second "as profit" (pur le guaain, 11:19), the third as "companion" (cumpain, 11:20), and the fourth "because *he* killed" the deer (kar *il* l'ocist, 11:22) – in contradiction of the plural verbs previously cited. The bullock and wolf neither resist nor protest but bow to the "law" (raisun, 11:22) of the strongest. Given how effortlessly he intimidates these relatively strong subjects, it is no surprise in the second half of the fable when the lion easily has his way over two weaker (and female) "companions" (cumpainuns, 11:28), a she-goat and a ewe. The epimythium linking the two adventures reads:

And so it is, do not doubt it, that if a poor man takes a stronger man as a companion, he will never reap any profit. *The rich* will want to have the honor, or the poor will lose his love.

---

[45] See also Fables 20 and 78.

And if they are to share any profit, *the rich man* will want to keep it all.

Autresi est, ne dutez mie,
si povres hum prent cumpainie
a plus fort hume qu'il ne seit:
ja del guain n'avera espleit.
Li riches volt aver l'onur,
u li povres perdra s'amur;
e si nul gain deivent partir,
li riches vout tut retenir. (11:41–8)

In courtly literature, "riche" indicates a combination of wealth and power, typically used as an attribute for nobles well placed in the hierarchy of feudal society. The fable, in explicitly equating "riches" and "plus fort" in direct opposition to "povres," unmasks the direct correlation between wealth and power. The powerful, exploiting their raw force, preemptively seize more than their fair share. Gone is any sense of the reciprocity or differentiation of feudal society; all its members are pitted against each other in a zero-sum competition for the same resources. In the real world, of course, neither a bullock nor a ewe would be found competing for its share of venison. Here, however, the exigencies of the fable override those of nature.

The flip side of this equation among force, power, and wealth is explored in the three fables devoted to a sick lion. In Fable 14, a goat, ass, and fox take advantage of his weakness physically to abuse the lord they formerly feared. As the lion laments:

It's a much greater case of baseness, it seems to me, on the part of those who were my intimates – those who remember nothing of how I honored and favored them – than of those whom I mistreated. Those without power have few friends/ feudal allies.

Mut me semble greinur vilté
de ces ki furent mi privé,
a ki jeo fis honur e bien,
ki n'en remembrent nule rien,
que des autres, que jeo mesfis:
li nunpuissant ad poi amis. (14:27–32)

We do not know whether this lion-king had (in contrast to his counterpart in Fable 11) genuinely shown honor and favor to his intimates (probably to be understood as members of his *maisnie*, or royal household). In any case, the loyalty of the weak toward the powerful is exposed as a simple matter of force. The sick and weakened lion-king of Fable 36 continues to abuse his authority: summoning his subjects to him on the pretext of delegating who is to fetch food for him, he kills and eats them one by one – all except the fox, who warily remains outside the lion's den.[46]

> So it is with a king's court: those who enter unreflectively would do better to stay put in order to hear news of what is going on.

> De curt a rei est ensement:
> tels i entre legerement,
> meuz li vaudreit ensus ester
> Pur les nuveles escuter. (36:25–8)

In startling contrast to courtly convention, the king's court is cast as a site of fear, danger, and caution. But given that commanding the presence of one's subjects is (as in the case of Arthur and the Round Table) a prerogative of royal power, the fox's refusal to obey the lion's summons, however reasonable a response to the lion's violent abuse of his power, radically challenges the legitimacy of the feudal order.[47] The theme of the sick lion reaches its culmination in Fable 70. Told that only a deer's heart can cure him, a lion sends for a deer, who hesitates, tries to flee, but is killed when it finally obeys the summons. Before its heart can be harvested, however, it is stolen by a crafty fox. Accused of the crime, the fox swears (jura par serement, 70:35) that he did not take it: if the deer came to court knowing he would be killed, he must not have had a heart anyway; moreover, it would have been "disloyal, bad, and false" (desleaus, … mauveis e faus, 70:61–2) of the fox knowingly to steal the lion's cure. The lion agrees: "Had he had a heart, he never would have come" (s'il queor eüst, ja n'i venist, 70:66). In this fable permeated by feudal vocabulary and procedures, a stag without a heart seems more plausible than the prospect of

---

46 In Fable 14, the fox had bitten his powerless master on the ears.

47 Summoning one's vassals to court thus functions as a collective ritualized performance of *consilium* – one of the obligations a vassal owes his *seignur*. In *Erec et Enide*, Arthur is bereft when "only" 500 knights remain with him at court (ll. 6410–15). Moreover, the idea that it is the vassal who should wait to hear "news" (nuveles) pointedly inverts the Arthurian topos of the king impatiently awaiting news from without in order to commence festivities at his plenary court.

an intentionally false oath.[48] The system is thoroughly corrupted by the use of undue coercion on the one hand and false reasoning on the other.

The most thoroughgoing critique of the corruption of the feudal system occurs in Fable 29. Announcing that he is leaving them "to go live in another land" (29:1–2), the lion-king instructs his subjects to choose a new ruler. They unanimously request "another lion" (29:8), only to be told that none is available: the reigning king "hasn't dared raise one" (ne nurri nul, kar il ne osa, 29:10) – a not-so-subtle indictment of the instability of a rule that cannot reproduce itself. So they turn to the wolf: though all "think him treacherous" (le teneient a felun, 29:16), he is bold and "had promised several of them that he would always love them" (a plusurs aveit premis / que mut les amereit tut dis, 29:17–18). "If he were as noble as he should be" (si...esteit si francs cum il devereit, 29:24–5), the lion concedes, the wolf would make a good choice; however, both he and the crafty fox he will undoubtedly select "as his counselor" (a cunseiller, 29:27) should be obliged in advance to "swear on holy relics" (sur sainz jurer, 29:31) never to harm them or to eat flesh again. The wolf complies (his oath fleetingly alluded to with the word "asseürez," 29:37), but no sooner has the old king left than the new king begins to crave meat. Summoning a roe deer to his presence, "he asked her, *in private*, to tell him truthfully, *for love*, if his breath stank" (en cunseil li ad demandé / que par amur veir li desist / De sa aleine si ele puïst, 29:44–6). When the deer admits that it does, the wolf, with a show of anger:

> sent for his men. He asked them, all together, what judgment each would mete out to one addressing his lord in a shameful, ugly, and dishonorable way.
>
> ... pur ses hummes ad enveiez,
> a tuz ensemble demanda
> quel jugement chescun fera
> de celi ki dit a sun seignur
> hunte, leidesce, e deshonur. (29:50–4)

---

[48] A variant of the sick lion and the wily fox occurs in Fable 68. When a fox summoned to cure the sick lion hesitates before entering his chamber, the provost, a wolf, threatens to have the fox killed "as a lesson to his relatives." In retaliation, the fox declares that at Salerno (site of a famous medieval medical school, mentioned in *Les dous amanz*), he has learned that a wolf's pelt will cure the lion's malady. The provost is skinned alive, occasioning a moral similar to that of *Equitan*: "He who seeks to do ill to others has the same return against him" (Tel purchace le mal d'autrui, / que cel meme revient sur lui, 68:57–8).

The assembled vassals immediately declare that the offending deer must die. Thus authorized, the wolf seizes and kills the hapless animal, eats the better part, then "to cover up his iniquity, had others share in it" (pur sa felunie coverir, / en fet as autres departir, 29:59–60). The ploy is soon repeated, but the second animal summoned to render judgment, "preferring to lie rather than to suffer death for the sake of the truth" (29:65–6), declares the wolf's breath to be the sweetest odor imaginable.

> The wolf assembled his council and asked his barons what judgment they should mete out to one who cheats and lies.
>
> Li lus ad concilie asemblé,
> a ses baruns ad demandé
> que il deit fere par jugement
> de celui que lui triche e ment. (29:69–72)

As before, the vassals vote for death; as before, the wolf kills and eats the offending animal, this time without sharing. In a third moment, a plump but clever monkey targeted by the wolf refuses to answer the fatal question, saying he doesn't know. Pretending to be sick, the wolf takes to his bed; when his doctors urge him to eat, he says his only desire is for monkey flesh, but "I must keep my oath – unless I were to have such a reason that my barons would grant [an exception]" (mun serement m'estut garder, / si jeo ne eüsse tele reisun / que l'otriassent mi barun, 29:104–6). On cue, his vassals collectively enjoin him to ensure his health. Acting on their counsel, he kills and eats the monkey as he had always intended: "Then all of them had their verdict; he kept no oath to them" (Puis eurent tut lur jugement, / ne tient vers eus nul serement, 29:113–14).

This fable, as the cited passages indicate, is replete with feudal-chivalric vocabulary.[49] What is so scandalous is less the wolf's manifest abuse of power than the way that abuse is given the cloak of due process through the manipulation of feudal institutions. To be sure, there are hints of the weakness of the system early on in the vacuum of power created by the lion's abdication and his failure to produce or select a suitable heir because he "did not dare."[50] But in the three cases where the

---

[49] Thus the wolf's animal subjects are referred to, in familiar feudal fashion, as "his men" (ses hummes, 29:50); feudal function unproblematically trumps species differentiation.

[50] Contemporaries may well have been reminded of the multiple revolts of Henry II's sons, beginning in 1173 and lasting until his death in 1189. Besides the long fable tradition of the lion as king of beasts, lions figured in the arms of both the dukes of Normandy and the dukes of Aquitaine. Henry II's symbol was a lion rampant.

new king violates his solemnly sworn oath, it is with the full consent of his council. Assembling his barons and duly consulting them as use and custom demand, he secures their assent to the execution of his first two victims. If their only crime was to render a judgment displeasing to their lord, it is their fellow subjects who decide their sentence. Their complicity makes a mockery of the fable's ostensible moral:

> Thus the wise man shows that one should under no circumstances take a treacherous man as one's lord nor put him in any position of honor. He will never remain loyal either to strangers or to intimates. He will conduct himself towards his people as with wolf did with his oath.

> Pur ceo mustre li sage bien
> que hum ne deüst pur nule rien
> felun hume fere seignur
> ne trere lë a nul honur:
> ja ne gardera leauté
> plus a l'estrange que al privé;
> si se demeine envers sa gent
> cum fist li lus del serement. (29:115–22)

Literally sharing in the spoils created by the judgments they render, they are guilty not simply of having knowingly chosen a *felun* (29:16) to rule over them, but of willingly endorsing his abuse of power and, for good measure, sharing in his *felunie* (29:59). In contrast to those examples in which a rapacious lord imposes his will by brute force, in Fable 29 the governed themselves knowingly collude in the abuse of power, undermining the structural ideal of the feudal system for their own advantage.[51]

Bad vassals, though fewer in number than bad lords, are equally to be scorned. Fable 23, "The Bat," imagines the animal kingdom divided into two parallel realms: that of four-footed beasts, ruled by the lion, and that of the birds, ruled by the eagle. As the two factions prepare to go to war, a hapless bat first throws his support to the animals, only to switch his allegiance to the birds when he realizes that they are more numerous.[52]

---

[51] An example of an honorable exchange is found in Fable 16, when a lion spares the mouse who inadvertently wakens him; soon after, when the lion falls into a hunter's trap, the mouse comes to his rescue, mobilizing his friends to gnaw through the rope netting in which he is caught: "Don't be afraid! Now I'll return the favor you rendered in pardoning me" (N'eiez poür! / Ore vus rendrai le guerdun / que a mei feïstes le pardun, 16:28–30) – one of the rare examples of a properly rendered *guerdon* in the *Ysopë*.

[52] For a further reading of this fable, see Chapter Five.

Amidst the looming battle encompassing all of the animal kingdom, the fable and its lesson focus on the dishonorable and self-interested behavior of the little bat.

> Thus it is with the traitor who acts unbecomingly toward his lord, to whom he should do honor and keep loyalty and faith. If his lord needs him, then he tries to make accommodations with others, failing him in his need and cleaving onto others. If his lord triumphs, he can't change his bad ways but wants to return to him. He acts badly all around. So he loses honor and wealth, and his heirs incur blame. He is forever shamed, like the bat, who never again can fly during the day nor ever again speak in court.

> Autresi est del traïtur
> que meseire vers sun seignur
> a ki il deit honur porter
> e leauté e fei garder;
> si sis sires ad de li mestier,
> as autres se veut dunc ajuster,
> a sun busuin li veut faillir
> e od autres se veut tenir;
> si sis sires vient el desus,
> ne peot lesser sun mauveis us;
> dunc vodreit a lui returner,
> de tutes pars veut meserrer;
> si honur en pert e sun aveir
> e repruver en unt si heir,
> a tuz jurs en est si huniz
> cum fu dunc la chalve suriz,
> que ne deit mes par jur voler,
> në il ne deit en curt parler. (23:49–66)

Throughout the *Ysopë*, the strong abuse the weak with impunity; rarely are they subject to *Equitan*'s "reap what you sow" logic of just returns.[53] Here, the consequences the bat suffers within the tale for acting out of fear and self-protection are reinforced in the epimythium, which cas-

---

[53] Exceptions include Fable 3 (a victimizer randomly victimized), in which a frog who tries to lure an unsuspecting mouse to its death turns into a tasty morsel for a passing kite whose attention had been drawn by the mouse's cry. Its epimythium says: those who "plot against others put themselves in danger" (as autres quident purchacer, / avient lur cors a periller, 3:91–2). In Fable 68, as we saw above in note 48, a similar moral sums up the case of a fox who turns the tables on the wolf who had threatened to kill him.

tigates him for his violation of the social contract so rarely respected by others. Though the *Fables* unmask the violence at the core of feudal society, they explicitly moralize at the "misbehavior" of the weak but not of the strong.[54] A corrective model of behavior is found in Fable 20, in the rectitude of the shepherd's guard dog who refuses the bread offered him by a thief on the grounds that he would be unable to "repay" (reguerduner, 20:9) the gift without betraying his lord (seignur, 20:19) in the process.

Fable 10, "The Fox and the Eagle," provides the sole example of the victim unleashing violence against his victimizer. When an eagle snatches one of its young, the fox takes up a burning brand and sets fire to the tree housing the eagle's nest. The eagle cries out for the fox to extinguish the flame before it consumes his offspring, but the tale ends there, with no hint as to its resolution. The epimythium, however, strikes an ominous note:

> From this exemplum we understand that this is what happens to the powerful and arrogant: never will their protests or cries win them mercy from the poor; rather, if the latter can take vengeance, you'll see the former beg soon enough.

> Par ceste essample entendum nus
> que si est del riche orguillus:
> ja del povre n'avera merci
> pur sa pleinte ne pur sun cri;
> mes si cil s'en peüst venger,
> sil verreit l'um tost suppleer. (10:17–22)

Across the *Ysopë*, the fox is hardly the quintessential victim; though occasionally bested by superior force, wit, or circumstance, in the majority of the fables in which he appears, the fox wins out by a combination of cunning and circumspection.[55] Thus in this case, the revenge of the "povre" is hardly that of the mouse or the lamb. Even so, in the epimythium, the question of revenge turns around the conditional "if" of line 21, as if the full consequences of unleashing the pent-up fury of the victimized remain not just unnarrated (as here) but perhaps unimaginable.

The prevalence of feudal vocabulary is all the more incongruous given

---

[54] More crudely, the moral of Fable 84 (on the oxen who protest at having to haul their own manure from the stable) inveighs against the ingratitude of the "bad servant" (mauveis sergant, 84:19) who complains about "how much he serves his lord" (sun grant servise a sun seignur, 84:21) while conveniently forgetting his own "frequent misdeeds" (de ceo qu'il mesfet suvent, 84:25).

[55] Compare Fables 13, 28, 36, 58, 60, 61, 68, 69, 70, 88, 98.

the lack of courtly and chivalric signifiers within the tales themselves. In the *Ysopë*, love is conspicuous by its absence; in striking contrast to the *Lais*, feudal relations are rarely articulated through forms of the word "love" (amur) or "to love" (amer).[56] Alliances are matters of status and mutual advantage; relationships are unstable and always prone to trickery and betrayal, all the better to illustrate the importance of self-reliance.[57] And though occasional fables show animals or peasants with their young, the *Ysopë* in general lacks the preoccupation with lineage that helps drive the plot of *Guigemar*, *Equitan*, *Le Fraisne*, and *Yonec*.

As might be expected in a world populated mainly by animals and peasants, objects play little role. Relationships among the protagonists tend to be raw and direct – unmediated by the exchange of belts, rings, or swords. Where two protagonists compete over a common object of desire, it is generally food – the whelk in Fable 12, "The Eagle and Crow (corneille)," or the piece of cheese in Fable 13, "The Crow (corbeau) and the Fox." Both are presented as cautionary tales on the perfidy of speech acts: "bad counsel" (mescunseille, 12:32) in the first instance and "false flattery" (faus losenge, 13:34) in the second. In contrast to the *Lais*, the world of the *Ysopë* is devoid of fine silks, delicately wrought reliquaries, and the other luxurious goods forming the backdrop of courtly society.

The exception that proves the rule is the very first fable in the collection: "The Cock and the Gem." A cock, scratching around on a dung-heap "according to [his] nature" (sulum nature, 1:3), uncovers a "precious gem" (chere gemme, 1:5), only to immediately scorn it:

> I'll never pay it honor! I know that if a rich man found you, he'd set you in gold; your beauty would be enhanced by the gold's brilliance. When it's left up to me, you'll never have any such honor.

> ... ja n'i ert pur mei honuree!
> Si un riche hum vus trovast,
> bien sai ke de or vus aürnast,
> si acreüst vostre beauté
> par l'or, que mut ad grant clarté.
> Quant ma volenté n'ai de tei,
> ja nul honur n'averas de mei. (1:10–16)

---

[56] Exceptions include Fable 29:18, 45, discussed above.

[57] "Self-reliance, suspicion, mistrust of others, [and] self-interest," Mann points out, are "traditional fable characteristics" that run counter to the feudal-courtly ethos of the *Ysopë*'s vocabulary. Mann, *From Aesop to Reynard*, pp. 67–76 (quotation on p. 76).

From the outset, the world of beautifully courtly riches is ruled irrelevant, of little interest. In contrast to the Ugly Cowherd in Chrétien de Troyes's *Yvain*, who lacks the vocabulary and social knowledge to distinguish gold from iron or emerald from plain stone, the cock knows full well what gold and gemstones are and the worth that others attach to them; it's simply that for him, having no use value, they have no exchange value. We might take the cock's dismissal of the gem and all it implies as a lesson in literary sociology: set in the barnyard rather than at court, drawing on a narrative tradition associated with the lowest orders of society, fables generically (as it were) bracket the world of the heroic epic or courtly romance. For Marie, on the other hand, the cock's indifference to the cultural capital condensed in the *chere gemme* exemplifies the waywardness of those who "value good(s) and honor very little, [who] choose the worst and despise the best" (bien e honur nïent ne prisent, / le pis pernent, le meuz despisent, 1: 21–2). This lesson, as Jauss and Mann tell us, depends on two significant alterations to Marie's source text in the *Romulus Nilantii*: first, the hypothetical finder of the gem is transformed from a miser to "a rich man" (un riche hume, 1:11); and the original focus on utility is transformed into a "fusion of social and moral" meaning through the repeated evocation of "honor" (ll. 10, 16).[58]

As Jill Mann points out, however, "the laws of Marie's fable world are more complex and comprehensive than Jauss allows." In particular, the *Ysopë* devotes substantial attention to *horizontal* relations – elective, often inter-species alliances captured under the theme of "companionship" (cumpainie). As in the case of the vertical feudal hierarchy, however, these relations, far from ideal, tend to be guided by "a self-interested isolationism."[59] "Almost invariably," she notes, "the companionship proves to be short-lived, its instability being already apparent in the disparate nature of the companions." These temporary alliances are

---

[58] See Jauss, *Tierdichtung*, pp. 32–3 and Mann, *From Aesop to Reynard*, pp. 57–8. On the way the *Ysopë*'s final fable, "The Woman and the Hen," bookends Fable 1 with Marie's vision of authorship and readership, see Sandra Hindman, "Aesop's Cock and Marie's Hen: Gendered Authorship in Text and Image in Manuscripts of Marie de France's *Fables*," in *Women and the Book: Assessing the Visual Evidence*, ed. Lesley Smith and Jane H. M. Taylor (London: British Library, 1997), pp. 45–56 (at 48–9).

[59] Mann, *From Aesop to Reynard*, pp. 67–72 (esp. 67, 69). Her examples include Fables 11 (the "booty-sharing tales of the lion, the buffalo, and the wolf, and the lion, the sheep, and the goat), 26 ("The Wolf and the Dog"), 37 ("The Man and the Lion"), 52 ("The Man and the Dragon"), 71 and 77 ("The Wolf and the Hedgehog"), 76 ("The Badger and the Pigs"), and 98 ("The Cat and the Fox"), which she quotes at length.

frequently ruptured by trickery or treachery (tricherie).[60] In this climate, "traditional fable values" such as self-reliance and an alertness to (or ability to mobilize) linguistic deception "not only survive…but are given a quite new force and vigour." [61] Words and reality diverge: "those who are so foolish as to put their trust in words are taught by experience to know better. The wise, on the other hand, fix their attention on physical reality."[62]

In the *Lais*, characters are caught between different social codes (like Guigemar and Equitan, hesitating between the demands of feudal loyalty and courtly love), and attempt to negotiate among multiple possibilities (Eliduc, poised between two lords and two wives) or rival interpretations (who is worse off? the lady who has lost four potential lovers or the knight who has survived his rivals but is unable to possess his lady?). In the *Ysopë*, choices are different and more limited. Repeated in several fables is the tension between nature and nurture. Nurture triumphs over nature in the case of the lamb who acknowledges the she-goat who "reared" her (nurri, 32:11) as her mother "rather than she who bore me and who cut herself off from me" (meuz que cele ke me porta / e qui de li me desevera, 32:15–16). Elsewhere, nature must out. This lesson is conveyed most succinctly in Fable 65b, of the grey wolf who will grow old "in [his] skin" (en cele pel, 65b:3) in a way that neither the instruction of a "good teacher" (bon mestre, 65b5) nor priestly training can alter. This point is elaborated in Fable 81, where a priest studiously drills a wolf in his ABCs; when asked what the letters spell, the wolf blurts out, "Lamb!" (Aignel, 81:12). The priest concedes that this "rings true" (verité tuche, 81:13), for, "as one thinks, so one speaks" (tel en pensé, tel en la buche, 81:14).[63]

Yet the *Ysopë* abounds with animals unsatisfied with their nature. In Fable 67, a crow plucks out all his feathers in order to array himself in peacock plumes – only to be shunned by real peacocks and then set upon

---

[60] Ibid., pp. 69–70.

[61] Ibid., p. 65.

[62] Ibid., p. 87. Mann's examples of the unreliability of speech include Fables 57 ("The Peasant and the Goblin"), 69 ("The Fox and the Bear"), 83 ("The Swallow and the Sparrows"), and 89 ("The Wolf and the Kid").

[63] This is the only tale from Marie's *Ysopë* discussed in the "Aesop's Fables and Their Afterlives" chapter in Seth Lerer's *Children's Literature: A Reader's History, from Aesop to Harry Potter* (Chicago: University of Chicago Press, 2008). Noting its popularity throughout the Middle Ages, he takes it as exemplary of the pedagogical context of Marie's *Fables* as well as of the wolf's frequent association with "*ingenium* gone wrong – wit and instruction pressed into the service of cupidity or vice." See Lerer, "Aesop's Fables," pp. 47–8. See also Fables 79 and 102.

by his fellow crows, who now fail to recognize him. In turn, the peacock in Fable 31 is unhappy despite his beautiful plumage because he cannot sing as sweetly as the nightingale. Yet the nightingale in Fable 66 proves unable to sing, silenced by his terror of the hawk who commands it. A sad counterexample occurs in Fable 87, "The Two Wolves," in which the titular protagonists set out to counter their poor reputation by "doing good, if we can" (bien a fere, si nus poüms, 87:6). When they attempt to help with the harvest, however, "men shouted at them" (les humes les escrïerent, 87:20). Seeing that good behavior gets them nothing, they abandon their effort and "swore and promised never to do good" (jurerent e pramistrent / jamés bien ne ferunt, 87:29–30). The epimythium criticizes the wolves, not for attempting to go against their nature but for being too readily discouraged: the scoundel "abandons the good he's started on the least provocation" (a mut petit d'acheisun / laisse le bien que il comence, 87:32–3). But any narrative of self-improvement is short-circuited in advance by equating the wolves with a "felun" (87:31) whose least effort is by definition doomed to failure. We are a world apart from *Bisclavret*, where "betrayal" resides in the failure to perceive the feudal and courtly nobility in a werewolf's behavior.

Espurgatoire seint Patriz

We began this chapter by calling attention to the resolutely secular atmosphere of the *Lais*, before turning to the feudal and social preoccupations more cynically developed in the *Ysopë*. In the case of the *Espurgatoire seint Patriz*, it may seem perverse to stress the secular nature of a text about the Christian afterlife. The heart of the text (some 1400 lines out of 2300) recounts the pilgrimage of a knight named Owein to Saint Patrick's Purgatory and the ten "torments" he undergoes there, his tour of the earthly paradise, and his glimpse of the celestial one. Preceding this narrative is a prologue and an account of Saint Patrick's mission to Ireland and discovery of the mouth of Purgatory. Yet behind this hagiographical subtext and theological vision, the text itself makes a compelling case for understanding its composition, intended audience, and even its content through the lens of twelfth-century secular society.

Purgatory, writes the historian Jacques Le Goff with startling precision, "did not exist before 1170 at the earliest."[64] Before that, "purgatoire" was

---

[64] Jacques Le Goff, *The Birth of Purgatory*, trans. Arthur Goldhammer (Chicago: University of Chicago Press, 1984), p. 135.

an adjective, referring to the punishments (often associated with fire) that purified sinners so that they could attain heaven. The concept of Purgatory as a third place between Heaven and Hell where souls were purged of their sins after death emerged in the last third of the twelfth century, at the intersection of two intellectual milieus: Paris (at the cathedral school of Notre-Dame, Saint-Victor, and Sainte-Geneviève) and the Cistercian order. Gathering up a number of theological problems and discussions that had been circulating since at least the time of Augustine, the notion of Purgatory arose to counter those doctrines that contested the possibility of souls' movement after death.[65]

Marie's vernacular *Espurgatoire*, speculatively dated to the 1190s, thus lays out for a non-Latinate audience a theological innovation that had first emerged little more than a generation before.[66] Designed to appeal precisely to the noble and courtly audience addressed in the *Lais*, its protagonist is a knight named Owein, whose visit to Saint Patrick's Purgatory is presented as the one formative spiritual episode in an otherwise worldly life.[67] The pilgrimage he subsequently makes to Jerusalem is alluded to in a scant six lines (ll. 1913–18); then he returns to court and, after narrating his life "tut en ordre" (l. 1921), asks the king's "advice" (conseil, l. 1923) on whether to become a monk. In no uncertain terms,

> the king replied that he should be a knight, just as he was. He advised him to stick with that; thus could he serve God. This is what he did with the rest of his life, not exchanging it for any other.

> ... li reis lui ad respondu
> chevaliers seit, si cum il fu.
> Ço lui loa il a tenir:
> en ço poeit Deu bien servir.
> Si fist il bien tute sa vie,
> pur autre ne changa il mie. (*Espurgatoire*, ll. 1927–32)

---

[65] From its first emergence in the late twelfth and early thirteenth century, interest in Purgatory, Le Goff notes, has peaked in moments of heretical crisis. In this sense, it was an establishment response to a crisis that on the Mediterranean rim was answered by a different sort of innovation – the rise of the mendicant orders of the Franciscans and the Dominicans.

[66] On dating the *Espurgatoire* to "the decade after the *Tractatus* and probably around 1190," see Bloch, *The Anonymous Marie de France*, pp. 215–16.

[67] The visit of a knight with the Welsh name of Owein to a remote site in Ireland would likely have evoked the 1171 Cambro-Norman campaigns to Ireland. R. Howard Bloch emphasizes the integral role the Cistercians played in this expansion: "the Cistercian colonization and ecclesiastical reform of Ireland represented the spiritual arm of invasion." Bloch, *The Anonymous Marie de France*, p. 284.

In contrast to the model of *Eliduc*, where a knight might expiate a life of violence by taking vows near the end of his life, this model accepts – and honors – a knight's place in secular society.[68] Owein quickly finds his calling as the translator for a Cistercian monk named Gilbert, dispatched by his abbot, Gervais, to claim land promised to their order by the king of Ireland. (Gilbert, we are told, "neither knew nor had learned the language of that country" [ne saveit ne n'out apris / le language de cel païs, ll. 1953–4].) Owein is happy to assist the Cistercians, even while (we are emphatically told) never relinquishing his lay status:

> Thus the knight remained with Gilbert, serving him well. *But he didn't want to change status; he didn't want to become a monk or conversus [lay brother]. He retained his knightly status, never taking any other habit.* The two of them founded the abbey and populated it with people of good morals. Gilbert was the cellerer, and Owein his translator.

> Issi remist od Gilebert
> li chevaliers e bien le sert,
> *meis ne voleit changer sun estre,*
> *moigne ne convers ne volt estre.*
> *En non de chevalier morra,*
> *ja autre abit nen recevra.*
> Cil dui funderent l'abbeïe
> e mistrent genz de bone vie.
> Gileberz en fu celerers
> e Oweins fu ses latimers. (*Espurgatoire*, ll. 1971–80)

As a translator, Owein, like Marie, is an intermediary between worlds, negotiating between Irish and Latin/Romance, the living and the dead, the sacred and the secular.

The startling innovation of Saint Patrick's Purgatory is drawn directly from the confluence of these worlds: that instead of being raised to Heaven or condemned to Hell on the basis of one's life, one's post mortem fate could be helped along by the actions of living friends and relatives. Though there may have been a long-standing popular tradition

---

[68] The efficacy of a late turn to the monastic life had already been called into question in *Le Moniage Guillaume*, in which the eponymous hero of the William of Orange cycle enters a monastery, only to prove incapable of shedding the outsized appetites and willfulness that had made him so successful a vassal and crusader.

predating the "birth" of Purgatory in the 1170s,[69] the *Espurgatoire* exudes a palpable sense of novelty, purveying an idea that needed to be broadcast and explained to the lay public.

> Therefore I exhort you to think about the torments and help your friends who are subjected to suffering there. As the knight was told: those who are there to be purged will be delivered from their suffering (excepting those who are completely damned). Truly: those who are in places of torment will be delivered by masses, prayers, alms, and gifts given to the poor in their name. All will be delivered, except for those who are in the mouth of hell: they will never receive God's mercy.

> Pur ço vus voil amonester
> que des tormens deies penser.
> E si aidez a vos amis
> qui laienz sunt en peine mis.
> Si com fud dit au chevaler,
> cil qui la sunt pur espurger
> serront de peines delivrez,
> fors ceus qui sunt del tut dampnez.
> Ceus qui par lius sunt en torment
> erent delivres veirement
> par messes e par oreisons
> e par almones e par dons
> qu'om done a povre gent pur eus.
> Tuit erent delivré, for ceus
> qui en la bouche d'enfer sunt;
> james de Deu merci n'avrunt. (*Espurgatoire*, ll. 1433–48)

Though repetition is by no means foreign to medieval verse, in the *Espurgatoire* it seems to respond to a sense that the poem's message must repeatedly be preached to an audience perhaps not quite ready to believe its ears.

> None of those who are in torment know how long they will be nor how long they have (already) been there; this is all according to God's will. When someone prays for them – offering masses, alms, and gifts – their torment is lessened:

[69] A. Ja. Gurevich, "Popular and Scholarly Medieval Cultural Traditions: Notes in the Margin of Jacques Le Goff's Book," *Journal of Medieval History* 9.2 (1983): 71–90.

either they are relieved of them altogether, or their pains are reduced, and they are given lesser ones.

Quant hom fait pur eus oreisons,
messes e almones e dons,
lur tormenz sunt amenusez
ou del tut en sunt aleggez;
ou l'om alege lur dolurs,
ou l'om les met enz en menurs. (*Espurgatoire*, ll. 1759–64)

Those thus purged by the efforts of their loved ones pass into "Earthly Paradise, from which Adam was expelled and exiled for his sins" (d'out Adams fud pur ses pechiez / getez e si fud eissillez, ll. 1691–2).[70]

Two things stand out in the *Espurgatoire*'s description of earthly paradise. The first is the sensory brilliance that overwhelms Owein as he approaches its jewel-encrusted precious metal portal: a wonderful odor with curative powers – "At the sweetness he smelled which filled his body, he completely recovered his strength" (A la douçur que il senti, / que tut le cors lui repleni, / tut en recovra sa vertu, ll. 1513–15) – and a dazzlingly intense light.[71] The second is the beauty, but also the familiarity, of the garments in which the denizens of the earthly paradise are arrayed. On setting foot inside the portal, Owein sees a procession of churchmen, "variously appareled according to their position" (Vestuz…diversement / solum l'ordre qu'a eus apent, ll. 1545–6), from archbishops, bishops, and abbots to priests, deacons, canons, subdeacons, acolytes, and conversi. Lest we miss the point, the text explicitly notes: "They were, you may be sure, dressed in the form and appearance they had while in God's service in this life" (En tel forme e en tel semblant / furent vestu aparissant / cum il furent, n'en dotez mie, / el Deu servise en ceste vie, ll. 1553–6).[72]

The following scene is calculated to appeal directly to the lay courtly audience to whom the *Espurgatoire* is addressed. Escorted by two archbishops, Owein is shown a locus amoenus "with a profusion of flowers and trees: there are sweet-smelling herbs and precious, noble fruits" (de flors

---

[70] In medieval cartographical and textual traditions, Earthly Paradise was a geographical place, located in the farthest or inaccessible East, but (like Saint Patrick's Purgatory) in a space contiguous with our own. See Paul Freedman, *Out of the East: Spices and the Medieval Imagination* (New Haven: Yale University Press, 2008), pp. 97–8.

[71] On the association between Eden and the odors produced by aromatic spices, see Freedman, *Out of the East*, pp. 76–103.

[72] Contrast the early-thirteenth-century parodic *chantefable Aucassin et Nicolette*, in which paradise is populated by old crusty priests and ill-dressed paupers, and hell by brave knights and beautiful ladies.

e d'arbres plenteïs: / herbes i out de bone odur / e gentilz fruiz de grant valur, ll. 1588–90) – a scene that might easily fit a courtly romance. In this resplendent light-infused scene, he finds "such a profusion of people that he firmly believed that no living being would be able to see as many in the world" (gens a si grant plenté / qu'il quidout bien ke nuls vivanz / el mund n'en peüst veeir tanz, ll. 1600–2). Earthly paradise, this vision tells us, is densely populated, not just reserved for the few. The people are divided "by community" (Par covenz, l. 1603) yet circulate freely and all come together "in one group" (communement, l. 1607) to sing in praise of their Creator. Like the clergy, they are splendidly dressed:

> Some [wore] pure gold, others green or purple; some hyacinth color, off-white or flower-white.

> Li uns l'orent tute d'or fin,
> e li autre vert ou porprin;
> li uns de jacinte colur,
> ou bloie ou blanche cume flur. (*Espurgatoire*, ll. 1617–20)

And, like the clergy, they retain the semiotic markers of their earthly identities:

> Owein recognized these people by their clothing – what they had been, what they were when they died. As the colors varied, there were diverse lights. The color of glory shone in all their clothing. Some went around crowned and bedecked like kings; some carried golden palm fronds, flowers, and branches in their hands.

> Cist Oweins sout de cele genz,
> par la forme des vestemenz,
> de quel mestier orent esté,
> en quel mestier orent finé.
> Si com variouent les colurs,
> aveient diverses luurs.
> Colur de gloire apparisseit
> sur tuz les dras k'il i aveit.
> Li uns alourent coroné
> cume rei e si atorné;
> li uns portouent en lur mains
> palmes orines, flors e rains. (*Espurgatoire*, ll. 1621–32)

From this earthly paradise, Owein is given a brief glimpse of the celestial paradise before being told by the two archbishops that it is time for him to return to the world. Distraught, Owein doesn't want to leave: not having quite understood the import of purgatory, "he doesn't believe he'll ever return, on account of the grievous sins encumbering those in the world" (ne quide jamés venir / pur les grevous pechiez del munt, / qui encombrent ces qui i sunt, ll. 1862–4). In the end, however, he finds his way, setting off, as we have seen, for the Holy Land – "In honor of God, his Creator, he took the cross, for great love" (En honor Deu, sun Creatur, / croiser se fist par grant amur, ll. 1913–14) – before following the king's advice to remain in the world. Having lived and recounted his adventure of Saint Patrick's Purgatory, he translates this theological innovation to a lay audience, just as he bridges the linguistic gap between Irish king and Anglo-Norman monk.

Marie de France and the *Vie seinte Audree*

In our Introduction, we posed the debate surrounding the attribution of the *Vie seinte Audree* to Marie de France as an issue that raises, or should raise, questions about the basic assumptions we make concerning medieval authorship and textual production. Arguments in favor of attributing the *Vie seinte Audree* to the presumed author of the *Lais*, the *Ysopë*, and the *Espurgatoire seint Patriz* cluster, as we saw in the Introduction and Chapter 1, around perceived continuities of vocabulary, style, and thematics – notably the concern for memory and remembrance, especially as linked to the preoccupation with authorship in the final line (l. 4625) of the text.

Among the works that have been attributed to Marie, the *Vie seinte Audree* pairs most obviously with the *Espurgatoire seint Patriz*. In contrast to the feudal-courtly setting of the *Lais* and the eminently worldly concerns of the *Ysopë*, both the *Vie* and the *Espurgatoire* are manifestly religious in inspiration and intent: directed at a lay audience, to be sure, but preoccupied with matters of salvation and spirituality. Given this commonality, it is also worth noting where the two texts diverge – specifically, in keeping with the theme of this chapter, in their treatment of feudal society.

Alongside the association of her cult with the monastery at Ely, the salient features of the hagiographical legend of Saint Audrey are the way she "abandoned kingdom and rank" (deguerpi regne et hautesce, l. 19) in setting aside her queenship (the secular world's highest female station), combined with her perseverance in maintaining not just one but *two* chaste marriages. Both the desire for a religious over a secular life and, failing that, for chastity in marriage are familiar to us from numerous saints' lives

from throughout the Middle Ages.[73] Audrey's canonization itself fits the
pattern prevailing roughly up until the millennium, by which female saints
were typically women of royal and noble lineage who founded monasteries.[74] In any case, Audrey's determination to embrace the religious life
presents a very different model from that of Owein in the *Espurgatoire*,
where the physical–spiritual ordeal undergone in Saint Patrick's Purgatory proves perfectly compatible with the continuation of a secular life.

Strikingly, the *Vie seinte Audree* shows no signs of the theological inno-
vations announced in the *Espurgatoire seint Patriz*.[75] Where that text goes
to great lengths to reassure its lay audience with images of the continuation of many earthly forms of life after death and that the intervention
of the living was crucial to the progress of the dead, the prologue to the
Vie seinte Audree insists that one's life on earth is the sole determinant of
one's ultimate fate:

> Little do a man's treasures avail him since/after the soul leaves
> the body if he has not shared it out for God and *during his*
> *lifetime* made sure that his goodness/goods overcome his ill
> deeds, pride, and bad vices. He is saved who serves/deserves
> God's grace and company *while alive.*

> Poy vaut a home ses tresors
> Puis ke l'ame se part del cors
> S'il ne l'ha por Deu departi
> Et *en sa vie* deservi
> Ke ses biens venquent ses malices,
> Son orguil, ses mauveises vices:
> Gariz est ki desert *en vie*
> La Deu grace et sa compaignie. (*Seinte Audree*, ll. 9–16)

In the *Vie seinte Audree*, "the faithful" (ses feus, l. 21) to whom God
promises "wealth" (la richesce, l. 20) are identified as:

> the clerics, monks, hermits who have disdained this life, [and]
> the glorious holy virgins who have made themselves God's
> wives.

---

[73] See Jocelyn Wogan-Browne, *Saints' Lives and Women's Literary Culture: Virginity
and its Authorizations* (Oxford: Oxford University Press, 2001).

[74] Venarde, *Women's Monasticism*, p. 125.

[75] This despite the fact that June Hall McCash uses the geographical proximity
of Saltrey and Ely – where the source texts of the *Espurgatoire* and *Seinte Audree*,
respectively, were produced – as an argument in favor of the attribution of the *Vie* to
Marie de France. See Introduction, *The Life of Saint Audrey*, p. 8.

> Li clerc, li moine, li hermite
> Ky ont ceste vie despite,
> Les saintes virges glorïuses
> Ky se firent a Deu espouses. (*Seinte Audree*, ll. 23–6)

In contrast to the *Espurgatoire*, no outlet is imagined for lay piety; here the cloistered life is not presented as an option for wives or widows seeking to leave the secular world – in contrast not only to *Eliduc* but to episodes within the narrative itself.

How do these discrepancies figure into the way we understand Marie de France as an author?[76] Certainly, nothing prohibits a single individual from authoring texts of seemingly disparate conception and vision. In our own times, such variation is likely to be positively coded under the name of versatility or experimentation. Can we imagine the same for a medieval author? The question reveals its fullest complexity in a case such as that of Marie de France, who exists only as an intratextual and intertextual reference, where the connections between the Maries of the *Lais*, the *Ysopë*, the *Espurgatoire*, and the *Vie seinte Audree* remain speculative and provisional. Do we think of Marie as a pen-for-hire, obliged to "seek pay" (soldees querre, *Eliduc*, l. 14) and patronage, like the unlooked-for commission proffered by "Count William" (*Ysopë*, epilogue, l. 9)? Or do we seek to integrate each component of Marie's presumed corpus into a legible biography, punctuated by turns of fortune and narratives of conversion, to imagine an authorial voice shaped by authenticity as well as artistry? The range of representations of feudal society surveyed in this chapter invites reflection on these larger historical and metaphysical questions.

---

[76] Our view here counters that of the text's editor, who, drawing on Virginia Blanton-Whetsell's observations on the differences between the *Vie seinte Audree* and its Latin source text in "St. Aethelthryth's Cult: Literary, Historical, and Pictorial Constructions of Gendered Sanctity" (Ph.D. dissertation, State University of New York at Binghampton, 1998), pp. 251, 255, 257, emphasizes the continuity of vision with the *Lais*. June Hall McCash, "*La vie seinte Audree*: A Fourth Text by Marie de France?," *Speculum* 77.3 (2002): 744–77 (at 751).

4

Movement and Mobility: Plot

Marie de France is a master of the episodic form.[1] Her works unfold in relatively short narrative segments that are defined less by temporality than by movement. In her collection of *lais*, stories are structured by travel between places as well as by movement among conflicting obligations, desires, and value systems. Time passes, but its passage is not usually described with any urgency or explanation – why does Guigemar's lady suffer for two years (and not one or three) before going to the shore to drown herself and instead finding the boat that takes her to the court where she will find her lover again? The *Ysopë*, a collection of episodic tales that move from forest to barnyard and from country to the city, mostly takes place in an unspecified present.[2] And although Owein's journey in the *Espurgatoire* is bounded by time, his progression through Purgatory is described in episodes that correspond to the places and tortures through which he passes. In all Marie's works, time seems less important than place, and movement among places is one of the primary motors of plot.

Movement, like many other themes, works on a variety of levels in Marie's works. It may recall *mouvance*, in the form of changes to texts not just through transmission and transcription, but also through translation. As we noted in Chapter 1, vernacular literature in Old French has its origins in transcription and translation, and Marie's works are no exception.[3] Yet in the *Lais*, the *Ysopë*, and the *Espurgatoire*, movement is more

[1]   Philippe Ménard similarly identifies an "esthétique de la brièveté" in Marie's *Lais. Les Lais de Marie de France: Contes d'amour et d'aventure du Moyen Age* (Paris: Presses Universitaires de France, 1979). Peter Haidu identifies brevity as a gendered choice in *The Subject Medieval/Modern: Text and Governance in the Middle Ages* (Stanford: Stanford University Press, 2004), pp. 124–5.
[2]   For a reading of the logic of the collection, see Matilda Tomaryn Bruckner, *Shaping Romance: Interpretation, Truth, and Closure in Twelfth-Century French Fictions* (Philadelphia: University of Pennsylvania Press, 1993), pp. 157–206.
[3]   While all of Marie's works are identified as translations, like all translations they are rewritings. Comparisons of the *Espurgatoire* and the first fables in her *Ysopë* with their Latin originals have shown that Marie changes her narratives, emphasizing different elements of the story, omitting or adding to the plot, omitting, shortening, or lengthening

than a theme. Movement generates meaning in all of Marie's narratives, though in different ways and to different ends in each. In this chapter, we take movement as a focus for thinking about how Marie uses characters' trajectories through space to generate story and meaning. Many of the *lais* describe protagonists whose travel to new lands leads to the discovery of love and adventure, or whose immobility is compensated by the exchange of objects that move between lovers. By contrast, protagonists in many of the fables must decide whether to stay at home or move out into new worlds, and after frightening forays into unknown places, most decide that the security of home is better than the risk of travel. The *Espurgatoire* also links travel and discovery, following the knight Owein as he moves through the spaces of Purgatory and glimpses the pleasures of paradise.

Mobility and adventure in the *Lais*

In the *Lais* characters travel between and among sites in England and Northern France, that is, in areas identified with a Celtic cultural sphere. Seven of the *Lais* are set in Brittany (*Guigemar, Equitan, Le Fraisne, Bis-clavret, L'aüstic, Chaitivel, Eliduc*) and four others are situated in what we might see as the interface between the Celtic and Anglo-Norman worlds: *Lanval* at Carlisle (Kardoeil, l. 5) on the English–Scottish border;[4] *Yonec* and *Milun* in South Wales; and *Chievrefueil* in Cornwall (l. 27). These locations correspond to Marie's claim to translate Breton tales, a claim twice repeated in *Les dous amanz*, the only *lai* that falls fully outside the Celtic cultural world. Set at Pistres in Normandy, *Les dous amanz* is presented as a tale that explains how a place got its name: a mountain outside Pistres is named "The Two Lovers" after the adventure of the only child of the region's first king and the would-be lover who carries her to

certain passages. On the *Espurgatoire*, see Rupert T. Pickens, "Marie de France, Translatrix," *Le Cygne* 1 (2002):7–24, and Michael J. Curley, trans., *Saint Patrick's Purgatory: A Poem by Marie de France* (Binghampton: Medieval and Renaissance Texts and Studies, 1993), pp. 19–37. On the *Ysopë*, see Charles Bruckner, ed. and trans., *Les fables* (Louvain: Peeters, 1991), pp. 6–19, and Rupert T. Pickens, "Courtly Acculturation in the *Lais* and *Fables* of Marie de France," *The Court and Cultural Diversity: Selected Papers from the Eighth Triennial Congress of the International Courtly Literature Society, the Queen's University of Belfast, 26 July–1 August 1995*, ed. Evelyn Mullally and John Thompson (Cambridge: D. S. Brewer, 1997), pp. 27–36, esp. 29–32.

⁴ The future Henry II was knighted on this northern border of England by King David of Scotland on Pentecost 1149. The castle was formerly held by the father of Ranulf, the powerful earl of Chester. W. L. Warren, *Henry II* (Berkeley: University of California Press, 1973), p. 36.

the top of the mountain and then dies. The first fourteen lines of the story proper insist on its intensely local grounding:

> The Lord of the Pistres had a city built and had it called Pistres after the Pistres people. The name has endured, and a city and houses are still found there. We know well this country called the Valley of Pistres.

> ... une cité fist faire uns reis
> ki esteit sire des Pistreis;
> de ses Pistreis la fist numer
> e Pistre la fist apeler.
> Tuz jurs a puis duré li nuns;
> uncore i a vile e maisuns.
> Nus savum bien de la cuntree
> que li vals de Pistre est nomee. (*Les dous amanz*, ll. 13–20)

If *Les dous amanz* explains the name of "an amazingly tall mountain" (un halt munt merveilles grant, l. 9) just outside the settlement of Pistres and locates it firmly "in Neustria, which we call Normandy" (en Neüstrie, / que nus apelum Normendie, ll. 7–8), the story itself is told by the Bretons, as we hear both in the prologue (Un lai en firent li Bretun, l. 5) and in the last line of the epilogue (li Bretun en firent un lai, l. 254).[5] Why would the Bretons have made a *lai* of this adventure? Unlike *L'aüstic*, set "around Saint Malo" (En Seint Malo en la cuntree, l. 7) near the border with Normandy, Pistres is located near the Seine, deep in the heart of Normandy. *Les dous amanz* thus shows the *Bretons* commemorating what is presented as a local *Norman* adventure.

The Breton story about a place in Normandy, recorded and translated by a woman living in Britain but originally from France, suggests a movement of stories among Brittany, Normandy, Britain, and even Scotland and Ireland. Such a literary circulation corresponds to what we know of travel and exchange among places that shared historical, linguistic, and cultural characteristics.[6] The movement of protagonists in the *Lais* suggests the

---

[5] Willem Noomen, "Le lai des deux amants de Marie de France," *Etudes de langue et de littérature du moyen âge offertes à Félix Lecoy* (Paris: Champion, 1973), pp. 469–81; and Jeanne Wathelet-Willem, "Un lai de Marie de France: les deux amants," *Mélanges Rita Lejeune* (Gembloux: Delthier, 1969), pp. 1143–57. On Google Maps, "Pîtres Normandy" gives a map showing a "Côte" and a "Lac des Deux Amants."

[6] Benjamin Hudson, *Irish Sea Studies 900–1200* (Dublin: Four Courts Press, 2000), pp. 212–29. Hudson also notes that the "Normans" responsible for the "colonization" of Wales and Ireland were descendants of the Vikings who had for several centuries been an integral part of the Irish Sea world.

even broader circulation of a shared European culture of chivalry. Guigemar, son of the lord of Leon (in Brittany), travels in pursuit of renown to Lorraine, Burgundy, Anjou, and Gascony (ll. 53–4), while Milun, the knight born in South Wales, earns his reputation on an international tournament circuit that takes him to Ireland, Norway, Gotland (or Jutland), Logres, Scotland (ll. 15–17), and, eventually, Mont Saint Michel (l. 385). Fraisne's father, a Breton lord, has been as far as Constantinople (l. 125).

If places may be described with geographical precision in the *Lais*, travel between places is less realistically described, and Marie's protagonists are sometimes characterized by a marvelous mobility. Yonec's mother travels from Brittany, on foot, apparently to Wales. Guigemar boards a marvelous boat that guides itself and takes him to an unknown ancient city. Characters move from place to place, usually with the intention of gain: knights like Guigemar and Milun travel to seek renown, the young man in *Les dous amanz* goes to Salerno in quest of a strength-giving potion, and Eliduc travels to a new land to serve another lord when he falls from his own lord's favor. Characters sometimes enter into movement without a precise destination, as does the lady in *Yonec* who follows a blood trail to her lover's tomb, or Guigemar, who boards a boat that steers itself (a voyage that his lady later repeats). In contrast, the plot of *Les dous amanz* is defined by a particular destination – the mountain top to which the lover must carry the king's daughter, though he takes a rather large detour to Salerno in preparation for the ascent. In *Bisclavret* and *Yonec*, mobility even extends to bodily form, as protagonists move between human and animal embodiment.

Travel from one place to another is a prominent way of showing change in the *Lais*. The text uses movement through space to define relationships, to resolve conflicts, and to put characters in unanticipated situations that require them to act in new ways. Like many other twelfth-century narratives, the *Lais* are reticent about interior motivations, and they more readily describe acts and movements than psychological complexity. Interiority is figured as isolating, even alienating, and the work of the narrative is to find a social matrix in which the characters can participate. This transition is often figured as a movement between places.

Movement also brings different places together, and since places are associated with values – the feudal hierarchies that structure courts are an example – travel between places brings different values and value systems into contact. Movement between places also puts different relations of loyalty into contact and sometimes into conflict, and this is key to the way that Marie constructs plot. Guigemar's indifference to love changes when he is transported to a mysterious otherworldly place in a marvelous boat, falls in love with the unhappily married woman he meets there, leaves her when they are discovered by the lady's husband, and later wins her back in a war against his feudal lord. When Lanval is neglected by his feudal lord, he rides into the forest where he finds a lady who offers him love and rich gifts; his status at court is restored through the lady's generosity, then threatened when his secret liaison brings him into conflict with the queen, and finally abandoned when he departs with his lady for Avalon. Eliduc travels between two lands, and maintains a different relationship to lords and ladies in each; the two worlds meet in the boat that brings the knight and his lady back to the land where he has a wife. As protagonists move from place to place they encounter and must resolve conflicts between love and fealty, and between loyalty and marriage.

Not all of Marie's *lais* describe mobile characters. In *Yonec, L'aüstic, Guigemar*, and *Milun*, ladies are imprisoned by jealous husbands and may not leave the rooms in which they are kept. They find happiness only when lovers come to them – in the form of a shape-shifting bird, or a knight who arrives in a marvelous boat – or send them secret messages and gifts. But although these *lais* may describe the pleasures of intimate enclosure,[7] all but *L'aüstic* end with the liberation of the lady and the reunion with a lover, albeit a dying one in the case of the lady in *Yonec*. Marie's stories about enclosed women emphasize the mobility of men. *Chaitivel* suggests that the gendering of mobility may apply even when the lady is not imprisoned, but it also suggests the contrasting values of movement and stasis in the *Lais*.

> There wasn't a knight in the land who did not ask for [the lady's] love after having seen her a single time. She could not love them all, but she did not want to kill them...If the lady had responded to them all, she would have had the good will of all; but even if she did not want to listen to them, she should not speak badly of them, but should hold them dear and honor them, and serve them willingly and thank them.

> N'ot en la terre chevalier
> ki alkes feïst a preisier,
> pur ceo qu'une feiz la veïst,
> que ne l'amast e requeïst.
> El nes pot mie tuz amer
> ne el nes volt mie tuër...

---

[7]   Cary Howie, *Claustrophilia: The Erotics of Enclosure in Medieval Literature* (New York: Palgrave, 2007), pp. 123–7.

> Se dame fait a tuz lur gre,
> de tuz a bone volunté;
> purquant, s'ele nes vuelt oïr,
> nes deit de paroles laidir,
> mes tenir chiers e enurer,
> a gre servir e merciër. (*Chaitivel*, ll. 13–18, 23–8)

The lady occupies a passive position of response that is dictated by her beauty.[8] She should not reject the many knights who love her, but willingly accept their love and thank them for it. The lady is thus fixed in a position from which she may not choose, and accordingly she loves equally the four knights who ask for her favors. When these would-be lovers decide to undertake a tournament, knights come from many regions to participate, and this influx emphasizes the static role of the lady. She is a spectator at the tournament. Instead of being the object of the gaze of all the knights of the country, she herself looks on her knights as they fight, but she is still immobilized in her position as the beloved lady. The tournament ends with the death of three knights, and the fourth is wounded between the thighs (nafrez e malmis / par mi la quisse, ll. 122–3). The tragic outcome of the story is emphasized in the description of the wounded knight's immobility. The move from the tournament before the city to the lady's room where he will convalesce isolates the knight from the mobility that defines adventure and chivalric identity and that leads to love. The knight can no longer kiss his lady or take her in his arms or do anything except speak with her (ne de baisier ne d'acoler / ne d'altre bien fors de parler, ll. 221–2). The intimate enclosure in the lady's room is far from the idyllic space of love that it represents in *Guigemar* or even *Yonec*. Here the knight's enclosure represents a stasis that defines the tragedy of the adventure and points to the importance of masculine mobility in making love and adventure possible.

Chaitivel recounts a story of rule-bound conduct. All knights who see the lady fall in love with her, and she should not refuse their love, the narrator tells us. The lady does not choose among them and she loses them all. By contrast with the other *lais*, *Chaitivel* points to the static sterility of social codes. This is a story played out in a single place, the city of Nantes, and within a single code of values. The narrator seems to point to the isolation of the lovers even before they hold their tournament. The arriving knights are named by their place of origin and marked as foreigners (et li Franceis e li Norman / e li Flemenc, et li Breban / li

---

[8]   See the discussion of beauty as a feudal and courtly value in Chapter 3.

Buluigneis, li Angevin, ll. 77–9). Their organization according to region when they take up arms (dous Flamens et dous Henoiers, l. 92) further emphasizes that they come from outside Nantes and from outside the closed world of love that the lady inhabits with her suitors.[9] The other stories in Marie's collection venture more widely. They recount movement between or among codes of behavior and values, and they portray characters who act in conflict with scripted social codes.

Guigemar, the first *lai* in the Harley collection, is exemplary of the way that movement constructs plot in the *Lais*. It begins with a conflict whose resolution comes through travel. The eponymous protagonist is a great knight from a noble family who is indifferent to love (de nule amur n'out cure, l. 58; il n'aveit de ceo talent, l. 64). Because of this, "both strangers and friends held him at fault/as lost/in peril" (Pur ceo le tienent a peri / e li estrange e si ami, ll. 67–8). The exact meaning of "a peri" is unclear. Marie uses "peri" as a past participle in the *Espurgatoire* to mean "condemned" (l. 132), and most translations offer related meanings: at fault, as given up for lost.[10] William Burgwinkle suggests the translation "in peril," and argues that the text indicates the danger of erotic attachments that do not conform to cultural norms.[11] Certainly the knight's unusual and much criticized refusal to love women must be understood in relation to the feudal politics of his position as a noble son. Guigemar's refusal to love (and, implicitly, to marry) is widely known, and when the narrator emphasizes that both friends and strangers hold the same view of the knight, she suggests that there is no secret or intimate truth to be discovered about why he does not love. Indeed, we never learn that his indifference is caused by anything in particular. Guigemar's lack of desire for love is simply the starting point of his story, and it is marked as a conflict to be resolved. That resolution comes in an encounter with a marvelous beast that leads to travel.

Guigemar may be indifferent to love, but he appears to be passionate about hunting: "this pastime pleased him greatly" (cil deduiz forment li

---

[9] In Chapter 6, we discuss the contrasting lack of differentiation among the lady's suitors.

[10] "Therefore both friends and strangers / gave him up as lost." (*The Lais of Marie de France*, trans. Robert W. Hanning and Joan M. Ferrante [New York: Dutton, 1978], p. 32); "[he was] considered a lost cause" (*The Lais of Marie de France*, trans. Glyn S. Burgess and Keith Busby [London: Penguin, 1986], p. 44); "ce refus lui était reproché comme une tare" (Laurence Harf-Lancner, trans., *Lais de Marie de France* [Paris: Librairie Générale Française, 1990], p. 29).

[11] William Burgwinkle, *Sodomy, Masculinity, and Law in Medieval Literature: France and England, 1050–1230* (Cambridge: Cambridge University Press, 2004), pp. 147–8.

plest, l. 80). A hunt in the forest takes him first into the familiar world of the chase, but he moves increasingly away from his companions until "deep in a thick wood" (En l'espeisse d'un grant buissun, l. 89), Guigemar sees a doe with her fawn. This deer is a marvelous animal: "the beast was completely white and had stag's horns on its head" (Tute fu blanche cele beste; / perches de cerf out en la teste, ll. 91–2). Guigemar shoots the deer, and his arrow rebounds and wounds him in the thigh. The doe-stag speaks to Guigemar and prophesies that the knight will fall in love and he will suffer for his love. Then the deer orders Guigemar to leave:

> The wound in your thigh will never be healed through herbs or roots, by a doctor or with a potion, until you are cured by one who will suffer more pain and hurt for your love than any woman ever suffered. And you too will suffer for her love, so much that all those who love, have loved, or ever will love will marvel at it. Go away from here! Leave me in peace!

> Ne par herbe ne par racine,
> ne par mire ne par poisun
> n'avras tu ja mes guarisun
> de la plaie qu'as en la quisse,
> de si que cele te guarisse,
> ki suferra pur tue amur
> si grant peine e si grant dolur,
> qu'unkes femme tant ne sufri;
> e tu referas tant pur li,
> dunt tuit cil s'esmerveillerunt,
> ki aiment e amé avrunt
> u ki puis amerunt aprés.
> Va t'en de ci! Lai m'aveir pes! (*Guigemar*, ll. 110–22)

Several reversals take place in this scene. The hunter is wounded along with his prey, and the deer speaks while the man is silent. The deer prophesies that Guigemar will suffer in love, when we have just learned that he is indifferent to love, and finally, the deer commands the knight to leave (Va t'en de ci!, l. 122) and sets the knight on a course that will change his destiny.

Guigemar was already mobile – he had traveled home to visit his family and he had gone into the forest to hunt. The deer's command does not so much launch Guigemar into movement as it defamiliarizes mobility. The well-traveled knight no longer knows where he is going. His adventures unfold not as the result of a trip to a tournament or an excursion into the forest, but after a sea journey in a boat that sails itself. This is a common narrative strategy in Marie's *Lais*. Boats sail themselves, excursions into familiar woods lead to encounters with unfamiliar beings, men fly in bird form or roam the forest on four feet. When characters move into the unknown, places and travel between places become unfamiliar and open to new possibilities.

Upon hearing the deer's prophecy, Guigemar understands that he must travel in order to be healed: "He began to ask himself in what land he could go to have his wound healed" (Comença sei a purpenser / en quel terre purra aler / pur sa plaie faire guarir, ll. 125–7). He sends his valet away and before his companions can return and retain him, he mounts his horse and rides away, following a winding trail through the forest. The landscape he finds is not just unfamiliar but strange, since he finds a rich boat in what had seemed an unnavigable branch of the sea: "he had never heard that a boat could dock there" (n'out unkes mes oï parler / que nes i peüst ariver, ll. 163–4). This is the marvelous boat that sails itself and it will take him to a place where he will be healed, as the narrator explains: "before vespers he will arrive in the place where he will be healed, at the base of an ancient city, the capital of this realm" (ainz la vespree arivera / la u sa guarisun avra, / desuz une antive cité, / ki esteit chiés de cel regné, ll. 205–8).[12]

In *Guigemar*, movement changes when the marvelous is introduced into the story. Guigemar's travels to earn chivalric renown and his trip into the forest to hunt give way to a journey in a boat without a pilot that takes the knight to a destination he does not know in advance. The ambiguously gendered speaking deer and the boat that guides itself are marvelous elements in the story, but the narrator does not explicitly describe them as marvelous or magical.[13] In this *lai* the verb "merveillier" is reserved for the extraordinary, but not the supernatural. Guigemar "marvels" at the rich interior furnishings of the boat (De ceo s'esteit il merveilliez, l. 187), the deer announces that all those who love will "marvel" at Guigemar's love for his lady (cil s'esmerveillerunt, l. 119), and when the lady sees the boat arriving without a pilot, the narrator tells us, "it is no wonder that she is afraid" (se ele a poür, n'est merveille, l. 271). But characters do not "marvel" at the boat that sails itself or the deer that speaks. It seems that

---

[12] On the deer as a figure of the narrator, see H. Marshall Leicester, "The Voice of the Hind: The Emergence of Feminine Discontent in the *Lais* of Marie de France," *Reading Medieval Culture: Essays in Honor of Robert W. Hanning*, ed. Robert M. Stein and Sandra Pierson Prior (Notre Dame: University of Notre Dame Press, 2005), pp. 132–61.

[13] On the definition of the marvelous narrative, see Edgard Sienaert, *Les Lais de Marie de France: Du conte merveilleux à la nouvelle psychologique* (Paris: Champion, 1978), pp. 15–48.

the narrative interest is in what the marvelous does, not what the marvelous is, and in *Guigemar* the marvelous moves characters between places. It sends Guigemar into movement (the deer's command) and transports him (the trip in the boat). The marvelous moves the protagonist toward love and toward adventure, that is, it moves him toward change. The marvelous and movement are narrative strategies that work in tandem in *Guigemar*, most obviously in the representation of the boat. They push the story toward its resolution by moving the indifferent protagonist to a new land where he can learn to love.

This new land is similar to what critics have identifed as "otherworlds" in Celtic folklore. Otherworlds are marvelous spaces continguous with but isolated from the worlds in which the protagonists live. When characters enter otherworlds, often by crossing over water, they enter an alternative reality. The constraints and restrictions of the world ordered by social hierarchies fall away, desires are fulfilled, and adversity is left behind. *Lanval* offers the clearest example of an Otherworld in the *Lais*. After his lover has revealed herself to Arthur's court and proven Lanval's innocence of slander against the queen, the knight leaps onto her horse behind her as she departs and accompanies her to the isle of Avalon, leaving the court behind. At this point in the story, Marie stresses the Breton origins of the *lai* and, perhaps, implicitly recalls the otherworldly spaces of Celtic folklore: "He goes with her into Avalon, as the Bretons recount, to a very beautiful island" (Od li s'en vait en Avalun, / ceo nus recuntent li Bretun, / en un isle qui mult est beals, *Lanval*, ll. 659–61). Otherworlds define an alternative reality for the protagonists who reach them, and this is certainly the case for Guigemar, who does not experience love until the marvelous boat takes him to the harbor where he meets his beloved lady. This unnamed lady lives in a walled enclosure that is bounded on one side by the sea. She is strictly guarded by her husband's servants and yet manages to keep the knight with her for a year and a half before they are discovered. The place where she is enclosed is both a prison and an isolated garden of love, a place where desires are both regulated by social and religious constraints and fulfilled in an adulterous liaison. Like the forest where Guigemar hunts the white doe-stag and finds the boat, the lady's enclosure is both familiar and marvelous. Marie's distinctive treatment of space defamiliarizes and then refamiliarizes the marvelous and makes it hard to label different spaces with certainty.

When the lady's husband discovers the lovers in the enclosure where the lady lives, Guigemar explains how he entered the space:

> [Guigemar] tells [the old man] how he came there and how the lady kept him close, and he told him all about the prophecy of the wounded doe and about the boat and about his wound.

> Cil li cunte cum il i vint
> e cum la dame le retint;
> tute li dist la destinee
> de la bisse ki fu nafree
> e de la nef e de sa plaie. (*Guigemar*, ll. 605–9)

Guigemar describes his voyage in terms of a destiny dictated by the deer, guided by the boat, and motivated by his wound. The boat and the wound (la nef e…sa plaie, l. 609) link the ancient city to which the boat takes him and the land where he was wounded.[14] Many readers have noted that *Guigemar* includes extensive word-play with the homonym plaie/pleit/plait.[15] Guigemar's wound in the thigh is a "plaie" (l. 609), and love is a "wound the heart" (plaie dedenz cors, l. 483). When he declares his love, Guigemar calls for the lady to leave aside debate (plait, l. 526) and grant her love to him, and, finally, the knot in the shirt that the lady gives her lover is called a "pleit" (l. 559). The homophony links wound, love, discourse, and the knot, and it also marks a continuity of movement. Just as the marvelous boat takes Guigemar from the site where he receives the wound (plaie) from his own arrow and leads him to the love that will heal him (called a wound, *plaie*, in the heart), so too the knot (pleit) takes the place of the healed wound (plaie), and, as a sign of the lovers' separation, extends the movement of the narrative to include the voyage that will unite the lady with her lover.

The knot represents the wound that motivated Guigemar's first voyage and introduced him to love, and it ties his first journey in the marvelous boat to the subsequent trips. Objects, as we saw in Chapter 3, often signify identity in the *Lais*.[16] The narrator uses them to focus attention on the essential elements of the story, and the development of episodic

---

[14] Sienaert, *Les Lais de Marie de France*, p. 54.

[15] Robert Hanning, "'I shal finde it in a maner glose': Versions of Textual Harassment in Medieval Literature," in *Medieval Texts and Contemporary Readers*, ed. Laurie A. Finke and Martin B. Shichtman (Ithaca: Cornell University Press, 1987), pp. 27–50 (at 35, n. 15); R. Howard Bloch, "The Medieval Text – 'Guigemar' – as a Provocation to the Discipline of Medieval Studies," *Romanic Review* 79 (1988): 63–73 (at 72); Robert M. Stein, "Desire, Social Reproduction, and Marie's *Guigemar*," in *In Quest of Marie de France, A Twelfth-Century Poet*, ed. Chantal A. Maréchal (Lewiston: Edwin Mellen Press, 1992), pp. 280–94 (at 283–6).

[16] Nancy Warren Bradley, "Objects, Possession and Identity in the *Lais* of Marie de France," *Romance Languages Annual* 6 (1994): 189–92.

scenes through descriptions of objects is a distinctive narrative strategy of the *Lais*.[17] Objects also connect places and provide continuity between apparently disjunctive spaces. Guigemar's failure to recognize his lady at Meriaduc's court because women look a lot alike (*femmes se resemblent asez*, l. 779) is not just a failure to know his beloved, but also a failure to see a transition between two unconnected places: "Where did she come from? Who brought her here?" (*Dunt vient ele? Ki l'amena?*, l. 776). The knot in the knight's shirt and the belt around the lady's waist establish a link between Meriaduc's court and the far-away land where Guigemar encountered his lady. Similarly, in *Chievrefueil*, as Queen Iseut rides in the forest she sees the hazelnut branch in her path, a signal that Tristan has used before, and recognizes that her exiled lover is nearby. In *Le Fraisne*, the silk coverlet that Fraisne places on her lover's marriage bed allows her mother's identification of her own noble daughter in the unlikely place of Gurun's court.

In *Guigemar* the knotted shirt and the belt that the lovers carry with them are identifying objects that allow them to recognize each other, but the boat is the object that brings them together. Two years after Guigemar's departure, the lady finds the marvelous boat when she resolves to drown herself in the spot where her lover was put to sea. She gets in the boat, thinking she will let herself fall over the edge to die, but the boat sails away too quickly for her to act. The rudderless boat takes her not to Guigemar, but to Meriaduc, who claims her as his lady and later refuses to relinquish her to Guigemar when he recognizes his lover and opens the belt he placed around her body. In the contest for the lady and the land, Guigemar values love over the bond with his feudal lord, as we have discussed above, and the end of the story shifts away from movement and travel to focus on the resolution of the knight's trials (*Ore a trespasse sa peine*, *Guigemar*, l. 882). The boat is lost to view as the story ends, but it is an essential agent of the plot. It carries the characters from place to place, marvelously connecting places that are otherwise not in contact. In *Guigemar*, the boat is a place of transition – nothing happens on the boat. In this respect, *Guigemar* is very different from *Eliduc*, the other *lai* in which a boat prominently mobilizes the plot. In *Eliduc*, we might say, everything happens on the boat.

---

[17] Micheline de Combarieu, "Les objets dans les *Lais* de Marie de France," *Marche Romane* 30.3–4 (1980): 37–48, esp. 47. For a study of objects in relation to a psychoanalytic understanding of fetishism, see Sarah Kay, *Courtly Contradictions: The Emergence of the Literary Object in the Twelfth Century* (Stanford: Stanford University Press, 2001), pp. 179–215.

In both *Guigemar* and *Eliduc*, the boat is a mode of transportation, but in *Eliduc* the boat does not guide itself; it is steered by sailors and it is vulnerable to storms. The boat takes the knight from Brittany to Britain, where he serves the king of Exeter after he has lost his privileged position in his own lord's court, and a boat takes him back to Brittany when his lord calls for him to return. *Eliduc* is one of the *lais* most firmly grounded in feudal social structures, as we have described in Chapter 3, and feudal relations define the protagonist's movements between two lands, two lords, and two ladies. Eliduc's mobility is also regulated by time, particularly once he arrives in Exeter. His stay there is defined by the year-long term for which the king has retained him (Un an entier l'a retenu, l. 267), but the length of the knight's service is a point of anxiety for the king's daughter, Guilliadun, who has fallen in love with him:

> "I want to show him how much love for him makes me suffer. But I do not know if he will stay here." The chamberlain responded, "Lady, the king has retained him for a year and he has sworn to serve him loyally. You will have plenty of leisure to show him your pleasure."

> "... jeo meïsmes li vueil mustrer
> cum l'amurs de lui me destreint.
> Mes jeo ne sai se il remeint."
> Li chamberlens a respundu:
> "Dame, li reis l'a retenu
> desqu'a un an par sairement
> qu'il le servira leialment.
> Asez purrez aveir leisir
> de mustrer lui vostre plaisir." (*Eliduc*, ll. 446–54)

Guilliadun does not need the "leisure" of a year to convince Eliduc of her love and to win his in return. The time before Eliduc's term of service ends may then be used to figure out a way for the knight to keep his lady, even though he must leave her father's lands:

> "I have agreed to stay with the king for a year, and he has my oath on that. I will not leave for any reason before I have brought his war to an end. Then I will go to my country, if I may have your leave, for I do not wish to remain." The maiden responded, "Thank you, friend. You are wise and courtly, and before that time you will have figured out what you wish to do with me. I love you and trust you above all things."

> "Un an sui remés od le rei.
> La fiance en a de mei prise;

> n'en partirai en nule guise,
> de si que sa guerre ait finee.
> Puis m'en irai en ma cuntree
> kar ne vueil mie remaneir,
> se cungié puis de vus aveir."
> La pucele li respundi:
> "Amis, la vostre grant merci!
> Tant estes sages e curteis,
> bien avrez purveü anceis
> que vus voldrez faire de mei.
> Sur tute rien vus aim e crei." (*Eliduc*, ll. 524–36)

When Eliduc's lord calls him home, the leisure to find a solution to his dilemma is cut short. He asks the king of Exeter for permission to leave his service, but he makes a new commitment to his lady:

> "I swear and promise loyally that if you will give me leave and grant a delay and name the day that you want me to return, there is nothing in the world that will keep me from you as long as I am living and healthy. My life is entirely in your hands." She loved him greatly and gave him a term and named the day when he should return and take her away.

> "Leialment vus jur e plevis,
> se cungié me volez doner
> e respit metre e jur nomer,
> se vus volez que jeo revienge,
> n'est riens el mund ki me retienge,
> pur ceo que seie vis e seins.
> Ma vie est tute entre voz meins."
> Cele ot de lui la grant amur;
> terme li dune e nume jur
> de venir e pur li mener. (*Eliduc*, ll. 690–9)

Eliduc uses a vocabulary of feudal allegiance when he promises Guilliadun a term of service similar to the one he promised to her father. Obligation is defined in terms of time, and time determines the characters' movements between places. However, the plot unfolds not according to the temporality of feudal and love contracts (after all, Eliduc cuts short his stay with the king of Exeter), but in response to travel between places that represent conflicting obligations and desires. Despite the time he has had to work out his dilemma, when Eliduc returns to Exeter at the appointed date to take Guilliadun away to his lands, he has not resolved what he will do with a lover from Britain once he lands in Brittany.

The two places are connected by the knight's travels between them by sea, and ultimately his two worlds confront each other in the space of the boat. When a storm threatens to capsize it, one of the sailors claims that Eliduc's adultery has brought danger upon them. When Guilliadun learns that Eliduc already has a wife, she falls into a faint and appears to have died. The boat reaches harbor safely, and Eliduc declares that Guilliadun must have a burial befitting the daughter of a king. He carries her to a hermit's chapel in the forest surrounding his castle, and here the story shifts its spatial focus. Eliduc no longer moves between two lords and two lands, but between the castle where he lives with his wife and the chapel where he has installed his lover's body.

The chapel is a place where Eliduc worships his lady. He goes there every day after mass to pray for her soul and although the text does not say so explicitly, we might assume that he prays before her body, since he has placed it on the altar. He marvels that Guilliadun remains white and rosy – she does not lose her color, except that she is a little pale (De ceo li semblot granz merveille / qu'il la veeit blanche e vermeille; / unkes la colur ne perdi / fors un petit qu'ele enpali, ll. 971–4). When Guilde-luëc finds her in the chapel, she too remarks on Guilliadun's beauty and, implicitly, on her color when she thinks that she looks like a new rose (resemblot rose nuvele, l. 1012). The body that does not lose its color and that does not become corrupt recalls a saint's body, and this implicit reference emphasizes the mixing of values in the space of the chapel.[18] Eliduc's daily prayers and laments before his lover's apparently dead and saintly body define the chapel as a space of religious and amorous devotion. By contrast, his castle is the site of feudal and marital obligation. Guildeluëc's discovery of Guilliadun's body brings Eliduc's two lives and two ladies into confrontation, and in this it is similar to the scene on the boat, though here the effect is reversed. Guildeluëc revives Guilliadun from her death-like state and immediately says that she will take the veil and free Eliduc to marry his lover. "I will take you with me and give you to your lover. I want to release him from all obligations, and I will take the veil." (Ensemble od mei vus en merrai / e a vostre ami vus rendrai. / Del tut le vueil quite clamer, / e si ferai mun chief veler, ll. 1099–102). This is a startling speech, both in its promise and in its abrupt resolve. Here Guildeluëc's choice to withdraw from her marriage is emphasized in her own words and in terms of her husband's obligation to his wife, but later it is characterized in indirect discourse as a way to allow Eliduc

[18] See Sarah Kay's exploration of the sublime body of the saint and the beloved lady in *Courtly Contradictions*, pp. 216–58.

to conform to the law: "it is not fitting to have two wives and the law should not allow it" (kar n'est pas bien ne avenant / de dous espuses meintenir, / ne la leis nel deit cunsentir, ll. 1128–30). This narrative shift may suggest the potentially controversial nature of Guildeluëc's withdrawal, since canon law required both spouses to abandon their marriage vows when one of them took an oath of celibacy (though it appears that in practice this law was not always observed and in some cases husbands rejected unwanted wives by forcing them into convents).[19] The narrative also stresses the resolution of Eliduc's dilemma in terms of place, through the description of the knight's gift of land for the abbey where Guildeluëc will live with thirty nuns (ll. 1139–44).

Whereas *Eliduc* could end with Guildeluëc's move to a convent and the marriage of Eliduc and Guilliadun, Marie adds a narrative coda in which she describes the couple's long years of perfect love in a single couplet, then recounts their entry into religion:

> They lived together for many days, and they shared a perfect love.... Near the other side of the castle, Eliduc built a church with great care and dedicated land and gold and silver to it, and he installed men and other people of good faith to keep the house and its order. When everything was prepared, he did not delay. He joined them and gave himself to the service of omnipotent God. He put his beloved wife with his first wife. She received her as her sister and accorded her great honor.

> Ensemble vesquirent meint jur,
> mult ot entre els parfite amur....
> Pres del chastel de l'altre part
> par grant cunseil e par esguart
> une eglise fist Elidus,
> e de sa terre i mist le plus
> e tut sun or e sun argent;
> humes i mist e altre gent
> de mult bone religiün
> pur tenir l'ordre e la maisun.
> Quant tut aveit apareillié,
> nen a puis guaires atargié:
> ensemble od els se dune e rent
> pur servir Deu omnipotent.

---

[19]   Sharon Kinoshita, "Two For the Price of One: Courtly Love and Serial Polygamy in the *Lais* of Marie de France," *Arthuriana* 8.2 (1998): 33–55 (at 48).

> Ensemble od sa femme premiere
> mist sa femme que tant ot chiere.
> El la receut cum sa serur
> e mult li porta grant honur. (*Eliduc*, ll. 1149–50, 1153–68)

Eliduc's construction of a church and abbey repeats Guildeluëc's action recounted a few lines earlier: "Near the castle in a wood, on the site of the chapel and the hermitage, she built a church and a convent" (Pres del chastel enz el boscage / a la chapele a l'ermitage, / la a fet faire sun mustier / e ses maisuns edifiër, ll. 1135–8). The story insists on the emplacement of the abbeys that seem to flank the castle, and on the placement of the protagonists in the abbeys. In a rather neat symmetry, the married couple's entry into religion realigns the shifting configuration of couples and unites the two women in a space outside of both the politics of feudal obligation and the feudal politics of marriage. It also adds a third space of circulation to the story. First Eliduc journeys between Brittany and Exeter, then he makes daily trips between his home and the chapel, and finally he enters into correspondence with his former wives: "He sent his messenger to them to learn how they were and to be sure they had found contentment" (Ses messages lur enveiot / pur saveir cument lur estait / e cum chescune cunfort ait, ll. 1174–6).

The end of *Eliduc* is unusual in its lengthy exposition of the lives of the protagonists after the crisis of the story has been resolved. It contrasts, for example, with the abrupt ending of *Guigemar*, where the plot of courtly love takes over and seems to preclude the resolution of the feudal conflict:

> [Guigemar] destroyed the castle and took it, and he killed its lord. With great joy he takes his lover. Now his trials are over.

> Le chastel a destruit e pris
> e le seignur dedenz ocis.
> A grant joie s'amie en meine.
> Ore a trespassee sa peine. (*Guigemar*, ll. 879–82)

Any feudal obligation that Guigemar may owe to Meriaduc is subordinated to love in the resolution to the contest over the lady. Meriaduc is dispatched quickly in the text, and Guigemar wins his lover. But although *Guigemar* uses brevity and *Eliduc* uses elaboration, both *lais* avoid dwelling on unresolved questions of feudal loyalty: Guigemar's renunciation of his feudal loyalty to Meriaduc in order to wage war against him and win his lady; Eliduc's questionable loyalty to the king of Exeter, whose daughter he abducts and then marries when his wife takes the veil. The confrontation and conflict of forms of social relations are resolved in terms of mobility and place. Guigemar takes his lady away; Eliduc sends his to a convent. The movement that avoids the conflict between love and feudal loyalty is also at stake in *Chievrefueil* but perhaps most obvious in *Lanval*, where the knight and his lover leave Arthur's court and escape into Avalon when Lanval must choose between feudal loyalty and love.

The *Lais* demonstrate a polyphony of vision in that the stories engage in different registers – religious, feudal, moral, and amorous. In the *Lais* different value systems are tied to place and they are put into contact with each other by the characters' movements between places. This is one way to understand Marie's organization of plot. But whereas in other courtly narratives, and notably in the romances of Chrétien de Troyes, the forest and the court are separate but contiguous spaces, each governed by distinct rules, in Marie's *Lais* spaces seem less consistently defined. Sometimes the court is a place of amorous intrigue, as in *Eliduc*, and sometimes it is dangerous for love, as in *Chievrefueil*. Sometimes the forest is like a courtly love bower, as in *Lanval*, sometimes it is a place of encounter with the marvelous, as in *Guigemar*, and sometimes it is a place where savage animals hunt, as in *Bisclavret*. Transitions between spaces articulate the values that define them. As protagonists move between and among places, they confront conflicting value systems, but the interesting thing about the *Lais* is that there is no one consistent resolution to conflict. In *Guigemar*, the jealously guarded lady escapes her old husband, but in *Milun* the lady lives with her husband for twenty years until he dies and she can wed her lover. Both of these *lais* end with the happy union of the lovers, but in others, like *L'aüstic* and *Les dous amanz*, the lovers are thwarted. *Bisclavret* valorizes feudal relations, whereas in *Guigemar* the abrupt ending of the story precludes an examination of Guigemar's turn against Meriaduc, and similarly in *Lanval* a knight chooses love over loyalty to his lord. If the collection of stories resists a common message, so too do the individual *lais*. Different values and different sets of rules map onto places, and movement and mobility in the stories foreclose any univocal reading.

The *Ysopë* and the *Espurgatoire* move away from this kind of mobility and offer a more univocal articulation of values associated with space. A reading of these texts in light of the values of space and the possibilities of movement in the *Lais* may suggest the ways in which the moral restriction of the fables and the pious didacticism of the *Espurgatoire* are articulated through representations of mobility.

Staying at home in the *Ysopë*

Marie's fables offer cautionary narratives about the dangers of change and they define mobility not as a movement toward opportunity and possibility, but away from the comforts of known social relations and hierarchies. The social isolation synonymous with mobility is particularly evident in one of the last fables in Marie's collection (Fable 100). An anxiously mobile knight seeks advice about where he should go to live from an old man who has visited many countries. The old man suggests that he should seek to live in a place where all men will love him. This response provokes a further question: if the knight can't find that land, where should he go? He should go to a place where people are afraid of him, the old man replies. The knight's questions are about place, but the old man replies in terms of social relations, and the continuing dialogue suggests that they are the same. When the knight replies with yet another question (what if he can't find the land where people will fear him?), the old man replies that if he can't find a place where he will be loved or feared, he should go to a place where no one will see him and no one will know where he is (Va la u nul humme ne veies, / que nul ne sacë u tu seies, 100:21–2). In other words, if the knight cannot find people who will love him or fear him, then he is nowhere; if he cannot enter into social relations, then it is as though he does not exist.

This fable is one of several in Marie's collection in which the protagonists are humans, not animals, and it describes mobility in terms of social relations. It seems that this knight has no lands of his own and no feudal bonds to honor; he may go to live where he pleases, yet this mobility represents not freedom, but a lack of grounding in the world. The knight's questions about where to live are answered by the old man in terms of how to live and what kinds of social relationships to cultivate. However, the fable's epimythium emphasizes not the knight's mobility, but his foolishness: "With this example, we learn how one should respond to a fool who asks more than he ought to and then often hears more than he wishes" (Par cest essample nus veut sumundre / que si deit hum a fol respundre, / ki plus enquert k'il ne devereit; / si ot suvent que ne vodreit, 100:23–6). The moral reveals the subject of the fable to be speaking rather than moving, but it describes speaking about mobility and it represents the perils and possibilities of mobility in relation to social identity. This foolish knight, as the fable characterizes him, asks questions that mobilize meaning in many of the fables: where should I live and, more implicitly, what will my life be like there?

The desire for movement and change is often described as a foolish desire in the fables, and a desire to change place is often represented as a desire to change social position. The fables reprimand such desires and teach an acceptance of the status quo as a natural order. Indeed, the impossibility of escaping one's nature is a fundamental characteristic of the genre and is often described as the impossibility of escaping social hierarchies.[20] Contentment with one's lot is expressed as the value of staying the same in the *Ysopë*, and in many fables the value of staying the same is represented as the value of staying at home. In this the *Ysopë* is very different from the *Lais*. Where the *Lais* describe movement as leading toward adventure and change, the fables value stability over change and stasis over movement. The foolish mobile knight of Fable 100 has animal counterparts in Fable 22. A group of hares wishes to escape the forest to find a safe place where they will not have to fear the men and dogs that hunt them. Wiser hares tell them they are foolish to leave the place they know and where they have been nourished since birth (Li sage lievre lur diseient / que folie ert ceo que quereient / a eissir de lur cunissance, / u furent nurri des enfance, 22:9–12), but, unbelieving, the hares venture forth. They reach a pond and their approach causes a group of frogs to leap into the water in fear. One of the hares takes a lesson from the frogs' flight:

> "Because of the frogs we have seen, and their fear, we should understand that we are questing after foolishness when we have left our forest to be more secure elsewhere. We will never find a land where one doesn't fear something. Let's go back, that is the best thing to do." With this, the hares turned around and went back to their country. Those who wish to move and leave their former place should understand what can happen afterwards. They will never find a kingdom or come to a land without fear and work and pain.

> "Par les reines que nus veüms,
> que poür unt, nus purpensums
> que nus alum querant folie,
> que nostre grave avum guerpie
> pur estre aillurs asseürez.

---

[20] Judith Barban, "*Lai ester*: Acceptance of the Status Quo in the *Fables* of Marie de France," *Romance Quarterly* 49.1 (2002): 3–11; Hans-Robert Jauss, *Untersuchungen zur mittelalterlichen Tierdichtung* (Tübingen: M. Niemeyer, 1959), p. 38; Jill Mann, *From Aesop to Reynard: Beast Literature in Medieval Britain* (Oxford: Oxford University Press, 2009), pp. 63–4.

Jamés tere ne troverez
u l'um ne dute aucune rien.
Ralum nus en! Si ferum bien."
Atant li lievre returnerent;
en lur cuntree s'en alerent.
Por ceo se deivent purpenser
cil ki se veulent remuer
e lur ancïen liu guerpir
que lur en put aprés venir.
Jamés regne ne troverunt
ne en cele tere ne vendrunt
que tut tens seient sanz poür
u sanz travail u sanz dolur. (22:23–40)

The hares learn that it is foolish to seek a land where there is nothing to be feared, and so they go back home. The lesson is that every place holds danger: "They will never find a kingdom or come to a land without fear and work and pain." Unlike the *Lais*, the fables teach that there is no reason to travel, since all places are alike. The productive nature of movement in the *Lais* – the confrontation of different spaces and different values through the movement of the protagonists – is not at play in the fables, where no place is ever better than home.

Fable 22 may offer further insight into the didactic structure of the fables. The hares learn the lesson about the futility of travel by observing the behavior of frogs. It is as if the hares are reading a fable – the other animals' behavior suggests a conservative course of action they should follow. A similar attention to the fate of other animals characterizes several other fables that offer cautionary tales about travel. In Fable 26, a wolf meets a dog and decides to go to town to share his life of ease, but then notices the chain around the dog's neck and decides that his own freedom is dearer than well-fed servitude. The dangers of domestication are described in terms of moving from the forest to the town, and the animal protagonist makes those dangers visible to another animal who learns the lesson. Fable 9 repeats the lesson in the familiar story about the country mouse who visits her city cousin. Terrified by the dangers of city life, the country mouse reproaches her cousin for boasting of the good and hiding the bad. She would rather be in her woods, alone and secure, than live fearful in her cousin's abode. The epimythium of the fable emphasizes contentment with what one has: "This fable teaches us that each one loves better that which he holds in peace and without fear, than others' riches that he will possess with unease" (Ceste fable dit pur respit / chescun aimt meuz le suen petit /

que il ad en pes e sanz dutance / que autrui richesce od mesestance, 9:53–6). The story about the city mouse and the country mouse valorizes the stability of belonging to a place and emphasizes the dangers of change and mobility. Whether travel is motivated by curiosity or by a desire for change, it inevitably leads back to an embrace of what was already known.

The return to home is linked to social status in Fable 74. A beetle sees an eagle flying in the sky and envies the bird's noble demeanor. Using the vocabulary of courtly identity, this beetle tells his fellows that whereas their Maker made the eagle courtly and beautiful (curteis e bel, 74:11), he left beetles in an in-between status: they are neither worm nor bird. This beetle particularly regrets the limited mobility of his species: when beetles are full, they cannot fly, and when they are hungry they cannot move at all. The beetle protagonist links privilege to mobility, and physical constraints to social constraints. His voice is as strong as an eagle's, the beetle claims, and his body glistens as much as the eagle's. He decides to imitate the eagle's flight, but when he tries to leap away he finds that he cannot get far, and soon he longs to return to his dunghill. The epimythium to this fable emphasizes not mobility, but pride and place. "This is what happens to the prideful," the moral teaches: "they judge themselves. They try what they cannot do, and then they have to turn back" (Issi avient des surquidez: / par eus meimes sunt jugez; / ceo enprenent que ne poënt fere, / dunc lur covient arrier retrere, 74:47–50). In the end, the beetle does not care whether he is taken for a worm or a bird; he wishes only to return to the pile of horse's excrement in which he lives.

The beautiful courtly eagle soaring in the skies suggests noble identity, and the beetle on the dunghill recalls the farmyard and the peasant who tends it. Like others in Marie's collection, Fable 74 maps social privilege and hierarchy onto space, and it valorizes acquiescence to social distinctions in terms of remaining within geographical limits. R. Howard Bloch situates the fables' collective caution about leaving social identities that are tied to place within what he describes as:

> the specific historical context of twelfth-century Anglo-Normandy [where] the metaphorics of natural places and newfound homes, and even changing bodily parts, are unquestionably linked to the anxieties of social promotion and the development of a professional administrative class – of *curiales* or *ministeriales* – at the Plantagenet and then the Angevin court of Henry I and that of his grandson Henry II. And almost all who comment on life at court praise or protest what was

perceived even at the time to be new opportunities for, and forms of, social mobility.[21]

The development of a new administrative class creates the possibility of social advancement through merit rather than birth, and gives rise to a wider anxiety about social transformation that is reflected in the changes associated with mobility in Marie's *Ysopë*.[22]

If Marie's fables sound a cautionary note about mobility and describe changing place as a potential loss of social relations and identity, it is because they emphasize other values. As Jill Mann has argued, "Self-reliance, suspicion, mistrust of others, self-interest, are...as much a part of the ethos of the *Fables* as the 'feudal' values of *lëauté* and *honur.* And these traditional fable characteristics at times run directly counter to the values implicit in Marie's *Lais*."[23] It is not only the fables' endorsement of different values from the *Lais* that makes the two texts so different from each other. In the *Ysopë* we find a relatively consistent and explicit articulation of values whereas in the *Lais* different value systems come into conflict and produce a variety of outcomes. If in the *Ysopë*, travel provokes fear and retreat, in the *Lais* movement leads toward new possibilities and change. This is not just a generic difference. Marie rewrites the fables' generic caution about change as a caution about movement. More important, especially by contrast with the *Lais*, she represents the valorization of a given social position as the advantage of staying in familiar places.

The passage through Purgatory

As in many of her *Lais*, movement organizes the plot in Marie's *Espurgatoire*, and, as in the *Lais*, movement is associated with risk and with adventure. Just as in her first work Marie claims to record and translate Breton *lais* composed to commemorate adventures, in her last she translates a book that records the "adventures" of pilgrims in Purgatory.

> If any one returned, he would be received with joy. He would spend fifteen days in God's service in the church, then he would recount his adventure and it would be put into writing.

---

[21] *The Anonymous Marie de France* (Chicago: University of Chicago Press, 2003), p.169.

[22] Ibid., p. 173.

[23] Mann, *From Aesop to Reynard*, p. 76.

> Si aucuns en fust revenuz,
> a joie serreit receüz;
> puis demurreit, el Deu servise,
> pleinement quinzeine en iglise,
> puis contereit de s'aventure
> e serreit mise en escripture. (*Espurgatoire*, ll. 495–500)

The feudal vocabulary of service and the chivalric notion of adventure are appropriated for a religious context and for a journey that is highly scripted, beginning with the rituals that precede the entry into hell, and ending in the service in the church.

Owein's trip is described as a journey of severe penitence (la plus grïeve penitence, l. 536). Its trajectory is known in advance through the recorded accounts of those who have returned. The voyage seems initially to be set out on a geographical, horizontal space, but as Owein moves into hell we learn that he moves through a vertical space organized by a hierarchy of sins. This hierarchical, vertical organization is radically different from the spatial organization of the *Lais*.

Time, too, is organized differently in the *Espurgatoire*. Chronology is strictly choreographed but at the same time it is intricately bound up with movement. This text references time in a way that Marie's other works do not.[24] The *Lais* unfold through time, but the characters' movements are not tied very strictly to chronology. The stories accommodate great leaps of time without comment (as in *Yonec* and *Milun* where sons are born and grow to be knights). When the passage of time is indicated it seems somewhat arbitrary – why do three months elapse between the time Equitan and his lady decide to kill her husband and the day when they put their plan into action? Even when time is a crucial part of the plot, as in the term Guilliadun sets for Eliduc's return, time motivates movement, but movement advances the story. In the *Ysopë*, the fables take place mostly in the present, and in their temporal structure they are like single episodes. But in the *Espurgatoire* time is defined through the ritualized sequence of acts and movements that structure the entry into Purgatory. Those who would undertake the journey must first confess to the bishop, who will try to persuade them to abandon it. If they insist, he will send letters to the prior asking him to receive them. The prior, too, will try to dissuade penitents from entering Purgatory. If he is not successful, he closes the penitents in the church, where they must spend fifteen days fasting, praying, keeping vigils, and practicing mortifications. Then they

---

[24] Bloch, *The Anonymous Marie de France*, p. 287.

must attend mass and receive the eucharist, and only then are they led to the door of Purgatory, accompanied by a procession of clergy. Penitents may spend only one day in Purgatory, and those who fail to return within this time are lost. Those who return are received by the clergy and must remain another fifteen days in the church. Finally, the returned penitents must tell their adventures, so that they may be recorded (ll. 435–500).

If in the *Lais*, the passage of time seems less important for the development of the plot than movement through space, in the *Espurgatoire* Owein's journey is strictly scripted by time; it is the passage through the spaces of Purgatory that defines the movement of the narrative. Moreover, the time of the living – the temporality in which one day's journey is counted – seems out of sync with the time of Purgatory, and the single day that Owein is absent in the world of the living seems to include a lifetime of experience in the world of Purgatory.

The *Espurgatoire* is explicitly about a journey in time and place, and it brings together different modalities of both time and place – the historical peregrinations of St. Patrick, the geographical location of St. Patrick's Purgatory, the anticipation of where souls go after death, and the story of Owein's descent into Purgatory. It also draws on the paradigm of chivalric adventure in the knight's journey through Purgatory. The tortures that Owein confronts and conquers through faith recall the adventures encountered by knights in chivalric romances, and just as the knight's prowess is tested and confirmed in the battles he encounters, so too is Owein's faith tested by the tortures through which he must pass.[25] The penitential pilgrimage motif would seem to propose movement through a geographical space toward a final destination, while the paradigm of chivalric adventure would suggest a wandering through an unmapped landscape. Both models suggest a horizontal movement through space, but in the *Espurgatoire* they are used to describe a journey organized vertically.

Just as heaven is on high and hell down below, so too the lightest torments of Purgatory are near its entrance and the most severe are in its depths, as the narrator explains when she describes the vertical hierarchy that organizes Purgatory's punishments:

---

[25] Bloch notes that the recording of Owein's adventures after his return recalls the transcription of knights' adventures in the Old French *Prose Lancelot*. "Other Worlds and Other Words in the Works of Marie de France," *The World and Its Rival: Essays on Literary Imagination in Honor of Per Nykrog* (Amsterdam and Atlanta: Rodopi, 1999), pp. 39–57, here 53.

According to God's foresight, the greatest torments and the
strongest, without doubt, are the furthest down, and the others
are less serious for those who expect forgiveness and will not
be completely lost. Likewise, the location of hell is below the
earth, deep and dark, like a shadowy prison, perilous to those
who do evil. On earth there is a paradise toward the east, where
God put it, and where souls are led when they are delivered
from punishment. According to our book they dwell there in
delight.

Tels est de Deu la purveance:
li greignurs turmenz, sanz dutance,
sunt plus parfunz e plus custus;
e li autres sunt meins grevus
pur cels ki atendent merci
e n'erent pas del tut peri.
Autresi est d'enfer li lius
desuz terre, parfunz e cius,
si cume chartre tenebruse,
a cels qui n'eissent, perilluse.
En terre ad il un parewis,
vers oriënt, u Deu l'ad mis,
u les almes sunt amenees,
quant de peine sunt delivrees.
Ici trovum en nostre escrit
ke'iluek demuerent a delit. (*Espurgatoire*, ll. 127–42)

The *Espurgatoire* thus recounts a vertical descent through the regions
of Purgatory and a subsequent return upward to a glimpse of paradise.
The pilgrim's trajectory is mapped in advance, and whereas in the *Lais*
movement is linked to the possibility of escaping social strictures, in the
Espurgatoire Owein moves through rigidly defined spaces in a voyage
through a spiritual world experienced as a material reality.

The material experience of the journey through Purgatory is both the
story recounted and the means by which the spiritual significance of the
journey is described. In other words, the physical experiences of the
protagonist as he moves through the regions of Purgatory map a spiritual
as well as a physical progress. The journey is thus the subject of the story
and the way in which the story conveys meaning. In her effort to disclose
spiritual truths for "the simple folk" (la simple gent, l. 36), the narrator
is careful to distinguish between the soul's journey out of the body after
death, when it is either taken to rest by good angels or to torment by
devils, and the souls that are carried away in visions before they leave the

body (ll. 49–68). The latter travel through spiritual landscapes that they see in physical form:

> Before their death, many souls are truly spirited away and see visions. Then they come back to their living bodies and each shows what it has seen of torments or of salvation, what comes to the good, and what the evil should fear. They see spiritually things that appear materially. They see water and drawbridges, fire and houses and woods and meadows, and men of various kinds, appearing either black or white, and they see many other things appearing either joyful or sorrowful.

> Plusurs des almes veirement
> veient, devan lur finement,
> avisïuns e sunt ravies;
> puis repeirent as cors en vies,
> e mustrent ço ke unt veü
> ou de turment u de salu,
> ço ke li bon deivent aver
> e ke li mal deivent cremer.
> Il veien espiritelment
> ço ke semble corporelment;
> il veient ewe e punz levez,
> feu e maisuns e bois e prez
> e homes de divers semblanz,
> ou neirs ou blans aparissanz.
> Autres choses veient plusurs,
> semblanz a joie u a dolurs. (*Espurgatoire*, ll. 69–84)

The idea that the ravished souls "see spiritually things that appear materially" (Il veien espiritelment / ço ke semble corporelment) is the grounding concept of the *Espurgatoire* and one that is articulated in terms of movement through space.

> Here we will show you the punishments that are full of every pain. They are described as though they were in physical spaces.

> Ici vus musteruns des peines
> ke de tute dolur sunt pleines.
> Aparillees sunt e tels
> cum fuissent en lius corporels. (*Espurgatoire*, ll. 123–6)

Spiritual truths are demonstrated through a story about physical movement through a place. The description of the pains of Purgatory as though they were in physical spaces (lius corporels) is a strategy of emplacement, literally of putting the narrative into a place.

Although Marie's other works (except *La vie seinte Audree*, if she is its author) do not claim to offer spiritual insights, this is essentially the same narrative movement we have identified for the *Lais* and the *Ysopë*, where psychological or emotional drama is represented through movement between or among places. In all these works, the journeys and physical movements that the characters enact have meaning as embodied experiences. In the *Espurgatoire*, the journey is not merely a figure for a spiritual experience, it is the physical experience of a spiritual truth. The narrator insists on this distinction in the final section of the *Espurgatoire*, where Gilbert responds to a man who did not believe that Owein ever really entered Purgatory:

> Gilbert responded to him that those people were unbelievers who said that those who enter the house of God's purgation see the great punishments and torments established there spiritually and not materially. The knight who saw it all materially disputed this view; he suffered the torments in his flesh and bones when he was there.

> Gileberz en respondi tant,
> k'il n'erent mie bien creant
> qui dïent k'espiritelment
> veient, e non corporelment,
> quant il entrent en la maison
> que est de Deu espurgacion,
> les granz peines e les tormenz
> qui sunt establez la dedenz.
> Li chevaliers tut ço desdit,
> qui tut corporelment le vit;
> en char e en os les tormenz
> suffri quant il fud la dedenz. (*Espurgatoire*, ll. 2003–14)

Otherworld journeys emphasize the allegorical and *literary* nature of the experience of movement.[26] But in the Middle Ages, Latin Europe conceived of an anamorphic relation between earthly and spiritual geography. As we noted above, Earthly Paradise is a geographical place in medieval

---

[26] See Bloch's detailed development in *The Anonymous Marie de France*, chps. 7 and 8, esp. 247–8.

cartographical and textual traditions.[27] This emplacement operates as well in Marie's *Espurgatoire*, where Gilbert insists that the experience of Purgatory's pains is a physical experience, not merely a spiritual allegory. The meaning of the pilgrim's journey is located in the movement through and experience of the punishments and tortures that Purgatory contains. In other words, if the story about what Owein sees and feels is only a story, and not an experience, its truth is not grounded in experience but in the narrative itself, and in storytelling. But in all of Marie's narratives, storytelling is related to travel. Plot is constructed through movement, and meaning is constructed through encounters with places and through the meeting of different places and different values. If in the *Lais*, travel leads to the possibility of adventure and change, and in the *Ysopë* staying at home is better than venturing into the dangerous unknown, in the *Espurgatoire* movement through Purgatory brings spiritual and material experience together and also into debate around the nature of meaning.

---

[27] Suzanne Conklin Akbari, *Idols in the East: European Representations of Islam and the Orient, 1100–1450* (Ithaca: Cornell University Press, 2009), pp. 58–66.

5

Bodies and Embodiment: Characters

Marie de France's works mobilize characters who seek love and adventure, learn to appreciate the safety of home, and undertake the physical experience of a spiritual journey through Purgatory. In all of Marie's texts, characters experience the world through their bodies. Each work also includes an exploration of the values of embodiment. Marie uses forms of embodiment to point to categories of identity – beauty is a quality of noble status, for example. But bodies are often changing and changeable in Marie's narratives, and the values associated with forms of embodiment may also change or come into contact with each other. In this the poetics of embodiment is similar to the narrative use of place and movement we examined in Chapter 4. But whereas in Marie's representations of mobility characters encounter different values, in her thinking about embodiment, they inhabit them. The difference is crucial for this chapter's shift of focus from plot to character. In Marie's works, characters experience the world through their bodies.

Each of her works draws on a different literary tradition for its representations of embodiment. The *Lais* use the conventions of beauty in courtly literature to imagine noble courtly bodies whose primary characteristics are beauty and prowess. They also represent marvelous creatures drawn from or inspired by Celtic folklore. The *Ysopë* follows Latin fable collections in using animal embodiment in the service of didacticism. Popular and learnèd understandings of how souls inhabit bodies structure the journey through the Christian otherworld that reveals the embodied suffering of human souls tortured by demons in the *Espurgatoire seint Patriz*.[1]

In this chapter we seek to understand Marie's characters through an examination of the values she associates with embodiment. We begin with a discussion of the varieties of animal and human embodiment in the *Lais*, then explore the relationship between embodiment and the prominent

---

[1]   *La vie seinte Audree* would add yet a fourth exploration of the values of embodiment in its exploration of martyrdom and miracles.

theme of belonging to a group in many of the fables, and then examine the relationship between the spiritual and the sexual in the *Espurgatoire*'s representations of bodies.

Embodiment and animality in the *Lais*

Embodiment and appearance are both important and unremarkable in the *Lais*. The stories describe noble courtly female bodies whose primary characteristic is their beauty – in fact, the question of just how beautiful a woman is motivates the plot of two of the *lais*. In *Lanval* a trial tests the knight's claim that his lady is more beautiful than the queen. This lady's arrival and display of her body before the court confirm Lanval's claim and lead to his flight with her into Avalon. In *Yonec*, a lady becomes more beautiful when she finds a lover, and her husband suspects and then discovers her liaison when he notices the change. But beauty is also unremarkable: in *Guigemar*, after a separation of two years, the knight doesn't know his beautiful lover when he encounters her unexpectedly, and only the belt that he gave her secures his recognition. Objects like this belt, the rings that circulate in *Milun*, and the silk coverlet in *Le Fraisne* provide continuity in the stories through the identifications they make possible, as we have discussed in Chapter 2. Objects distinguish bodies for the characters in the *Lais* since apart from the beauty contest in *Lanval* and the lady's changing appearance in *Yonec*, forms of human embodiment seem relatively unremarkable. Unless, that is, they involve animals.

Marie's *Lais* explore embodiment most obviously in stories about marvelous animals: the speaking doe-stag in *Guigemar* and the animal–human transformations in *Bisclavret* and *Yonec*. These marvelous animals have been studied for what they can tell us about Marie's definition of human identity, her understanding of gender and sexuality, her sources, and her poetic project.[2] Critics have also attended to the more ordinary animals in the *lais* – the nightingale in *L'aüstic*, the swan in *Milun*, and

[2]   See, for example, Emma Campbell, "Political Animals: Human/Animal Life in Marie de France's 'Yonec' and 'Bisclavret,'" in *The Other Within: Imposing, Imposed and Self-Imposed Identities in Medieval French Narrative*, ed. Adrian Tudor and Kristin Burr (forthcoming); William Burgwinkle, *Sodomy, Masculinity, and the Law in Medieval Literature: France and England, 1050–1230* (Cambridge: Cambridge University Press, 2004), pp. 138–69; Peggy McCracken, "Animals and Translation in Marie de France's *Lais*," *Australian Journal of French Studies* 46.3 (2009): 238–49; Robert R. Edwards, "Marie de France and *Le Livre Ovide*," *Mediaevalia* 26 (2005): 57–81.

the weasels in *Eliduc*.[3] These ordinary animals play extraordinary roles in the stories, and along with the marvelous animals, they may suggest the interactions and the intimacies that define embodied values in the *Lais*. That is, because animal bodies interact with human bodies, and because animal bodies are explicitly invested with varying forms of agency, they may point to some of the ways in which the values of human bodies and human agency are both assumed and questioned in the *Lais*.

Here we will focus on the three *lais* in which a bird is featured as a protagonist.[4] *Yonec*, *L'aüstic*, and *Milun* are grouped together in the Harley manuscript and they share a number of plot elements: each features an unhappily married woman as a protagonist, each lady receives a bird in her room, and each has a secret liaison with a lover who is literally or metaphorically embodied by a bird. Both animality and gender are instantiations of embodiment; here they work together to suggest Marie's interest in animal and human bodies, in the categories that keep them apart, and in the spaces in which they come together.

In *Yonec* a rich old man takes a very beautiful (forment bele, l. 22) young wife so that he can engender an heir. He loves this lady for her beauty (pur sa bealté l'a mult amee, l. 24), and because of her beauty he makes sure she is watched carefully (Pur ceo que ele ert bele e gente, / en li guarder mist mult s'entente, ll. 29–30). The young wife's beauty earns her imprisonment in a tower where she is closely guarded by her husband's sister. After seven years of this life the lady is so sad that she loses hope of happiness and her beauty begins to fade (sa belté pert en tel mesure / cume cele ki n'en a cure, ll. 51–2). One spring day her guardian leaves her alone, and the lady laments her situation. She reproaches the parents who married her to the old man and regrets her inability to leave her tower. Then she remembers stories about marvelous adventures in which ladies found handsome courtly lovers whom they alone could see, and she prays that God will grant her wish for such a lover (Deus, ki de tut a poësté, / il en face ma volenté!, ll. 107–8). As soon as the lady has

---

[3]   See, for example, June Hall McCash, "The Swan and the Nightingale: Natural Unity in a Hostile World in the *Lais* of Marie de France," *French Studies* 49.4 (1995): 385–96; Pierre Jonin, "Le bâton et la belette, ou Marie de France devant la matière celtique," *Marche Romane* 30 (1980): 157–66.

[4]   Critics who have studied the three bird *lais* include Matilda Tomaryn Bruckner, "Speaking Through Animals in Marie de France's *Lais* and *Fables*," in *A Companion to Marie de France*, ed. Logan E. Whalen (Leiden: Brill, 2011), pp. 157–86; Denyse Delcourt, "Oiseaux, ombre, désir: Ecrire dans les *Lais* de Marie de France," *MLN* 120.4 (2005): 807–24; and Rupert T. Pickens, "Marie de France and the Body Politic," in *Gender and Text in the Later Middle Ages*, ed. Jane Chance (Gainesville: University Press of Florida, 1996), pp. 135–71 (149–55 on *Yonec* and *Milun*).

finished her prayer, a hawk appears at her window. He comes into her room, changes into a man, and offers her his love. The lady responds that she will accept and return his love only if this mysterious being believes in God.

The focus of the story then shifts from appearance to belief. The knight's profession of faith will take away any anxiety produced by his avian body. Christian belief and marvelous folklore meet in this *lai*, and many critics have noted the extent to which Marie uses Christian ritual and symbolism in the representation of the marvelous.[5] The lady's prayer to God brings the shape-shifting lover to her window, and she will accept his love only if he will profess his own religious orthodoxy. It seems that the knight's Christian credo will domesticate his animality. Religious and bodily orthodoxy are somehow linked, and the hawk-man's belief in the spiritual truth of Christianity aligns his ability to change form with a belief system that the lady shares and that seems implicitly to sanction her liaison with the unknown lover. Indeed, since this story is set in Wales, a place known in the twelfth century for heterodox Christian practices, the lady may well have reason to be concerned about the orthodoxy of the Welsh hawk-man's belief, since she certainly has evidence of the heterodoxy of his form.[6] It is clear, though, that the lady's request for a profession of faith is linked to embodiment. Perhaps she wants to be sure that the shape-shifting man is not a demon, since demons were known for their ability to change form. That is, she may wish to verify that she is not being tempted into a love affair by a demon who will steal her soul once she offers her body. Or it may be that confirmation of the hawk-man's Christian humanity makes his animal embodiment somehow secondary and acceptable. The narrator does not explain the lady's reasoning. It seems that she identifies a danger in the movement between forms of embodiment, but also perhaps in the movement between forms of narrative: the hawk-man's profession of belief will suture the legendary stories about marvelous lovers to the Christian story of salvation and belief.

Muldumarec, the hawk-man, cites his credo in response to the lady's requirement ("Jeo crei mult bien al creatur," l. 153). This declaration of belief in God may be seen as a proof of his humanity – if he is a Christian, he is a man and not a demon or an animal. However, Muldumarec never

⁵ See, for example, Susan Johnson, "Christian Allusion and Divine Justice in *Yonec*," in *In Quest of Marie de France, a Twelfth-Century Writer*, ed. Chantal A. Maréchal (Lewiston: Mellon, 1992), pp. 161–74.

⁶ Sharon Kinoshita, *Medieval Boundaries: Rethinking Difference in Old French Literature* (Philadelphia: University of Pennsylvania Press, 2006), p. 116.

says that he is not a hawk. In fact, when he appears before the lady and she is afraid, he emphasizes the nobility not of his human body, but of his avian form:

> "Lady, do not be afraid," he says. "The hawk is a noble bird, even if its secrets remain obscure to you."

> "Dame," fet il, "n'aiez poür,
> gentil oisel a en ostur,
> se li segrei vus sunt oscur." (*Yonec*, ll. 125–7)

Muldumarec reassures the lady not by denying his hawk form, but by locating the animal in the value-system of the aristocratic culture in which the lady lives (the hawk is noble, *gentil*) and in the marvelous secret world to which the lady has appealed in her call for a lover (its secrets are obscure).[7] The lady's memory of stories in which women summoned secret lovers recalls Marie's own memory of *lais* she heard, written by those who wished to preserve them, and the "obscure secrets" of the hawk hearken back to Marie's characterization of the meaning of ancient authors who wrote obscurely (oscurement diseient, *Prologue* l. 12), so that those who came after them could gloss their meaning.[8] The implicit reference to the *Prologue* of the *Lais* suggests that embodiment invites glossing and that embodiment is something to be understood, not merely observed.

Subsequent representations of bodies further invite an interrogation of the meaning of embodiment in the story, since the animal–human transformation is only one in a series of bodily metamorphoses in *Yonec*. When the lady says that she will take Muldumarec as her lover if he believes in God, the hawk-man confirms his faith and then suggests a further proof of his belief, one that offers expanded evidence of his ability to change appearances. The knight tells the lady to pretend to be gravely ill and call for a priest to hear her confession. He will take her appearance, he says (La semblance de vus prendrai, l. 165), and receive the eucharist in her place. In this way he will allay the lady's fears. She agrees, and pretends that she is dying.

---

[7] Dafydd Evans, "The Nobility of Knight and Falcon," in C. Harper-Bill and R. Harvey (eds.), *Ideals and Practice of Medieval Knighthood III: Papers from the Fourth Strawberry Hill Conference, 1988* (Woodbridge: The Boydell Press, 1990), pp. 70–99.

[8] For a reading of Marie's own obscurity, see Alexandre Leupin, "The Impossibility of Manifesting 'Literature': On Marie de France's Obscurity," *Exemplaria* 3 (1991): 221–42.

> [The priest] came as quickly as possible, bringing the *corpus domini*. The knight received it and drank the wine from the chalice. The chaplain left and the old woman closed the doors. The lady lay next to her lover: I never saw so fair a couple. When they had laughed and played and exchanged confidences, the knight took his leave, for he wanted to return to his own country.

> ... e cil i vint cum plus tost pot,
> corpus domini aportot.
> Li chevaliers l'a receü,
> le vin del chalice a beü.
> Li chapeleins s'en est alez,
> e la vieille a les us fermez.
> La dame gist lez sun ami:
> unkes si bel cuple ne vi.
> Quant unt asez ris e jué
> e de lur priveté parlé,
> li chevaliers a cungié pris;
> raler s'en vuelt en sun païs. (*Yonec*, ll. 189–200)

The bodily transformations recounted here are multiple. Presumably the knight changes into the lady's likeness and receives the eucharist, then transforms into a man and makes love, then metamorphoses into a hawk and flies away. The transubstantiation of the host into the body of Christ in the eucharistic ritual adds yet another layer of metamorphosis to this already complex series of transformations. But the text does not explicitly describe the changes; they remain "obscure secrets" that invite a gloss – or at least some questions. Are there *two* bodies that look like the lady on the bed when the priest arrives? If not, where is the lady while the man receives the eucharist in her form? When they make love after the religion test, does the knight change back into a man? Or does he transform back into a bird? Or does he remain in the lady's *semblance*?[9] The fantasy-like erotic pleasure that the lady will receive from the lover who appears whenever she calls him is a pleasure derived from a body that morphs across at least three forms or appearances: the human lover's body, the noble bird's body, and the lady's own appearance, her "semblance." This

---

[9]   On the separateness of the lovers, see Cary Howie, *Claustrophilia: The Erotics of Enclosure in Medieval Literature* (New York: Palgrave Macmillan, 2007), p. 127. For a different view that sees the scene as one in which bodies are fused in a way that emphasizes continuity rather than identity and difference, see Stephen G. Nichols, "Deflections of the Body in the Old French Lay," *Stanford French Review* 14.1–2 (1990): 27–50.

series of transformations emphasizes not the value of one bodily form over another but the movement among three forms or *semblances*.[10]

Yonec mixes the Celtic marvelous and Christian mystery in the representation of hawk-man's transformations, and it suggests a fluidity of embodiment that corresponds to a fluidity of values. The stories the lady has heard about marvelous secret lovers inspire her to pray to God for such a lover, and she requires the shape-shifting being that appears to her to prove his Christian faith. The mixing of Christian belief and the pleasures of adulterous love is not unusual in the *Lais*: Eliduc's worshipful placement of his lover's body on the altar of a chapel is another example. In *Yonec*, shifts between Christian belief and marvelous presence, and between shifting forms and bodily pleasures, permit the intimate intersection of the animal and the human. But if the "obscure secrets" of the hawk-man invite an interpretive gloss, in *Yonec* any questions the lady may have had about her lover's metamorphosis are answered in advance in the stories she cites when she prays for a lover, and in the hawk-man's profession of Christian faith. The narrative itself also forecloses questions about the hawk-man as a progenitor, since the son he engenders shares his father's sword and his chivalric prowess, but none of his marvelous nature. When the bird first appears and transforms into a knight, the lady "thinks it is a marvel" (chevaliers bels e genz devint. / La dame a merveille le tint, ll. 119–20), but it is not clear whether she marvels at the metamorphosis or at the immediate answer to her prayer in the form of a handsome noble knight. In any case, when the hawk-man tells the lady that he has long loved her from afar, she is quickly reassured (La dame se raseüra, l. 139), and asks for his profession of faith. The animal–human nature of the hawk-man is not given much scrutiny, and a gloss on the relationship between the avian body and the human body is elaborated not in *Yonec* but in the two *lais* that follow it in the Harley manuscript: *L'aüstic* separates the bodies of the bird and the lover, making the bird a metaphoric stand-in for the beloved, and *Milun* offers a "realistic" rewriting of *Yonec* that literalizes the use of the bird as a mediator in the love relationship.

In *L'aüstic*, Marie's introduction names the Bretons as the source of the *lai*, and in a display of her translation skills she gives the French and English translations of the Breton name "l'aüstic":

---

[10] *Semblance* refers to appearance, but seems also to refer to form. When the bird first flies through the lady's window he is described as looking like a hawk (ostur sembla, l. 114), and here the bird's form and its identification as a kind of hawk seem both to be described by the verb "*sembla*."

I will tell you an adventure about which the Bretons composed
a lay. It is called "L'aüstic," I believe, or so they call it in their
country. In French it is "rossignol" and "nightingale" in correct
English.

Une aventure vus dirai,
dunt li Bretun firent un lai.
L'Aüstic a nun, ceo m'est vis,
si l'apelent en lur païs;
ceo est russignol en Franceis
e *nihtegale* en dreit Engleis. (*L'aüstic*, ll. 1–6)

Marie's translations of "l'aüstic" offer alternative forms of the word. They
are transformations of a kind, and they are like a gloss in that they refine
the meaning of "l'aüstic" for the reader by giving the word in French
and English. The only other prologue in which Marie gives translations
for a *lai*'s title is *Bisclavret*, another story about an animal.[11] She tells
us that "Bisclavret" is the Breton name for the story and "Garulf" is
the French (Norman) translation ("Bisclavret a nun en Bretan, / Garulf
l'apelent li Norman," ll. 3–4). Animals are associated with translation in
Marie's *Lais*, with movement between languages and between forms.[12]
The alternate linguistic forms of "l'aüstic" may recall the literary forms
that the nightingale takes in courtly literature and lyric poetry. The story
also contains echoes of the Pyramus and Tisbé legend, which Marie could
have read in Latin or in Old French, or simply known as a story in circulation among courts.[13] In other words, although Marie claims to have
recorded a Breton *lai*, *L'aüstic* references other literary forms. Read as
a gloss on *Yonec*, it extends the imbrications of animality, embodiment,
and love found there.

    In the closed world of *L'aüstic* the lady appears even more isolated
than her counterpart in *Yonec*. Both women are unhappily married, but
whereas in *Yonec* the lady is married to a rich old man (uns riches huem,
vielz e antis, l. 12) and she curses her parents and all those who gave her
to the jealous man and married her to his body (Maleeit seient mi parent
/ e li altre comunalment, / ki a cest gelus me donerent / e a sun cors me
marïerent!, ll. 85–8), in *L'aüstic* the lady's husband is one of two knights

---

[11] She translates "Chievrefueil" ("gotelef," the English goatleaf) in the epilogue of
Chievrefueil, ll. 115–16.

[12] See McCracken, "Animals and Translation."

[13] On classical references, see Delcourt, "Oiseaux, ombre, désir," 821–2; Kristine
Brightenback, "The *Metamorphoses* and Narrative *Conjointure* in 'Deus Amanz,' 'Yonec,'
and 'Le Laüstic,'" *Romanic Review* 72.1 (1981): 1–12.

whose valor contributes to the reputation of their city (Pur la bunté des dous baruns / fu de la vile bons li nuns, ll. 11–12). The second knight falls in love with the lady and she returns his love, both because of his reputation and because of his proximity – he lives beside the lady and her husband (ele l'ama sur tute rien, / tant pur le bien qu'ele en oï / tant pur ceo qu'il ert pres de li, ll. 26–8). Although the lover is described as young and unmarried (uns bachelers, l. 17), we don't learn that he is any younger than the lady's husband. She is closely guarded while her neighbor is in the country (la dame ert estreit guardee, / quant cil esteit en la cuntree, ll. 49–50), but this is the only initial indication of her husband's jealousy at the beginning of the story, and the lovers are separated at least in part by their own prudence:

> They loved each other wisely and well. They hid their love carefully and took care that they were not seen or disturbed or suspected. And they could do this because their houses were close beside each other.

> Sagement e bien s'entramerent.
> Mult se covrirent e guarderent
> qu'il ne fussent aparceü
> ne desturbé ne mescreü.
> E il le poeient bien faire,
> kar pres esteient lur repaire. (L'aüstic, ll. 29–34)

As in *Yonec*, the lady's lover appears at a window, but in *L'aüstic* only the lovers' words and the small presents they toss each other pass through the opening. And as in *Yonec*, a bird makes the lovers' encounters possible, but in *L'aüstic* the bird is separate from the man.

The bird in *L'aüstic* is a nightingale, not a hawk. The nightingale is associated with poetry and the pursuit of love rather than with hunting, and its song gives the lady an excuse to go to her window to meet her lover. The bird is at first a figural part of the story, a fiction that the lady invents to explain why she goes to the window at night. Although the bird that bears secret meaning may recall the bird-man whose secrets remain obscure, the nightingale becomes an embodied presence in the story only as a corpse, after the husband, like the jealous old man in *Yonec*, kills the bird. In both *lais* the bird is entombed, Yonec in a rich tomb in his own land and the nightingale in a rich coffer. But in *L'aüstic*, the bird's death is not followed by a marvelous journey to an unknown land. The bird itself travels – its dead body is enclosed first in an embroidered silk by the lady when she sends it to her lover, and then in the coffer that her lover carries with him. The constant presence of the enshrined bird substitutes and perhaps compensates for the lovers' inability to meet, the only thing that displeased the knight and the lady about their love affair before it was put to an end by the nightingale's death (N'unt guaires rien ki lur desplaise / … fors tant qu'il ne poeent venir / del tut ensemble a lur plaisir, ll. 45–8). The sealed golden coffer that holds the dead nightingale and that the knight keeps with him suggests that the love affair is transformed into a commemorative story that circulates with the knight. It also points to a persistent association of animal embodiment and intimacy in the *Lais*, especially when read alongside *Yonec*, a story in which a lover's body is also a bird's body, and *Milun*, a story in which lovers use a swan to arrange secret meetings.

Like the unhappily married women in *L'aüstic* and *Yonec*, the *malmariée* in *Milun* is closely guarded by the jealous old husband to whom her father has given her, but we learn that despite the surveillance, she and her lover manage to meet:

> They met several times. None can be so constrained and tightly guarded that he does not often find a way.

> Ensemble vindrent plusurs feiz.
> Nuls ne puet estre si destreiz
> ne si tenuz estreitement
> que il ne truisse liu sovent. (*Milun*, ll. 285–8)

The narrator's suggestion that even the tightest supervision cannot prevent lovers from meeting recalls the lovers' trysts in *Yonec*, where the birdman comes to his lady any time she wishes for his presence. In fact, *Milun* rewrites *Yonec* in several ways. The lady conceives a child with her lover, but gives birth before her marriage, rather than after, as in *Yonec*. In both *lais*, the sons unite their mothers with their fathers, but in *Yonec* this is a reunion in death, since when the son kills his mother's jealous husband, she dies on her dead lover's tomb. In *Milun*, the lady's husband conveniently dies just as her son finds his father and vows to unite him with his mother. Whereas in *Yonec*, the hawk-man's ability to change shape allows him to meet his lady, in *Milun* the marvelous elements are absent, and the lovers communicate and plan their meetings through messages carried by a swan that flies back and forth between them.

Milun is certainly one of the most realistic of Marie's *lais*, particularly in its detailed descriptions of customs and practices. The story begins with a description of Milun, a great knight who has never been defeated in battle. A beautiful courtly young woman hears of him and sends a

messenger to offer him her love. Milun accepts and swears he will always
be faithful to her. Messages between the lovers allow them to arrange
meetings in the garden beside the lady's chamber. Milun comes there so
often and loves the lady so well that she becomes pregnant (Tant i vint
Milun, tant l'ama / que la dameisele enceinta, ll. 53–4). This is the only
one of Marie's *lais* in which an unmarried woman becomes pregnant,
and it fully details the consequences of pregnancy for the unwed noblewoman.

> When she understood that she was pregnant, she sent for Milun
> and spoke her lament. She told him what had happened: she
> has lost her honor and her well-being because of it. She would
> be judged severely, and tortured with a sword or sold as a slave
> in another country. That was the ancient custom that they still
> followed at this time.

> Quant aparçut qu'ele est enceinte,
> Milun manda, si fist sa pleinte.
> Dist li cument est avenu,
> s'onur e sun bien a perdu,
> quant de tel fet s'est entremise;
> de li iert faite granz justise:
> a glaive sera turmentee
> u vendue en altre cuntree.
> Ceo fu custume as anciëns
> e s'i teneient en cel tens (*Milun*, ll. 55–64)

The lady's anticipation of the loss of honor may recall the importance of
lineage in noble families, but her fear of violent torture is somewhat surprising. Perhaps even more surprising is the way that the language of her
complaint echoes the *Prologue* to the *Lais*, and puts the torture of unwed
pregnant women into relation with Marie's poetic project. The phrase "it
was the custom of ancient people ..." (Ceo fu custume as anciëns ...,
Milun, l. 63) recalls Marie's statement in her *Prologue*, "It was the custom
of ancient people ..." (Custume fu as anciëns ..., *Prologue*, l. 9). Both
references to "ancient people" (anciëns) name customs that continue: in
Milun, the violent punishment of unwed mothers, and in the *Prologue* the
obscure writing that continues to invite interpretation. This repetition may
draw attention to a relationship between bodies and writing in the *Lais*
and, like the reference to obscurity in *Yonec*, it calls for an interpretation,
or gloss, of embodiment.

The link between bodies and writing is figured repeatedly in *Milun*.
First, the lady sends her child with an identifying ring and letter to her

sister in Northumbria, as she explains to Milun: "I will hang your ring at his neck and I will send a letter to her. I will write there the name of his father and the adventure of his mother" (Vostre anel al col li pendrai / e un brief li enveierai; / escriz i iert li nuns sun pere / e l'aventure de sa mere, ll. 77–80). The lady's letter repeats the very form of the *lai* itself, which bears the name of the baby's father and tells of his mother's adventures. This letter is the first of many to follow, attached not to the baby's neck, but to a swan's.[14]

This bird is not a pretext for the lovers' reunion, as in *L'aüstic*, nor is it a marvelous animal, as in *Yonec*. Its role in the story is defined by the use of its body: it can be made to carry letters between the lovers. In his first letter to his lady after her marriage, Milun explains how to make the swan carry a letter back to him:

> First she should take good care of it, then she should let it starve for three days without being fed. Then she should hang the letter around its neck and let it go. It will fly to the place where it first lived.

> Primes le face bien guarder,
> puis si le laist tant jeüner
> treis jurs que il ne seit peüz;
> li briés li seit al col penduz;
> laist l'en aler: il volera
> la u il primes conversa. (*Milun*, ll. 241–6)

Milun and his lady communicate through the swan for two decades, and in the repeated description of the treatment of the swan, the narrator emphasizes that the swan flies because it is hungry.

> Milun and his lover lived this way for twenty years. They made the swan their messenger, and they had no other intermediary. They starved it before they let it fly, and you can know that the one to whom the swan came fed it well.

> Vint anz menerent cele vie
> Milun entre lui e s'amie.
> Del cigne firent messagier,
> n'i aveient altre enparlier,

---

[14] On the swan (cisne) as a *signe*, and on the theme of writing, see R. Howard Bloch, *The Anonymous Marie de France* (Chicago: University of Chicago Press, 2003), pp. 98–103.

e sil faiseient jeüner
ainz qu'il le laissassent voler;
cil a qui li oisels veneit,
ceo saciez, que il le paisseit. (*Milun*, ll. 277–84)

Where we have translated "jeüner" as "to starve," we might just as accurately have translated as "to let go without eating." That is, to insist on the lovers' "starving" of the swan may suggest an imposition of modern understandings about the treatment of animals on a story in which the main point is that the lovers managed to communicate for twenty years through the intermediary of a messenger-swan. But here the narrator does seem to insist on the lovers' use of the swan in a way different from the use of the nightingale as a pretext in *L'aüstic*, or even from the use of animal knowledge in *Eliduc*, where Guildeluëc has her servant strike a weasel to make it drop the flower with which it has revived its stricken mate. The narrator tells us repeatedly that the swan is disciplined to carry letters. In other words, since the swan does not learn to carry the letters without first being starved, the detailed insistence on withholding food suggests not training but discipline. This distinction is worth noting because it calls attention to other disciplined bodies in the story.[15]

Perhaps because of its realist tone, *Milun* includes several descriptions of the social constraints that apply to bodies. As we noted above, the lady fears that she will lose her honor and be chastised and tortured if her pregnancy is discovered. Later she fears that she will lose her status as wife and be treated as a servant when the husband her father has chosen for her discovers that she is not a virgin (Ja ne sui jeo mie pucele; / a tuz jurs mes serai ancele!, ll. 135–6). The lady and the swan are aligned in the representation of their use-value. The lady's father gives her to a rich and powerful nobleman of the country (Sis pere li duna barun, / un mult riche hume del païs, / mult esforcible e de grant pris, ll. 124–6), and although the text does not say so explicitly, it would be reasonable to understand that the lady's father profits from the alliance and that the new husband will wish for an heir. The terms of the marriage exchange are more explicit in *Yonec*, where the narrator tells us that the lady's husband is very old and has taken a wife so that he can have a child who will inherit his wealth (Mult fu trespassez en eage. / Pur ceo qu'il ot bon heritage, / femme prist pur enfanz aveir, / ki aprés lui fussent si heir, ll. 17–20). *Milun* rewrites *Yonec*, putting the lady's pregnancy before her

---

[15] On the submission of animals as constitutive of the human, see Karl Steel, "How to Make a Human," *Exemplaria* 20.1 (2008): 3–27.

marriage and substituting mastery over a swan for the marvelous transformation into a bird that allows the lovers to meet, and the story describes animal subordination as an alternative to marvelous animal incarnation.

The changing, metamorphosing body meets the disciplined body in the other *lai* that recounts an animal–human metamorphosis. The protagonist of *Bisclavret* is equally at home in the forest and at court. When in his wolf form, he hunts in the forest and, as he tells his wife, he lives by killing prey (En cele grant forest me met / al plus espés de la gualdine, / s'i vif de preie e de ravine, ll. 64–6). Even after he is imprisoned in his animal form, he retains the courtliness of the knight, and he willingly submits to the king, kissing his foot in a gesture of homage (Des que il a le rei choisi, / vers lui curut querre merci. / Il l'aveit pris par sun estrié, / la jambe li baise e le pié, ll. 145–8).

Characters whose bodies defy categorization are imperiled in the *Lais*, and danger comes to them while they are in animal form. Bisclavret's wife steals his clothes while he is a wolf, and in *Yonec* the lady's jealous husband kills the hawk-man as he flies through her window in his bird form. Yet animal form is also attractive. The hawk-man's noble avian body is also the form in which the lady encounters her lover, and although Bisclavret's wife betrays him when she learns that he is sometimes a wolf, the king has a more intimate relationship with the wolf than he had with the knight. Bodies that move between worlds and participate in different value-systems structure the plots in Marie's *Lais*, as we suggested in Chapter 4, and the values of embodiment are defined by the social relations into which they enter. Many of Marie's *lais* recount what happens when love runs afoul of the social relations that define noble bodies. The old husband's desire for an heir and his wife's desire for a lover offer an example of this conflict in *Yonec*, and we cited above the use-value of marriage illustrated in the old husband's desire for an heir and in the severe punishments imagined for a woman who becomes pregnant with a lover before her family can arrange an advantageous marriage in *Milun*.

Conflicts between social roles for bodies and the relations of desire that draw bodies out of such scripted roles subtend most of the *Lais*. Noble succession and inheritance are guaranteed through marriage and legitimate childbirth, and female bodies are closely guarded with the intention of guaranteeing both, though usually with little success in Marie's stories. Male bodies, too, are also disciplined to their roles in feudal society, though also with mixed success. *Milun* and *Guigemar* offer examples of knights who leave home to participate in tournaments and win chivalric glory, but *Chaitivel* recounts the dangerous conflation of chivalry and the pursuit of love – when the four lovers organize a tournament to determine

which will have the lady's love, three are killed and the last is wounded
in the thigh, unable to love or to fight. The consequences of adultery
are also played out on men's bodies. Although they are not subject to
confinement or violent punishment, as are women, they are vulnerable
to vengeance. The hawk-lover is killed by the jealous husband in *Yonec*,
Guigemar is discovered in his lady's enclosure and sent out to sea, and
Equitan is killed in the boiling bath that he and his lover prepared for her
husband. In *L'aüstic*, as we have seen, vengeance is displaced onto the
body of the nightingale.

The starved swan is a figure that makes the discipline of bodies visible
in the *Lais*, and examples of the conflict between desire and the constraints
of social institutions point to the many stories in which characters try to
escape the contracts, conventions, and laws that define their place in the
world. *Les dous amanz* tells a different kind of story. Here the young
would-be lover must overcome the impossible conditions under which he
may win his beloved as his wife:

> He knows that her father loves her so much that if he asks him
> for her hand, he will not want to give it unless he can carry her
> in his arms to the top of the mountain.
>
> S'a sun pere la demandot,
> il seveit bien que tant l'amot
> que pas ne li voldreit doner,
> se il ne la peüst porter
> entre ses braz en sum le munt. (*Les dous amanz*, ll. 87–91)

The young woman sends her lover to an aunt in Salerno who fortifies
him with her medicines (Par mescines l'a enforcié, l. 143) and prepares a
potion that will reinvigorate him if he becomes tired or weakened as he
climbs the mountain. But although the story stresses the promised effects
of the potion, it also describes the lovers' bodily preparations for the
ordeal. The Salernitan aunt uses her drugs to strengthen the young man,
and his beloved – like the swan? – starves:

> The young woman prepares herself: she does not eat and
> deprives herself of food to help her lover by becoming lighter.
>
> La dameisele s'aturna;
> mult se destreinst, mult jeüna
> a sun mangier pur alegier,
> qu'a sun ami voleit aidier. (*Les dous amanz*, ll. 173–6)

The tragedy of the story comes from the young man's trust in his body and his failure to drink the strengthening potion. Like her lover, the young woman dies at the end of the story (Ilec murut la dameisele, / ki tant ert pruz e sage e bele, ll. 237–8). The brief account of her death gives no reason for it, and we assume that she dies from grief, but the earlier emphasis on her bodily discipline may suggest that it extends to an ultimate mastery: she does not wish to outlive her lover, so she dies.

The *Lais* invent forms of embodiment that escape the constraints scripted by social relations and institutions, and they make possible forbidden or unimagined relationships. The tension between forms of embodiment sanctioned by social institutions and forms of desire that subvert those institutions produces both narrative and pleasure. But if in the *Lais* bodies cross boundaries between worlds and species, and characters constantly seek to escape or redefine the categories that confine their mobility and discipline their bodies, in the *Ysopë* embodiment defines identity and identity is defined as belonging to a group.

The limits of the body in the *Ysopë*

In the *Lais* animal bodies usually belong to beings that demonstrate the qualities of the human. The hawk and the wolf that transform into men in *Yonec* and *Bisclavret* are distinguished by their nobility and courtliness even in their animal forms. In *Eliduc* the weasel's devotion to its mate resembles a lover's care for a beloved, and in *Guigemar* a deer speaks. But whereas the human-like animals of the *Lais* may suggest the fragility of the human–animal boundary, in fables the function of speaking animals is not to comment on the animality of humans or the anthropomorphic qualities of animals. Rather, as Jill Mann has argued, the usefulness of animals to the fable is a resistance to moral evaluation that is located in their very animality.[16] Mann argues that:

> Animals are chosen as the main actors [of fables] because – from the negative point of view – they remove any expectations of psychological individuality or moral complexity. From the positive point of view, they are chosen because their actions can be assumed to be dictated by nature, and this lends a quasi-inevitability to their actions, even when they are not such as the "natural animal" would commit.[17]

[16] Jill Mann, *From Aesop to Reynard: Beast Literature in Medieval Britain* (Oxford: Oxford University Press, 2009), pp. 31–3.

[17] Ibid., p. 39.

The animal's behavior is cast as somehow "natural," even when the animal protagonist demonstrates emotions or sentiments shaped by human social values. Then in the bipartite construction of the fable, the story of animal behavior and its consequences is transferred to human behavior and subject to a moral judgment in the epimythium.[18]

While the "nature" of animality may be assumed in the genre, the extent to which identity is natural is debated in many of the individual fables in terms of domestication and species identity. For example, in Fable 26 a wolf considers adopting the easy life of a dog. Then the wolf notices the chain around the dog's neck. The dog explains:

> It is my chain, and I am tied with it all week, because often I would bite and do damage to others. My lord wants to protect them, so he has me chained and restrained. At night I go around the house to protect it from thieves.

> ... C'est ma chaene,
> dunt homme me lie la semaine;
> kar suventefeiz je mordreie
> e a plusurs riens mesfereie
> que mes sires veut garantir;
> si me fet lïer e retenir.
> La nuit vois entur la meisun
> que n'i aprisment li larun. (26:25–32)

The wolf prefers freedom to the luxuries of the dog's life, and so returns to his life in the forest.

This fable lacks a true epimythium. It ends with the wolf's departure into the woods and the explanation that "because of the chain their love and their companionship were lost" (Par la chaene est departie / lur amur e lur cumpaignie, 26:41–2). The story seems to valorize freedom, but it does not condemn the dog's lot. Rather, like other fables it endorses stasis and the acceptance of one's place in the world. Species determines one's place in the world, it seems, and species is defined by domestication. This circular logic is at play in the fable: the wolf could have the dog's life, but he would have to give up his freedom. The chain domesticates the dog; it prevents him from biting and from doing damage – from being wild and from being a wolf.

Because fables use animal acts to speak about human behavior, we might say that they domesticate animal figures to didactic use. Certainly

---

18 Ibid., p. 35.

utility is associated with domesticity in the story of the dog whose tendency to bite is curbed during the day but freed at night so that he may guard his master's house. Domesticity is based on unnatural alliances, some of the fables suggest. The dog's defense of its master causes him to lose the love and companionship of the wolf, and in Fable 17 domesticity makes a sparrow the ally of a peasant in the slaughter of other birds. This swallow has seen the peasant planting linseed and counsels the birds to eat the seeds before they mature and the peasant can make nets and snares from the flax. The peasant strikes a bargain with the swallow and allows her to nest in his house (En sa meisun suffri sun ni, 17:21). In return, she and her relatives will not disturb his harvest, but the peasant makes nets and snares the other birds. The swallow's bargain with the peasant guarantees her safety at the price of the lives of other birds, and like the chains that control the dog's tendency to bite, it suggests the mastery and violence that subtend the relationship. Domestication aligns animals and humans, and makes animals' links to humans more important than ties to other animals. Domestication also defines animal difference from the human, to the extent that animal difference is constructed through the domination and subjugation of the animal.[19] In their representations of the alliance with humans that some animals embrace and others reject, and in their suggestion of the violence that subtends domestication, Marie's fables point to distinctions among species based on relationships with people.

The basic narrative strategy of the fable is to use animal behavior to illustrate a moral lesson for humans, but occasionally these stories about animal actions also debate the nature of species and of the behavior proper to species. That is, some fables debate the transferability of animal behavior from one species to another in a way that may reflect on the genre's use of animal actions to illustrate a lesson about human behavior. For example, Fable 23 is about a battle between creatures who walk on four feet and those who fly in the air, and about the bat who does not know which side to take (ne sot as quels se deust traire, 23:12). She chooses to join the four-legged creatures, but then when she sees the strength of the birds, she decides to change sides:

> She hides her feet in a foolish act, for when she opens her wings, she shows them to all. Her betrayal is obvious, and her treachery revealed.

---

[19] Steel, "How to Make a Human."

Ses piez musça, si fist folie:
mes, quant les eles *entreovri*,
par devant tuz les *decovri*.
Dunc est sa felunie *overte*
e sa traïsun *tut descuverte*. (23:28–32)

The repetition of the verbs *ovrir* (open, reveal) and *decovrir* (uncover, discover) emphasizes a link between uncovering the bat's body and discovering her betrayal of one side for a perceived advantage on the other. When she reveals her body, she exposes her four feet, and the text insists more on the display of the bat's beastly identity (the feet she tried to hide) than on the bodily ambiguity of a winged animal that has four feet. The beasts complain to their creator about the bat's failure to keep her word (ele ad sa fei mentie, 23:38). Although the fable does not comment on the bat's ability to speak and swear allegiance, her betrayal of species loyalty is condemned and the bat is forbidden ever to appear where beast or bird might see her – she may never again see the light of day. This story is taken to illustrate the imperative of loyalty to a lord. It explains that the traitor loses his honor and his wealth, and – in a conclusion that recalls the fate of the wife and her daughters in *Bisclavret* – his descendants will share his blame (si honur en pert e sun aveir / e repruver en unt si heir, 23:61–2). The fable is not sympathetic to the bat's bodily indeterminacy and it values loyalty over any identification of essential identity – in this, too, it may echo *Bisclavret*. The fable does not make a judgment about whether the bat is properly a bird or a beast, but teaches the importance of keeping one's word. Yet the initial implicit question about the bat's bird-like and beast-like body opens the story and defines her dilemma. She does not know which side to choose, "ne sot as quels se deust traire" (23:12), and the narrator's use of the verb "traire," which can mean "to lean toward" as well as "to betray," suggests that choice includes betrayal for this bird-like, beast-like being.[20]

A similar story about hiding one's identity is told in Fable 76, where a badger who sees pigs foraging in the woods decides that he is and should have been a pig (que porc esteit e estre dut, 76:6). He hides his paws (ses piez musça, 76:11), and follows the pigs home, but when he sees that they are to be slaughtered he reclaims his identity as a badger. In Fable 74 (also discussed in Chapter 4), the protagonist is a beetle who claims that his species was badly made by its creator since beetles "are neither worm nor bird; when they have eaten they cannot fly, and when hungry,

---

[20] For a discussion of *traire* in relation to translation, see Chapter 1.

they cannot walk" (il n'esteient ver ne oisel; / saül ne poeient voler, / a jeün ne sorent aler, 74:12–14). Like the bat in Fable 23, this beetle tries to imitate a bird, and when he fails to fly like an eagle he longs only to return home and no longer cares how he is perceived: "I don't care anymore if I am taken for a worm or a bird, I only want to return to the horse manure pile, for I am sick with hunger" (Ore ne chaut quë hum me tienge / verm u oisel, mes que jo vienge / dedenz la fiente del cheval; / kar de feim ai dolur e mal, 74:43–6) The epimythium condemns the pride of those who would reach too high, like the beetle who thinks he can fly like an eagle. Just as the fable cautions against leaving home, it also chastises those who are overconfident in their abilities, and locates a grounding of identity in embodiment. The beetle's desire to be something he is not fails because of bodily limitations:

> He leaped after the eagle because he believed he could fly higher. Before he had gone very far he was dizzy and stunned. He could not climb higher, and he could not return to his manure pile.

> Derere l'egle prist un saut,
> car il quida voler plus haut.
> Ainz que gueres fust luinz alez,
> esturdi fu e esturnez;
> ne poeit mie haut munter
> ne a sun femer puis asener. (74:31–6)

Here essential identity is located in embodiment, and the beetle's pride is the cause of his downfall. He claims that he can fly as high as an eagle, but his body limits his abilities and he literally falls short.

Fable 15, about the ass who envies the dog's favored position with their master, is also a story about knowing one's place in the world, but it polices species identity in a more pointed way than the fables about the ambiguously embodied bat who is neither beast nor bird and the beetle who is neither worm nor bird. Here the ass thinks that because he is better than a dog, he will also be better at playing with his master:

> After much deliberation, the ass decided that his goodness and size made him worth much more than the dog, and that he would know better how to play with his master than the dog, and that his cries would be more willingly heard. He would know better how to jump up on his master and how to strike him with his feet.

Mut s'est li asnes purpensez
que meuz del chien vaut il asez
e de bunté et de grandur,
meuz savereit a sun seignur
jüer que li chenez petiz
e meuz sereit oï ses criz,
meuz savereit a sun seignur
meuz savereit des piez ferir. (15:11–18)

The ass who aspires to show his superiority to the dog is thoroughly beaten after he frightens his master with his loud cries and knocks him to the ground when he tries to jump on him as the little dog does. The moral chastises those who would try to rise above their station in life, here defined according to a hierarchy of animal being that is indexed to embodiment. It further cautions those who would act in ways that are not suited to their bodies or their origins (que ne avient pas a lur corsage, / ensurketut a lur parage, 15:47–8).

Fable 65b also describes embodiment as destiny in a brief moralizing comment about the impossibility of escaping the skin one is born in:

According to an old example, I recount here that wolves grow old in the skin they are born in. They wear them all their lives. You can teach a wolf to be a priest, but he will still be a wolf, sly and cruel, ugly and hideous.

Par veille essample recunte ici
que tuit li lu sunt enveilli
en cele pel u il sunt né;
la remainent tut lur eé.
Ki sur le lu meïst bon mestre,
quil doctrinast a estre prestre,
si sereit il tut dis gris lus
fel e engrés, leiz e hidus. (65b:1–8)[21]

The fable suggests that you can't teach a wolf new tricks – a wolf is always a wolf.

Fable 87 recounts a similar story, but from the perspective of the wolf. Two wolves complain that no one seeks their company, even when they have no intention of robbing them. They decide to do good deeds in order

---

[21] Bruckner suggests that this text (cited here in full) may be the epimythium of a lost fable. Charles Bruckner, ed. and trans., *Les fables* (Louvain: Peeters, 1991), p. 255, n. 1.

to gain friends, so they go to help some peasants harvest their wheat. The men shout at them and chase them away, and the wolves conclude that doing good gets them no more company than doing evil: "Let us go back to the woods and live as we always have" (Hastivement al bois alums, / seüms si cum nus sulïums, 87:27–8). This fable offers a different perspective on identity from Fable 65b about the inability of wolves to change their skins. In yet another echo of *Bisclavret*, it suggests that bodies and appearance may deceive, and that actions can matter more than appearances.

Contradictions among the various implicit and explicit lessons of the fables are not uncommon, and the richness of Marie's collection, like those she draws on and translates, is located in the multiplicity of views and the complexity of the stories' engagements with social contexts and constraints. While drawing on a vocabulary of feudal relations and hierarchies to structure the social hierarchies they describe (see Chapter 3), the fables also draw lessons about social relations from the bodily capacities and limitations they describe. Although they situate their lessons within a moral universe, Marie's fables make little appeal to explicitly Christian values. In fact, the very different value systems from which Marie's works draw their ethical framework – courtly love and feudal relations for the *Lais*, the moralizing world of fables, the explicitly Christian didacticism of the *Espurgatoire seint Patriz* – make it difficult to generalize about the shared values of her narratives. The three works certainly do not represent the values of embodiment in the same ways. If the *Lais* experiment with the idea that bodies might cross species boundaries and imagine the possibility of intimate relationships shared with and through animals, the *Ysopë* takes embodiment as a firm indication of identity and belonging, and extends it in a lesson about knowing one's place in the world. The *Espurgatoire* gives much less importance to the values of embodiment, as might be expected in a story about the afterlife, but bodies are at stake in its dramatization of the punishment and temptation of human souls as an assault on Christian bodies.

Bodies and souls in the *Espurgatoire seint Patriz*

The *Espurgatoire seint Patriz* recounts the bodily experience of the pains of Purgatory – the pilgrim Owein sees and is threatened by the punishments demons inflict on embodied souls. We do not know how much Marie de France knew about theological understandings of demons, or even of the soul. She could read Latin, so if she were part of a monastic

community, as some have surmised, she could have read theological trea-
tises, though we cannot identify the libraries to which she may have had
access. We know that Marie was interested in stories. If she wrote *La vie
de seinte Audree*, we also know that she was interested in saints' lives, and
she may have known the stories of desert fathers in which these holy men
grappled with demons in graphic stories of temptation and resistance. We
know with certainty that she knew the *Tractatus* of H. de Saltrey, and
that her translation modifies and rewrites the narrative she finds there.
Our goal here is not to evaluate Marie's theology, but to understand the
poetics of embodiment that shapes her representation of Purgatory and
penance. The insistence on embodiment in the description of Owein's trip
through Purgatory may offer a context for understanding representations
of embodiment in the later sections of the *Espurgatoire*.

In its emphasis on spiritual things seen in material form, the *Espurgatoire* theorizes a thinking about bodies that is not simply an orthodox
repetition of medieval theology. The narrator explains that some souls
are taken from their bodies and they see spiritual truths in physical form:
"They see things spiritually which appear corporally" (Il veien espiritelment / ço ke semble corporelment, *Espurgatoire*, ll. 77–8). She further
explains:

> With God's help they return to their lives and recount that they
> see spiritual things through their demonstration in *corporeal*
> likeness. And they tell us that mortal *embodied* men have
> seen this in the form and appearance of *embodied corporeal*
> substance.

> Par Deu revenent a lur vies
> e dïent bien, par la mustrance
> de cele espiritel substance
> ke semblable est a *corporel*
> co k'il veient espiritel.
> E si nus dit k'home mortel
> unt ço veü e *corporel*
> si cume en forme e en semblance
> de home *corporel* sustance. (*Espurgatoire*, ll. 172–80)

The emphasis on corporeality in this passage insists on the embodied substance of spiritual things. Bodies, seeing, and understanding are brought
into relation, and the "corporel sustance," the corporeal substance that
represents truth, identifies embodiment as a medium of understanding. In
the *Lais*, bodies may represent change, sometimes marvelous change, and
in the *Fables* embodiment is a sign of identity, but in the *Espurgatoire*

embodiment is a method of explanation, a medium through which visitors to Purgatory understand the spiritual lessons to be learned there, and it is also the terrain on which spiritual battles are waged.

In Marie's other works, the values of embodiment are debated in representations of animals. In the *Espurgatoire*, marvelous animals are accomplices of the demons who torture souls. In the third scene of purgation that Owein enters, fire and terrible animality converge:

> In the field he entered he saw some of those [souls] lying face down. Flaming dragons attacked and tormented them and devoured them with flaming teeth. Some of them were cinched and strangled around the arm or the neck by flaming serpents. These were dolorous bonds! With their forked tongues they pierced their bodies and their chests, and it seemed to him that they pulled out their hearts with the tip of their tongues. Marvelously huge toads, all aflame, sat on the chest of each one and were intent on pulling out the hearts of the punished ones with their horrible beaks.

> Dedenz cest champ ou est venuz
> plusurs de ces i ad veüz
> qui adenz esteient gisanz;
> sur els veeit draguns ardanz,
> quis poigneient e turmentouent,
> od denz ardanz les devorouent.
> Plusurs i vit qui erent ceint
> e de serpenz ardanz estreint
> e par les cols e par les braz.
> Mult i aveit dolereus laz!
> Od lur langues qui sunt fuïnes,
> percent lur cors e lur peitrines;
> od l'agüesce traient fors,
> ço lui ert vis, les quers des cors.
> Crapouz i vit, merveilles granz,
> ço lui ert vis, trestuz ardanz.
> Sur les piz des asquanz seient,
> od lur becs qu'horribles aveient,
> a grant force erent ententis
> de traire les quers des chaitis. (*Espurgatoire*, ll. 993–1012)

The tortures are intensified by the horrible forms of the monstrous animals who inflict them. More common (and more benign) animals enter the narrative in rhetorical form. As Owein exits Purgatory and moves toward Earthly Paradise, Marie tells us that the pains of Purgatory can no more be compared to the pains of this world than the eagle can be compared to the finch (n'i avreit il comparison / plus ke de l'egle e del pinçon, ll. 1409–10). Marie adds the comparison to her translation of the *Tractatus*,[22] and it recalls the *Ysopë*'s emphasis on the radical difference that embodiment imposes: the beetle cannot be an eagle, the ass cannot be a dog, and the eagle cannot be a finch.

In the *Espurgatoire* spiritual truths are represented corporeally, through embodied corporeal substance (corporel sustance, l. 180), but the lesson to be learned in Purgatory is the rejection of the body's appetites and desires. In fact, the first part of the *Espurgatoire* may resemble many fables in its use of negative exemplarity. Owein experiences the physical tortures of Purgatory as a warning, and the tormented souls he sees in the form of bodies tortured by demons demonstrate the failure to repent. However, in the final sections, where the narrator seeks the testimony of living people to confirm Owein's experiences, the narrative shifts to an account of the actions of demons in the world of the living. Here the descriptions of spiritual punishments in corporeal terms give way to spiritual contests played out on living human bodies.

The final exemplary story in the *Espurgatoire* may serve as an illustration. A hermit recounts the tale of a demon who planned to corrupt a priest by using a woman to deceive him (Par une femme ai purveü / que donc l'avrai tost deceü, ll. 2211–12). He arranges for the priest to find a baby girl abandoned at the foot of a cross. The priest adopts the girl and raises her as his daughter, teaching her to read and to serve God. Inspired by the demon, the priest falls in love with the beautiful girl. He asks her to do his will, and she agrees. The demon and his fellows rejoice when the priest tells the girl to go and lie in his bed. He will come to her, he says, to take his pleasure (Ore alé, bele, / laenz cucher desur mun lit, / si acomplirai mun delit, ll. 2258–60). When the priest joins the girl he begins to think about the consequences of the act the demon wants him to accomplish and he understands that he will lose all that he has gained through virtue. He renounces his intentions by the grace of God, the hermit who tells the story reveals:

> The grace of God was at work in it: he went out of the room and left the girl. He took a knife that he carried and cut off his genitals. He threw them outside and said to the demons, "Hear

---

[22] *L'espurgatoire seint Patriz*, ed. Yolande de Pontfarcy (Louvain and Paris: Peeters, 1995), p. 203.

this, evil spirits! You will not rejoice in our perdition because
of this evil act."

La grace de Deu i ovra:
hors s'en issi, cele i leissa,
un coutel prist ke il porta
e ses genitailles trencha.
Hors les geta demaintenant
e puis dist as dïables tant:
"Oez, espiriz maufeisanz!
Jamés ne serrez joïssanz
de la nostre perdicïon
par ceste malveise achaison." (*Espurgatoire*, ll. 2269–78)

The demon who failed to corrupt the priest is roundly beaten by the other
demons, and the priest puts the young woman in a convent where she
serves God (La meschine dedenz l'iglise / mist li prestrë al Deu servise,
ll. 2295–6).

The account of the priest's self-castration and the young woman's
enclosure in a convent is the last narrative development in the *Espurgatoire*, and it is followed directly by Marie's epilogue. The narrative
thus ends with an inscription of repentance on the body, the "corporel
sustance" that is the instrument of sin. As in Owein's progress through
Purgatory, spiritual truths are represented in embodied form, but the
demon's assaults on the body take the subtle form of seduction rather
than the fiery tortures of Purgatory.

Embodied categories of identity

In all of Marie's works, embodiment has to do with groups rather than
individuals. The *Ysopë* is perhaps the text that most clearly articulates
the relationship between embodiment and belonging to a group, and it
does so in cautionary terms. The ridiculousness of the ass that tries to
act like a dog is perhaps the most vivid example of the futility of trying
to leave one's own group to join another, but many of the fables demonstrate the link between embodiment and group, particularly in terms
of species identity. The *Espurgatoire*, too, divides its protagonists into
groups – sinners and those who repent of their sins – and the demonstra-
tion of individual merit is subsumed into the exemplary embodiment of
virtue. Even the priest who castrates himself is an exemplary figure, an
embodied lesson in piety.

The thinking about categories of identity that spans Marie's works may lead us back to the *Lais*, and specifically to *Bisclavret*. The *lai* opens with a display of Marie's translation abilities, as in *L'aüstic* and *Chievrefueil*, but here the narrator not only names but defines the subject (and title) of her *lai*:

> Since I have set to writing *lais*, I do not want to forget *Bisclavret*. "Bisclavret" is its Breton name, the Normans call it "Garulf." One used to hear that men often transformed into werewolves and lived in the forest. The werewolf is a wild beast. When it is enraged it eats men and does great damage. It inhabits great forests. But I leave this subject aside, for I want to tell you the story of [the] Bisclavret.

> Quant des lais faire m'entremet,
> ne vueil ubliër Bisclavret.
> Bisclavret a nun en Bretan,
> Garulf l'apelent li Norman.
> Jadis le poeit hum oïr
> e sovent suleit avenir,
> hume plusur garulf devindrent
> e es boscages maisun tindrent.
> Garulf, ceo est beste salvage;
> tant cum il est en cele rage,
> humes devure, grant mal fait,
> es granz forez converse e vait.
> Cest afaire les ore ester;
> del Bisclavret vus vueil cunter. (*Bisclavret*, ll. 1–14)

Marie's introduction to the story first gives the Breton and Norman names for the *lai*. Then she describes the man who changes into a wolf as being a common figure in the past, and she describes it under the Norman name, "garulf." Finally, she says that she will leave "this subject" (cest afaire, l. 13) to speak about the Bisclavret. She turns from the species to the individual, but she also turns from the collective history of the (implicitly Norman) werewolf (garulf), to a story about a being whose individuality is marked both by the article that precedes his name and the change from "garulf" to "le bisclavret."[23]

---

[23] There are a number of werewolf stories in medieval literature. See Laurence Harf-Lancner, trans., *Lais de Marie de France* (Paris: Librairie Générale Française, 1990), p. 117, n. 1. For a reading of werewolf stories in relation to ideas about change, see

We usually take "Bisclavret" as the proper name of the protagonist in this story, and modern editors inscribe this interpretation into the typography of the text by capitalizing "Bisclavret" when in its manuscript context it could, like all proper names, be written with a lower case letter.[24] In *Bisclavret*, the distinction between the name of the category and the name of the individual is ambiguous because of the article that accompanies "bisclavret" in the story – is this the story of a werewolf or of Werewolf? In other words, is it a story about a member of a species or is it a story about an individual?[25] This distinction is centrally at play in the *lai*. The wife recognizes a category, a species. When her husband tells her about his transformations, she is frightened, and she seeks to separate from the shape-shifting man because she doesn't want to lie with him (De l'aventure s'esfrea. / En maint endreit se purpensa / cum ele s'en peüst partir; / ne voleit mes lez lui gisir, ll. 99–102). The wife's understanding of identity seems close to that of Marie's fable: "You can teach a wolf to be a priest, but he will still be a wolf, sly and cruel, ugly and hideous" (Ki su le lu meïst bon mestre, / quil doctrinast a estre prestre, / si sereit il tut dis gris lus / fel e engrés leiz e hidus, 65b:5–8). This lady fears that her husband will inhabit the skin of the savage *garulf* even in his human form; she does not imagine that his wolf form might be changed by his humanity.

By contrast, the king (another character identified as a singular member of a category in the story) recognizes Bisclavret as an extraordinary example of his species precisely because he does not act like a wolf. When the king meets Bisclavret in the forest and the wolf kisses the king's foot in a gesture of homage, the king proclaims that this beast has "the intelligence of a man" (Ele a sen d'ume, l. 154), and, further, he has reason and intelligence (Ceste beste a entente e sen, l. 157).[26] The extraordinary qual-

---

Caroline Walker Bynum, *Metamorphoses and Identity* (New York: Zone, 2001). For a claim about the difference between the *bisclavret* and the *garulf*, see Joyce Salisbury, "Human Beasts and Bestial Humans in the Middle Ages," in Jennifer Ham and Matthew Senior (eds.), *Animal Acts: Configuring the Human in Western History* (New York: Routledge, 1997), pp. 9–21.

[24] Matilda Tomaryn Bruckner, "Of Men and Beasts in *Bisclavret*," *Romanic Review* 81.3 (1991): 251–69 (at 255–6).

[25] Ibid., 253–4.

[26] The wolf's apparently rational behavior might also signal a lack of danger, and it might make the wolf seem more dog-like than wolf-like. Robert Bartlett notes the fascination that medieval people felt for animal behavior that mimics rationality and he points to dogs as prime examples of animals whose apparently rational behavior provoked affection and admiration from humans. *The Natural and the Supernatural in the Middle Ages* (Cambridge: Cambridge University Press, 2006), pp. 91–4.

ities the king recognizes correspond to the traits that make the wolf less recognizable as a wolf, and in particular the king marvels at the beast's submission to him: "'Lords,' he says, 'come forward and see this marvel, how this beast humbles itself!'" ("Seignur," fet il, "avant venez / e ceste merveille esguardez, / cum ceste beste s'umilie!" ll. 151–3). The king identifies Bisclavret as a courtly wolf, that is, as a wolf whose intelligence and submission make him suitable for the court. In fact, his recognition of the wolf as an individual different from his species is also a recognition that the wolf is like another species, the man whose intelligence he demonstrates. This understanding of Bisclavret as a wolf who is like a man allows the discovery of the wife's betrayal when the wolf attacks her. When the wolf acts most like an animal, or at least like the werewolves of old who "devour men and cause great harm" (humes devure, grant mal fait, l. 11), he does not act like a man, and there must be some reason for it. "He must have some grudge against her" (alkun curuz a il vers li, l. 249), a wise man at the court proclaims, and he advises the king to have the woman tortured to learn if she knows why the wolf acted as he did. The lady tells her story, but she still does not recognize Bisclavret. We don't know if the lady ever saw her husband in his wolf form, but she is certain that he has not been seen in his own country. She thinks that this wolf must be Bisclavret, the text reports in indirect discourse: "tresbien quidot e bien creeit / que la beste Bisclavret seit" (ll. 273–4). There are several different ways to read this verse, however. First, as above, "she thinks that this wolf must be Bisclavret." Or as "she thinks that Bisclavret must be this wolf." Or, taking "bisclavret" as a common noun rather than a proper noun, "she thinks that this wolf must be a werewolf." All these translations, and especially the last, reveal the wife's categorical thinking. For her, categories (bisclavret, wolf) are more important than individual identities (Bisclavret). In this her thinking may align with that of the text itself, where all the characters except Bisclavret are identified by social status: the wife, the knight, the king, the wise man at court. Even Bisclavret's name, "Werewolf," is a category taken as a proper name.

Embodiment identifies characters according to group, in Marie's works, but what is notable about them is the extent to which the relationship between body and identity is debated in her narratives. For the animal protagonists in the *Ysopë*, the body's limitations define the boundaries of experience and ambition; to a fallen humanity in the *Espurgatoire* the truths of salvation are figured in bodily form and the battle for souls is played out on vulnerable human flesh. In the *Lais*, characters are defined by social relations that discipline bodies and desires, but that are subverted by unexpected encounters that often lead to love. The story of these encounters is what the wise man in *Bisclavret* describes when he says that, "We have seen many marvelous adventures happening in Brittany" (Meinte merveille avum veüe / ki en Bretaigne est avenue, ll. 259–60).

6

Repetition and the Art of Variation:
Narrative Techniques

As has been evident throughout this book, the project of interpreting medieval texts often throws into question many of the basic assumptions modern readers bring to the study of literature. Questions of authorship, as we saw in Chapter 1, run up against issues such as the uncertain or hypothetical attribution of many works and our authors' absence from the historical record; meanwhile, questions of what constitutes a medieval work are complicated by textual variation across manuscripts and recensions. In this chapter we turn to repetition and variation, not as accidents of history and textual transmission but as a fundamental aspect of medieval aesthetics. In the Middle Ages, as Peter Haidu long ago pointed out, repetition is not simply "tolerated" but is "positively valued," while conventionality is an essential and distinguishing characteristic of medieval literary practice – "a formal embodiment of the shared consciousness between writers and audience."[1] This chapter revisits Marie's corpus while attempting to put aside the expectation and, especially, the privileging of singularity of all kinds: the distinctiveness of authorial voice, characters, and plots.[2] As we have seen, the manuscript evidence makes clear that in the Middle Ages, the *lais* we now attribute to Marie de France were not always associated with her name. From the standpoint of their transmission and reception, the boundaries between her *lais* and the texts we today call "anonymous Breton *lais*" were much more fluid.[3] Exploring some of the consequences of that insight, this chapter turns to repetition,

---

[1] Peter Haidu, "Repetition: Modern Reflections on Medieval Aesthetics," *Modern Language Notes* 92.5 (1977): 875–87 (at 880).

[2] Compare R. Howard Bloch's *The Anonymous Marie de France* (Chicago: Chicago University Press, 2003) on the singularity of Marie's authorial self-consciousness or Logan Whalen, *Marie de France and the Poetics of Memory* (Washington, DC: Catholic University of America Press, 2008) on the distinctiveness of Marie's focus on remembrance.

[3] *Les lais anonymes des XII et XIII s.*, ed. Prudence Mary O'Hara Tobin (Geneva: Droz, 1976); repr. in *Lais feeriques des XII et XIIIe s.*, presentation and trans. Alexandre Micha (Paris: Garnier-Flammarion, 1999).

multiplication, and variation both as themes and as structural and narrative principles. Focusing first on the *Lais*, we shall examine the themes of multiplication and (the threat of) non-differentiation; structural variations as a medieval mode of composition; and *Guigemar* as a composite text juxtaposing plot structures from different *lais*. In a second moment, we take up *Lanval* as a kind of master text linking Marie's *Lais* and several of the Breton *lais anonymes*. Next, we consider the collected fables of the *Ysopë* as a strategy for exploring the simultaneous continuities across and variations among social experience. Finally, we turn to the *Espurgatoire seint Patriz* and the *Vie seinte Audree* to assess the structural consequences of the shift from short narrative forms to extended ones.

Reduplication, multiplication, and the crisis of non-differentiation

Common understandings of courtly love center on an intense, overpowering, and immutable devotion – the fatalistic passion binding Lancelot and Guenevere in Chrétien de Troyes's *Le chevalier de la charrete* or Tristan and Iseut (at least until, in some versions of the text, the effects of the love potion wear off).[4] However conventionalized the players – the jealous or ineffectual husband, the *mal-mariée* or the *belle dame sans merci*, the intrepid or hapless lover – the strength of the emotion and the singularity of the object of desire combine to imply the uniqueness of each instance of courtly passion.

In contrast, one thing that renders the *Lais* of Marie de France at once puzzling and compelling is the way they explore, in different ways, the consequences of multiplying the bonds ideally posited as singular. *Le Fraisne* and *Eliduc* are both structured by a logic of reduplication – not incidentally, since both feature a male protagonist who exchanges one wife for another. *Le Fraisne* presents this problem in its most stylized form.[5] Its plot, as we have seen, is set in motion by the birth of twin daughters. Here, the threat posed by multiple births is, significantly, not the religious–ontological dread produced by twins in some cultures. Rather, the scandal it unleashes is eminently *social*: the suspicion of adultery created by the rebound effect of the lady's own words, in a verbal instantiation of *Equitan*'s logic of just returns. Yet overall, the tale makes surprisingly

---

[4]   On the complexity of courtly love and its vocabulary, see Chapter Three, p. 000.

[5]   In her excellent article, "*LeFresne*'s Model for Twinning in the *Lais* of Marie de France," *Modern Language Notes* 121 (2006): 946–60 (at 946), Matilda Tomaryn Bruckner shows the *lai*'s engagement with two differing views of twins: "duality (a competition of opposites)…and dualism (or complementarity to form a whole)."

little of the girls' twinship: when Fraisne is finally recognized, it is not by (say) an uncanny resemblance to her twin sister but by the silk swaddling cloth that signifies not just her noble birth but the singularity of her family's history.[6] Any potential scandal attaching to the exchange of wives is defused, as we have seen, by the archbishop of Dol's conspicuously legitimizing presence. In *Eliduc*, the prologue's introduction of Guildeluëc and Guilliadun, the two heroines of nearly identical name, seems to suggest a crisis of differentiation. In fact, as the story unfolds, the two are so clearly differentiated by location and status that no confusion arises between them: the plot is galvanized, rather, precisely by the clarity of Eliduc's choice.

The thematics of reduplication recur more subtly in the lai of *L'aüstic*. Ostensibly the tragic but charming tale of the memoralization of an unrealized love, it is (along with *Chaitivel*) the *lai* in which Marie seems to take the least sympathetic view of the lovers. The tale opens with two knights living side by side in two apparently interchangeable houses:

> In the region of Saint Malo there was a well-known city. Two knights lived there, in two fortified houses. The city enjoyed a good reputation on account of the worthiness of these two barons. One had married a woman who was wise, courtly, and well turned-out; she kept herself up to a surprising degree, according to custom and practices. The other was an unmarried knight – well known among his peers for his prowess and great valor, and the way he always strove to behave honorably.

> En Seint Malo en la cuntree
> ot une vile renumee.
> Dui chevalier ilec maneient
> e dous forz maisuns i aveient.
> Pur la bunté des dous baruns
> fu de la vile bons li nuns.
> Li uns aveit femme espusee,
> sage, curteise e acesmee;
> a merveille se teneit chiere
> sulunc l'usage e la maniere.
> Li altre fu uns bachelers,

6   This sense of disambiguation may have been stronger for a medieval audience, more intimately familiar with the differences between the ash tree – prized for its strong but flexible hardwood used to make bows and spears – and the hazel, valuable for its edible nuts. In a romance development of the plot in *Galeran de Bretagne*, the resemblance of the sisters is emphasized (see Chapter 7).

> bien coneüz entre ses pers,
> de pruësce, de grant valur
> e volentiers faiseit honur. (*L'aüstic*, ll. 7–20)

To this point, the two neighbor knights very much resemble their counterparts in *Le Fraisne*:

> Once upon a time in Brittany, there were two knights; they were neighbors. They were rich and well-established, brave and valiant knights. They were close, from the same region. Each of them had taken a wife.

> En Bretaigne jadis maneient
> dui chevalier; veisin esteient.
> Riche hum furent e manant,
> e chevalier pruz e vaillant.
> Prochein furent, d'une cuntree.
> Chescuns femme aveit espusee. (*Le Fraisne*, ll. 3–8)

Where *Le Fraisne* maintains the parallelism, *L'aüstic* distinguishes between the two knights by the simple fact that one is married and the other is not. As a bachelor, the latter lives the quintessential life of a youth (*jovens*), exemplifying all its ideal, if not to say stereotypical, qualities: "He took part in many tournaments and spent freely, giving away whatever he had. He loved his neighbor's wife" (Mult turneiot e despendeit / e bien donot ceo qu'il aveit. / La femme sun veisin ama, ll. 21–3).[7]

What motivates desire in a world where all women – and here, men – "look very much alike" (se resemblent asez, *Guigemar*, l. 779)? Unlike the *mal-mariées* of *Guigemar* or *Yonec*, the first knight's wife has no particular reason to be unhappy in her marriage; nothing marks her husband as in any way undesirable: neither old age, nor jealousy, nor a secret life as a werewolf. She is not, like the seneschal's wife in *Equitan*, being tempted by the prospect of a lover of much higher rank than her husband. In similar circumstances, the wife of Bisclavret had long discouraged the attentions of her aspiring lover. Here, however, the bachelor's assiduously waged campaign pays off: the lady is finally seduced by his reputation, his persistence, and – perhaps most of all – his propinquity:

---

[7] See Georges Duby, "Youth in Aristocratic Society," in *The Chivalrous Society*, trans. Cynthia Postan (Berkeley: University of California Press, 1981), pp. 112–22.

> So much did he beg and importune her and so fine were his
> qualities that she loved him more than anything – as much
> for the good she heard about him *as for the fact that he was*
> *close by.*

> Tant la requist, tant la preia
> e tant par ot en lui grant bien
> qu'ele l'ama sur tute rien,
> tant pur le bien qu'ele en oï,
> *tant pur ceo qu'il ert pres de li.* (*L'aüstic*, ll. 24–8)

Standing at their respective windows, the two easily exchange words and
small objects. The impression we get here is less of a tragic, ineluctable
love than one born of convention and opportunism:

> Their dwellings were close together; their houses, their rooms,
> their towers were adjacent. There was no barrier or separation
> except a high wall of dark stone.

> ... pres esteient lur repaire,
> preceines furent lur maisuns
> e lur sales e lur dunjuns;
> n'i aveit barre ne devise
> fors un halt mur de piere bise. (*L'aüstic*, ll. 34–8)

It is surely no accident, then, that *L'aüstic* is one of only two *lais* not to
be titled after at least one of its protagonists,[8] or that, as in *Les dous amanz*
and *Chaitivel*, both the male and female protagonists remain anonymous.[9]
What is at stake is positionality rather than identity. In Chapter 2, we
saw how *Equitan* inverted the prototypical scenario of adulterous love,
replacing the conventional triangle of a married woman with an old, high-
ranking husband and a young, socially subordinate lover (Arthur–Guenevere–Lancelot or Marc–Iseut–Tristan) with that of a married woman
poised between a husband of modest station and a high-ranking lover.
L'aüstic explores a third variant: the woman poised between two men of
equal station, for all intents and purposes indistinguishable, except for

---

[8]   The other is *Chevrefueil*, whose protagonists are two of the most famous names
in medieval literature and amply attested elsewhere, freeing up the *lai* to focus on the
symbolic object that serves as the medium of their communication.
[9]   Contrast *Guigemar, Yonec, Lanval*, and *Milun*, where the male protagonist is named
but the female protagonist is not.

their marital status. Together, the three are cast in a structural scenario of triangulated desire.[10]

Compared with those better-known adulterous tales, the plot of *L'aüstic* has literally nowhere to go. Chrétien de Troyes's *Le chevalier de la charrete* and the various texts of the early Tristan tradition all range widely over space (from Arthur's court through to the land of Gorre in the former, from Cornwall to Ireland to Morois forest in the latter) in a loosely linked episodic structure that generates continuations and variants well into the following century. *L'aüstic*, in contrast, is one of the shortest and one of the most lapidary of Marie's twelve *lais*. Generated less by difference than by sameness, its highly condensed plot is (as we saw in Chapter 2) more about the *signifier* of the lovers' "passion" (the hapless nightingale) than its *signified*. So it is hardly surprising that they quickly abandon their love once its pretext is killed off and enshrined in its jeweled casket.[11] Where Lancelot will go to any lengths to pursue his love for Guenevere, the protagonists of *L'aüstic* will go exactly the short distance separating one mansion from the other. The casket encasing the dead nightingale not only memorializes the protagonists' lost love but "entombs" the plot variation of the married woman and the two unremarkable men.

Marie's most thoroughgoing exploration of the problematics of non-differentiation, however, is *Chaitivel*, the *lai* structured by the lady's inability to decide among four excellent suitors of apparently comparable worth. If the conventional scenario of courtly love presents one lover's devotion to his lady, *Chaitivel* (whose alternate title is *Les quatre doels*) asks what happens when one lady is the object of multiple aspirants' desire. In Nantes, there lives a lady of such beauty and accomplishment that:

> In the land there was no knight of any worth who, once having seen her, didn't fall in love with her and begin to court her.

> N'ot en la terre chevalier
> ki alkes feïst a preisier,
> pur ceo qu'une feiz la veïst
> que ne l'amast e requeïst. (*Chaitivel*, ll. 13–16)

Guenevere, in a similar situation, has eyes only for Lancelot.[12] In contrast,

---

[10] On triangulated desire, see Rene Girard, *Violence and the Sacred*, trans. Patrick Gregory (Baltimore: Johns Hopkins University Press, 1977).

[11] See Chapter 5 for a discussion of the nightingale and embodiment.

[12] In the tournament episode in Chrétien de Troyes's *Le chevalier de la charrete*,

this lady wallows – if not to say revels – in her indecision: "*She could hardly love them all* but neither did she want to kill them" (*El nes pot mie tuz amer* / ne el nes volt mie tuër, ll. 17–18). Here the isomorphism of courtly love and feudal allegiance falls apart: for where a lord can routinely "love" – maintain political and affective ties with – multiple vassals, a courtly lady cannot. A somewhat enigmatic saying calls attention to the awkwardness of the situation:

> If a lady gratifies all of them, she maintains the good will of all; however, if she does not wish to heed them, she should not speak to them in an ugly way but should cherish and honor them, willingly serve them, and thank them.[13]

> Se dame fait a tuz lur gre,
> de tuz a bone volunté;
> purquant, s'ele nes vuelt oïr,
> nes deit de paroles laidir,
> mes tenir chiers e enurer,
> a gre servir e merciër. (*Chaitivel*, ll. 23–8)

This ideal, however, turns out to be easier to maintain in theory than in practice:

> In Brittany there were four nobles (though I don't know their names). They weren't very old, but they were very handsome: brave and valiant knights – generous, courteous, and free-spending. These local nobles had the most superlative reputation. The four of them loved the lady and strove to perform goodly feats; each one tried his best to get her and her love.

> En Bretaigne ot quatre baruns,
> mes jeo ne sai numer lur nuns.
> Il n'aveient guaires d'eé,
> mes mult erent de grant bealté
> e chevalier pruz e vaillant,
> large, curteis e despendant;

combatants flock from all around because they are all in love with the queen. Her attention, however, is focused on the anonymous knight whose identity she uncovers by sending him secret instructions to do "his worst" and then "his best."

[13] Alternatively, we could read the lady's inability to decide as structured by the gendered position she occupies. She cannot love them all, and yet, the narrator tells us, she should not reject any of them, but cherish and honor them.

mult par esteient de grant pris
e gentil hume del païs.
Icil quatre la dame amoënt
e de bien faire se penoënt;
pur li e pur s'amur aveir
i meteit chescuns sun poeir. (*Chaitivel*, ll. 33–44)

In medieval romance, "identity" is often constituted less by personalized traits that serve to distinguish a unique individual than around a collocation of qualities suited to one's social station.[14] For knights, these include the noble attributes summed up in a term like *chevalerie*: wealth, power, and birth; military virtues such as courage, loyalty, and skill in arms; and courtly accomplishments, like politeness and refinement of speech.[15] If the protagonist is defined not by his individuality but by his exemplarity, then his singularity is necessarily a singularity of degree rather than kind.[16]

In their beauty, courage, generosity, and courtesy, the four suitors figure as reproductions of a protagonist like Lanval, whose bravery, generosity, beauty, and prowess (*Lanval*, ll. 21–2) had made him the envy of King Arthur's court.[17] However, in contrast to the conventional hero of romance, nothing sets any of them apart. This is the lady's dilemma: unable to decide among the four undifferentiated claimants, she dispenses/ withholds her favor equally to/from them all:

> All of them were so valorous that she could not choose the best. She didn't want to lose three of them for the sake of choosing one. She was gracious to each of them: she gave them love tokens, sending them messages. All considered her their *amie*: all of them wore a token of hers – a ring or a sleeve or a banner – and each of them used her name as a rallying cry.
>
> Tant furent tuit de grant valur,
> ne pot eslire le meillur.

---

[14] See Zrinka Stahuljak et al., *Thinking Through Chrétien de Troyes* (Cambridge: D. S. Brewer, 2010), pp. 114–15.

[15] Individualizing characteristics – like Guigemar's rejection of love – are provocations that drive the plot forward toward their resolution or eradication. See William E. Burgwinkle, *Sodomy, Masculinity, and Law in Medieval Literature: France and England, 1050–1230* (Cambridge: Cambridge University Press, 2004).

[16] Stahuljak et al., *Thinking Through Chrétien de Troyes*, pp. 114–15.

[17] In Chrétien de Troyes's *Erec et Enide*, "beauty" functions as the master signifier – a shorthand for this collection of chivalric values. See Stahuljak et al., *Thinking Through Chrétien de Troyes*, pp. 113–15.

> Ne volt les treis perdre pur l'un:
> bel semblant faiseit a chescun,
> ses druëries lur donout,
> ses messages lur enveiout ...
> Tuit la teneient pur amie,
> tuit portouent sa druërie,
> anel u manche u gumfanun,
> e chescuns escriot sun nun. (*Chaitivel*, ll. 53–8; 67–70)

In feudal society, it is the mark of a good lord to avoid favoritism. If Arthur in the *lai de Lanval* had shown this lady's judiciousness, it would have short-circuited the entire plot of the underappreciated outcast knight. Granting her "favors" to all but her love to none, the lady's reluctance to choose reflects her "mult grant sens" (l. 49) – not what one expects in a lover, but exactly what one desires in an equitable lord.

When an Easter tournament is convened in Nantes, the four would-be lovers – as if to highlight this divergence between the feudal and erotic – function as one, their shared passion binding them together in a collective identity:

> Frenchmen, Normans, Flemings, Brabançons, Boulognais, Angevins came from abroad, along with those from nearby lands. All eagerly came to confront *the four lovers....* The foreigners recognized them from their insignias and shields; they sent two knights from Flanders and two from Hainaut to challenge them.

> Pur aquointier *les quatre druz*,
> i sunt d'altre païs venuz:
> e li Franceis e li Norman
> e li Flemenc e li Breban,
> li Buluigneis, li Angevin
> e cil ki pres furent veisin,
> tuit i sunt volentiers alé ...
> Cil de fors les unt coneüz
> as enseignes e as escuz.
> Cuntre els enveient chevaliers,
> dous Flamens e dous Henoiers. (*Chaitivel*, ll. 75–81; 89–92)

The contrast here is interesting: the four knights' lack of individuation, compounded by the lady's own refusal to choose among them, pulls them together in a collective bond distinct from the *regional* identities (familiar to us from the enumeration of Charlemagne's troops in the *Chanson de Roland*) of those who come to challenge them.[18] Though the *lai* had insisted on its Breton setting (ll. 9, 33), the four knights confronting the teams of visiting Frenchmen, Normans, Flemings, and so forth are never referred to as Bretons; in contrast to the rest of the feudal world, they are defined not by their allegiance to a territorially based lord but by their shared devotion to the anonymous lady of Nantes.

Even in the midst of battle, the four function as one; watching from her tower, the lady easily distinguishes "hers" from "theirs" (les suens e les lur, l. 108) but still "does not know which to esteem the most" (ne set le quel deit plus preisier, l. 110) – a stark contrast to the romances of Chrétien de Troyes, where the most chaotic *mêlées* only serve to highlight the superiority of the (frequently disguised) protagonist. In *Chaitivel* what finally distinguishes the knights, literally at the end of the day (a l'avesprer, l. 117), is a battlefield mishap: because of their own rashness, "three were killed and the fourth badly wounded in his thigh and body" (li trei i furent ocis / e li quarz nafrez e malmis / par mi la quisse e enz el cors, ll. 121–3).[19] This abrupt, tragic turn instantly unites the two opposing teams in a "shared grief" (doels comuns, l. 139), even as it forever divides the three dead rivals from their surviving companion.

As the lady takes the measure of her sudden loss, there is a momentary glimmer of differentiation: "When she recovers from her swoon, she mourns each one *by name*" (Quant ele vient de pasmeisun, / chescun regrete *par sun nun*, ll. 145–6), though these names are never communicated to us, the audience.[20] Instead, the three dead and one maimed suitor are reincorporated into one as the common source of her new unhappiness:

---

[18] Sharon Kinoshita, *Medieval Boundaries: Rethinking Difference in Old French Literature* (Philadelphia: University of Pennsylvania Press, 2006), pp. 29–30. In Marie's other *lais*, Breton or Welsh protagonists circulate abroad, to rounds of tournaments in Flanders, Lorraine, Burgundy, Anjou, Gascony (*Guigemar*, ll. 51–4), Ireland, Norway, Gotland, England, and Scotland (*Milun*, ll.15–17), while a tournament held at Mont Saint Michel draws Normans, Bretons, Flemings, and Frenchmen but, unaccountably, few "Englishmen" (*Milun*, ll. 385–8). See the discussion in Chapter 4.

[19] A wound in the lower body is a medieval euphemism for a disabling wound to the genitals, as in the case of Chrétien de Troyes's *Le conte du graal*, where both Perceval's father (par mi les anches navrez, l. 408) and the Fisher King (navrez ... [p]armi les anches, ll. 3450–1) are "wounded between the hips," with all the attendant associations of sterility and impotence. It also cruelly mocks the common metaphor of love as a wound "inside the body that shows no outward signs" (dedenz cors / e si ne piert nient defors, *Guigemar*, ll. 483–4), as described at length by the narrator of *Guigemar*. See also *Guigemar*, ll. 379–84.

[20] As is frequent in Old French, the narrative here shifts into the present tense in order to highlight the vividness of the action – and the better to set up the direct discourse that immediately follows.

"Alas," she said, "what shall I do? I'll never be happy. I loved
these four knights and desired each one individually.... I didn't
want to take one and lose them all; I don't know which one I
should pity the most. But I can no longer hide or pretend: one
I see wounded, and the three others are dead: I have nothing
in the world to comfort me!"

"Lasse," fet ele, "que ferai?
Ja mes haitiee ne serai!
Cez quatre chevaliers amoue
e chescun par sei cuveitoue; ...
nes voil tuz perdre pur l'un prendre.
Ne sai le quel jeo dei plus pleindre;
mes ne m'en puis covrir ne feindre.
L'un vei nafré, li trei sunt mort:
n'ai rien el mund ki me confort!"

(*Chaitivel*, ll. 147–50; 156–60)

These are the first words in the *lai* spoken in direct discourse, in a formulaic lament common (as we shall see shortly) to a number of characters
across Marie's *Lais*. Greatly afflicted, the lady stints neither on the honors
she bestows "nobly, and with great love" (a grant amur e noblement, l.
167) on the corpses of the three dead suitors, nor on the care and attention
she lavishes on the wounded survivor. As her lament indicates, however,
her attention is riveted less on her hapless lovers than on herself. This
comes explicitly to the fore one day as she sits with her maimed lover:

She *remembered* her great grief: she lowered her head. She
began to *think* very hard. And he began to look at her; he could
see that she was *thinking*.

De sun grant doel li *remembrot*:
sun chief e sun vis en baissot;
forment comença a *penser*.
E il la prist a reguarder;
bien aparceit qu'ele *pensot*. (*Chaitivel*, ll. 183–7)

When the knight asks what she is thinking about and begs her to cease
her mourning, she responds:

Friend, I was *thinking* and *remembering* your companions.
Never has a lady of my rank – however beautiful, valiant,
and wise – loved four [knights] together and lost them in
one day (except you alone, who were wounded – you really
almost died!). Because I loved you so, I want my grief to be

remembered. I'll compose a lai about the four of you; I'll call it "The Four Sorrows."

> Amis ... jeo *pensoue*
> e voz cumpaignuns *remembroue.*
> Ja mes dame de mun parage
> tant nen iert bele, pruz ne sage,
> tels quatre ensemble n'amera
> ne en un jur si nes perdra,
> fors vus tut sul ki nafrez fustes,
> grant poür de mort en eüstes.
> Pur ceo que tant vus ai amez,
> vueil que mis doels seit *remembrez.*
> De vus quatre ferai un lai
> e Quatre Doels le numerai. (*Chaitivel*, ll. 193–204)

Evocations of thinking and remembrance, in other words, set the scene for the lady's decision to memorialize her lovers' adventure in song. Throughout Marie's *Lais*, pensiveness is the state characteristic of lovers separated from the object of their desire. When Guigemar is first left alone after being struck by love for his lady, "He was pensive and anxious" (Pensis esteit e anguissous, l. 394); later, when his lady languishes in captivity before her reunion with Guigemar, "she was pensive and downcast all the time" (tuz jurs est pensive e murne, l. 718).[21] And remembrance is, of course, *the* key concept critics have privileged not just in the *Lais* but across the texts associated with Marie's name.

Marie's use of these terms here, however, departs dramatically from conventional norms. For if lovers are typically "pensive" when separated from their loves, this lady becomes pensive in the presence of one of the very lovers she is contemplating. Remembrance, furthermore, is usually associated less with characters within the *lais* than with their composers: the Bretons who compose the original oral songs "pur remembrance" (*Lais, Prologue,* l. 35) or the author-translator who wants to perpetuate their memory. Tristan, in *Chievrefoil*, is the exception that proves the rule: making a *lai* "to remember the words" (pur les paroles remembrer, l. 111) he and Iseut have exchanged both in writing and in person, his turn to composition signals the resolute pastness – not of their love (which is ongoing) but of their transient forest rendezvous. As in other *Lais*, concern with memory is oriented toward the future: the present act of composi-

---

[21] In *Lanval*, the titular protagonist is pensive (ll. 34, 51) at being neglected by the king.

tion preserves the past so that future readers and listeners will retain it in memory. In *Chaitivel*, on the other hand, both the lady's pensiveness and her concern for memorialization negate the ongoing present in order to focus on the past: it is the "four [knights] together" (quatre ensemble, l. 197) who constituted the object of her desire, so that her love is necessarily cast in the past tense: "I loved you all so much" (tant vus ai amez, l. 201).[22] No wonder her remaining lover objects so strongly to her appropriation.

Like the reduplication of male figures in *L'aüstic*, the multiplication of (aspiring) lovers in *Chaitivel* results in a narrative dead end: once again, but even more resoundingly, the "plot" of courtly love has nowhere to go except to dispute the title of the *lai* recording it. Arguing that his fate – being able to see and converse with her day and night without being able to "kiss and hug" her (de baisier ne d'acoler, l. 221) or enjoy the "surplus" (*Guigemar*, l. 533) of her love – is worse than death, the surviving suitor insists that the *lai* be named "The Wretched One" (Le Chaitivel, l. 208) after him, not "The Four Sorrows" (Quatre Doels, l. 204) as she had first proposed. And the lady readily agrees. We have already noted the anomaly of Marie's insistence in this *lai* that "there is nothing more" (il n'i a plus, l. 238) to be heard or told of the story. It is as if, having so thoroughly explored the perils of multiplication and non-differentiation, she seeks quickly to put the issue to rest once and for all.

Repetition and variation

The turning point of *Chaitivel*, as we have just seen, is the moment when the lady turns from living and loving in the present to lamenting the past, marked by her sudden exclamation, "Alas, … what shall I do?" (Lasse … que ferai?, l. 147). As novel as her specific lamentation may be, the phrase in which she expresses it is not. Highly formulaic in nature, it closely echoes similar speeches found in no fewer than four other *Lais*. Since in Marie's works, as in all medieval literature, much of the virtuosity lies in the art of variation, a look at the way this exclamation functions across the five tales reveals something of the aesthetics of repetition at work in the *Lais*.

---

[22] Pensiveness and remembrance are combined in Chrétien de Troyes's *Le conte du graal*, where the sight of three drops of red blood on the white snow trigger Perceval's reverie-stupor at his memory of Blanchefleur.

Breaking into the story well past its halfway point (line 147 of 240) with the force of an interjection, the lady's histrionic "Lasse...que ferai?" is in fact the first line of direct discourse spoken in *Chaitivel*. In this, it parallels the initial occurrence of the formula in the *Lais*, near the outset of *Guigemar*:

> Oh alas! I am slain! And you, vassal, who have wounded me, let this be your destiny: may you never be cured, either by herb or by root, by doctor or by potion. You will never be cured of *the wound in your thigh*, except by she who will suffer greater pain and sorrow for your love than any woman ever suffered; and you will do the same for her, such that all those who love, have loved, or will love will be amazed.

> Oï, lasse! Jo sui ocise!
> Et tu, vassal, ki m'as nafree,
> tels seit la tue destinee:
> ja mais n'aies tu medecine!
> Ne par herbe ne par racine,
> ne par mire ne par poisun
> n'avras tu ja mes guarisun
> de *la plaie qu'as en la quisse*,
> de si que cele te guarisse,
> ki suferra pur tue amur
> si grant peine e si grant dolur,
> qu'unkes femme tant ne sufri;
> e tu referas tant pur li,
> dunt tuit cil s'esmerveillerunt,
> ki aiment e amé avrunt
> u ki puis amerunt aprés. (*Guigemar*, ll. 106–21)

In its drama, this passage typifies the vividness of Marie's dialogues – one of the features that lend such a sense of immediacy to the *Lais*. What is unusual, of course, is that these – the very first lines of direct discourse in the collection, likewise occasioned by a debilitating (though in this case curable) wound in the male protagonist's "thigh" – are spoken by the white antlered doe whom Guigemar has shot in the forest.[23] For all

---

[23] This example is also unusual for its use of a broken couplet – unlike the other four cases we examine here. On the resonance of the doe's presence and speech, see H. Marshall Leicester, "The Voice of the Hind: The Emergence of Feminine Discontent in the *Lais* of Marie de France," in *Reading Medieval Culture: Essays in Honor of Robert W. Hanning*, ed. Robert M. Stein and Sandra Pierson Prior (Notre Dame: University of Notre Dame Press, 2005), pp. 132–61; and Burgwinkle, *Sodomy, Masculinity, and Law*.

of its curiosity (beginning with the fact of the speaking beast, though this is treated as if it were no curiosity at all), this passage, as in all the other cases except *Chaitivel*, occurs early in the story, pointing to a social or other kind of dilemma that triggers the subsequent action of the *lai*. In *Equitan*, it is the king who utters the fateful words:

> "Alas," he said, "what destiny led me to this land? On account of having seen this lady, anguish has wounded my heart and made my whole body tremble."

> "A las," fet il, "quels destinee
> m'amena en ceste cuntree?
> Pur ceste dame qu'ai veüe
> m'est une anguisse el quer ferue,
> ki tut le cors me fet trembler." (*Equitan*, ll. 69–73)

Like the doe, he is wounded, but his wound is metaphorical. This is the lone example of a male character crying "Alas!" Typically, it is women who bemoan their powerlessness before a fate that has befallen them. But that is exactly the point: in attributing to Equitan an exclamation normally attributed to women, the tale emphasizes the inversions set in motion by courtly love. The similarity between the king's opening lines and those uttered by Enide in her first direct speech only serves to highlight the element of play-acting in *Equitan*: "Alas, woe that I ever left my own country. Why did I come here?" (Lasse, con mar m'esmui / De mon païs! Que ving ça querre?, ll. 2492–3). Though both characters lament having physically moved to their present location, there is a world of difference between the king's intentional pursuit of his seneschal's wife and the plight of the poor vassal's daughter given in marriage by her father.[24] In that sense, his exclamation here anticipates the verbal abasement he deploys in wooing the seneschal's wife later in the text.

The first direct discourse in *Le Fraisne* is the anonymous lady's exclamation at their neighbor's "shame" and "dishonor" in announcing the birth of twins, since everyone knows this means the mother has lain with two men. Thus when she herself gives birth to twin daughters, she has ample cause to lament:

---

[24] Chrétien de Troyes, *Erec et Enide*, ed. and trans. Jean-Marie Fritz (Paris: Librairie Générale Française, 1992). For a reading of this scene, see Stahuljak et al., *Thinking Through Chrétien de Troyes*, pp. 122–3.

"Alas," she said, "what shall I do? I will never be esteemed nor honored. I am shamed – that's the truth. My lord and all my relatives will, I am certain, never believe me when they hear what has happened. For I passed sentence on myself [when] I spoke ill of all women."

"Lasse," fet ele, "que ferai?
Ja mes pris ne honur n'avrai!
Hunie sui, c'est veritez.
Mis sire e tuz mis parentez
certes ja mes ne me crerrunt,
des que ceste aventure orrunt;
kar jeo meïsmes me jujai,
de tutes femmes mesparlai." (*Le Fraisne*, ll. 73–80)

Her dilemma, of her own making, exactly fits the moral of *Equitan*, which directly precedes it: "He who seeks to do ill to others has all the ill return against him" (tels purchace le mal d'altrui, / dunt tuz li mals revert sur lui, ll. 315–16); in seeking to distinguish herself from her neighbor, she exposes herself to the vulnerability of "all women" (tutes femmes, *Le Fraisne*, l. 80), in keeping with the *lai*'s thematic of (non-) differentiation. We can easily imagine a variant tale with the lady as its protagonist, facing the consequences of her rash words. Meanwhile, the slightly eccentric nature of her lament – the dramatic rejoinder to the quandary created by her own rash speech – prepares us in advance for the unusual turns the plot will subsequently take.

Perhaps the most classic instance of our lament occurs in *Yonec* with the verbal protest of the beautiful young woman locked up in a tower by her old, jealous husband:

"Alas," she said, "that I was ever born! My fate is very hard. I am imprisoned in this tower, and won't get out until I'm dead. This jealous old man – what is he afraid of that he keeps me so imprisoned?"

"Lasse," fait ele, "mar fui nee!
Mult est dure ma destinee.
En ceste tur sui en prisun,
ja n'en istrai se par mort nun.
Cist vielz gelus de quei se crient,
ki en si grant prisun me tient?" (*Yonec*, ll. 71–6)

Of the *Lais*' six repetitions of "Lasse," this one, the closest to Enide's in tone, is the most pathos-laden.[25] Unlike those of the ladies in *Le Fraisne* and *Chaitivel*, her lament does not open up onto the question of what to *do* (que *ferai*?). Rather, as in the parodic case of *Equitan*, it casts her dilemma as the consequence of fate (destinee) – a situation immediately answered by one of the most striking moments in all twelve *lais*: the appearance of the wished-for lover in the form of a hawk at her window. But as is apparent from examining these five cases, Marie's use of this formulaic expression is far from merely conventional. Viewed synoptically in their kaleidoscopic variation, they exemplify the artful interplay of repetition and variation characterizing medieval literature in general and Marie's *Lais* in particular.

Apart from their shared use of the "Alas" lament, the adjacent tales of *Equitan* and *Le Fraisne* ostensibly have little in common. The first features protagonists playing at courtly love at the highest end of the social hierarchy while the second follows the fortunes of a foundling displaced from her rightful, if modest, position in feudal society. Yet each involves a male protagonist who lives happily with a mistress of much lower station until his vassals insist he give her up in order to contract an appropriate marriage. Accordingly, both *lais* contain similar scenes of the confrontation between lord and vassals, differing one from the other less in substance than in the degree of expansion or compression of their component parts.

Equitan	*Le Fraisne*
The king...	**The knight** who had brought her away **greatly loved** and cherished **her**, as did all his vassals and servants; there was not a one, little or great, who didn't love, cherish, and honor her for her nobility [of spirit].
... **loved her a long time** and had no desire for another woman. He didn't want to marry anyone, And never allowed it to be spoken of. His people **held this against him.**	She had been with him for **a long time** until the knights who held fiefs from him **began to hold this against him.** They often spoke to him about marrying a woman of noble birth and getting rid of *her*.

---

[25] The sixth occurs in *Eliduc*, ll. 387–92 (cited above in Chapter 3, p. 86), where the king of Exeter's daughter laments having fallen in love with a knight of unknown rank.

They would be happy
if he had an heir
who after him
would hold his land and patrimony.
Too much harm would result
if, on account of his concubine, he were
not to have a legitimate child;
they would never hold him as their lord
nor willingly serve him
if he didn't abide by their will.

Li reis...

Li chevaliers ki l'en mena
mult la cheri e **mult l'ama,**
e tuit si hume e si servant;
n'i out un sul, petit ne grant,
pur sa franchise ne l'amast
e ne cherist e honurast.

... l'ama mult **lungement,**
que d'altre femme n'ot talent.
Il ne voleit nule espuser;
ja n'en rovast oïr parler.
Sa genz li tindrent **mult a mal ...**

Lungement ot od lui esté,

tant que **li chevalier fiefé**
a mult grant mal li aturnerent.
Soventes feiz a lui parlerent,
qu'une gentil femme espusast
e de cele se delivrast.
Lié sereient, s'il eüst heir
ki aprés lui peüst aveir
sa terre e sun grant heritage;
trop i avreient grant damage,
se il laissast pur sa suignant
que d'espuse n'eüst enfant;
ja mes pur seignur nel tendrunt
ne volentiers nel servirunt,
se il ne fait lur volenté.

(*Equitan*, ll. 203–7)   (*Le Fraisne*, ll. 317–37)

This juxtaposition reveals the brief five-line passage in *Equitan* to be the germ of a larger discourse, more expansively developed in *Le Fraisne*, in which the political and social ramifications of the protagonist's behavior are fully spelled out. In the first case, Equitan, being king, shows little concern for his vassals' discontent, which is registered in one elliptical line. Rather, it is the lady's fear that he will drop her that eventually leads him to suggest – more as a gesture of devotion to her than as the resolution of a political crisis – that he would marry her if he could, thus precipitating the *lai*'s tragic ending. *Le Fraisne*, on the other hand, significantly expands this socio-narrative kernel: first, in distinguishing between the reactions of Gurun's household and his external vassals (as we saw in Chapter 3), it highlights the structural gap between Fraisne's personal qualities and those required in a lord's wife; secondly, it calls attention to the central role that lineage and inheritance play in the maintenance of political stability. As in her variegated repetitions of the lamentation "Alas," Marie's deployment of theme and variation exposes the complexity of the interface between the chivalric imagination and feudal ideologies.

From these cases of the strategic repetition and variation of discrete lines, we turn to the way the multiepisodic *Guigemar* juxtaposes and recombines plots developed separately in other tales. The *lai* unfolds as a kind of triptych, its narrative "panels" linked by the abrupt or magically engineered shifts in venue we examined in Chapter 4.

Knight excels at arms and wins a maid's attention (*Milun*)	Old man, young wife, young lover (*Yonec*)	Two men love same lady (*Equitan, L'aüstic*)

The opening segment (through the wounding of the white doe) presents the adventures of a typical youth winning fame on the tournament circuit, much like the titular protagonist of *Milun*. They are distinguished, however, by social rank: where Milun is a simple knight with nothing more to his name than the reputation he has won by his sword, Guigemar is the son of a landed baron well loved by his king (ll. 29–33). Thus their destinies diverge: though Milun wins the attention of a lady above his station, he is understood by all to be ineligible for her hand (thus exploding one of the most cherished myths of courtly-chivalric society), sparking off their clandestine twenty-year affair.[26] Conversely, Guigemar, as the son of a baron, has reached the point where it behooves him either (in feudal terms) to take a wife or (in courtly ones) to fall in love (mutually or unrequitedly) with a married and therefore unavailable woman. That he does neither is, as William Burgwinkle observes, a cause for general consternation – a pointed rejection of the heterosexual imperative governing twelfth-century feudal society. Thus when Guigemar is himself

---

[26] Compare the middle segment of *Eliduc*, in which the knight is married and a seasoned warrior rather than a youth, and the maid whose attention he wins is a princess, the daughter of the knight's employer.

wounded and boards the ship that mysteriously appears, he undergoes "a coercive process of interpellation: the boat knows him, waits for him, transports him toward a pre-existing identity that he has only to take up in fulfillment of destiny."[27]

That destiny takes shape in the second panel of our narrative triptych, set in an "ancient city" (antive cite, l. 207) whose lord, an "old man" (vielz huem, l. 210), is married to a young woman "of high lineage – noble, courtly, beautiful, and wise" (de halt parage, / franche, curteise, bele e sage, ll. 211–12) whom he keeps locked up out of jealousy. This is of course a classic scenario of adulterous love, closely anticipating the inaugural situation in *Yonec*, in which "a rich/powerful old and ancient man" (uns riches huem, vielz e antis, l. 12) marries a girl "of high rank … wise, courtly and extremely beautiful" (De halte gent … sage e curteise e forment bele, ll. 21–2). But for the accommodation of different rhyme words (parage/sage, pucele/bele), the descriptions are virtually identical, revealing the high degree of conventionality (and anonymity) defining Marie's standard-issue courtly heroine. Into the midst of this unnatural situation comes Guigemar – structurally parallel to the bird-man Muldu-marec, but coming and going in a magical ship rather than through the window in the form of a hawk (see Chapter 4). The love that develops between the lady and the stranger is almost immediate, but it requires the intervention of her companion (daughter of the old man's sister), who encourages each of them individually and diagnoses their love-sickness for what it is. The strength of the love between them is expressed in the syntactic parallelism structuring both the *pucele*'s exhortation to Guig-emar – "You are beautiful, and she is beautiful!" (Vus estes bels, e ele est bele!, l. 453) – and the lady's cry of desperation as they are about to be parted: "If *you* die, *I* want to die" (Se *vus* murez, *jeo* vueil murir, l. 549); in each, poetic compression signals a fatefulness like that of Tristan's famous line, "neither you without me or I without you" (ne vus senz me ne jeo senz vus!, *Chievrefueil*, l. 78). Except perhaps for the wife and husband's contrasting reception of Guigemar's tale of *aventure*, this episode remains largely conventional.[28] Its most important and compelling

---

[27] Thus for Burgwinkle, Guigemar's slaying of the antlered doe is a symbolic initiation, an overcoming of a former self that is hermaphroditic, marked as double and different, psychically bipolar – "the sacrificial sodomite put to rest in the forest." Burgwinkle, *Sodomy, Masculinity, and Law*, pp. 154, 156.

[28] Guigemar recounts his adventure (l. 313) and asks the lady's counsel (ll. 333–5) on where to go; she answers his question (l. 338), telling him he is welcome to stay with her (ll. 355, 357), but not until unfolding her long and arguably irrelevant story (ll. 341–52) of the jealous husband who has confined her against her will. Later, after the lovers have

element is its conclusion, when the lovers, just before parting, exchange the belt and knotted shirt meant to guarantee the singularity – and recoverability – of their love in the future.

The triptych's final panel is more conflicted and troubling. On the one hand, moving the lovers to a different setting confirms that their love was not simply "situational," the result of the lady's May–December marriage. On the other, it leaves material objects to carry the burden of identity: since "women look very much alike" (femmes se resemblent asez, *Guigemar*, l. 779), there seems to be a threat of displacement from "The lady I love is wearing a belt" to "I love (whichever) lady is wearing the belt." Equally ambiguous, as we saw in Chapter 3, is the relationship between the two male rivals. Having decided to launch a tourney against the neighbor with whom he is at war, Meriaduc assembles a team that includes his "friend and companion" (ami e cumpaignun, l. 750), who, as we have seen, owes him "repayment" (gueredun, l. 749) for an unspecified service previously rendered. In response to the summons, Guigemar "came richly equipped, bringing more than 100 knights" with him (Alez i est mult richement; / chevaliers meine plus de cent, ll. 753–4). If the lady's arrival at Meriduc's castle in Guigemar's magical ship is a mysterious act of fate, Guigemar's is determined by reciprocal feudal bonds of obligation.

Together, these two narrative strands – the magical and the feudal – bring the lovers together in a new courtly triangle. This time, however, the two men are of roughly the same age (as in *L'aüstic* and perhaps *Equitan*); more unusually, neither of them is her husband. In Chapter 3 we looked at the way this episode hints at feudal scandal, only to occult it in the *lai*'s abrupt conclusion. At the same time, it must contain the displacement evident not only in the *lai*'s shifts in geographical setting and in the chain of substitutability implied by Guigemar's pronouncement that "femmes se resemblent asez" (l. 779). Only after she succeeds in untying the knot in his shirt (as Meriaduc's sister has failed to do) is he convinced that she is his love:

> "Lords," he said, "hear me. In [this lady] I have recognized the friend I thought I had lost. I ask and beseech Meriaduc to return her to me, by his mercy!"

> "Seignur," fet il, "or m'escultez!
> Ci ai m'amie cuneüe
> que jeo quidoue aveir perdue.

been caught, Guigemar repeats his tale to the jealous husband, who disbelieves him (ll. 605 ff.).

Meriadu requier e pri,
rende la mei, sue merci!" (*Guigemar*, ll. 838–42)

Meriaduc will do no such thing, for of course he loves the lady himself. We have seen how the extreme compression of the *lai*'s conclusion forces this narrative to a happy ending while suppressing the feudal irregularity of Guigemar's rupture with Meriaduc. Structurally, on the other hand, this episode represents a fully (if not to say overly elaborated) response to the middle episode of the *mal-mariée*. By moving the lovers from a setting in which their love, however justified in courtly terms, remains morally suspect to a setting in which Guigemar can champion the lady against Meriaduc's unwanted attentions, the *lai* provides a delayed and compensatory resolution to the previously unresolved triangle.[29] As in *Equitan*, the tension between the feudal and the courtly is resolved in favor of the latter, but this time in a way that allows the lovers to escape the consequences of their action.

Marie's *Lais* and the *Lais anonymes*

Thus far we have examined instances of repetition and variation across several of Marie's *Lais*. But the twelve *lais* of Harley 978, as we know, represent only some of the surviving corpus of *lais* in vernacular French. Moreover, other manuscripts containing *lais* we recognize (from Harley 978) as "Marie's" do not consistently associate them with her name, telling us something about the fluidity of the tradition.[30] The *lai* of *Lanval* in particular strongly resembles several of the so-called "anonymous" Breton *lais*. As in the cases we examined above, reading it in relation to those variants both illuminates what remains implicit or understated in Marie's text while bringing the distinctiveness of her version into better focus. The *lai* of *Guingamor* features a knight who, like Lanval, leaves court and finds a beautiful woman in the forest. In Marie's version, the encounter is courtly and chaste: riding away from court, Lanval dismounts by

---

[29] A similar, even more complicated displacement occurs in the Gorre episode of Chrétien de Troyes's *Le chevalier de la charrete*. Lancelot fights a judicial duel against the queen's unwanted suitor, Mélégant, over the (false) accusation that Sir Keu is her lover. In this way, the charge of adultery is aired, but in such a way that Lancelot can fight all-out to prove it false. This (overly) neat resolution is itself deferred, hinting in advance at the difficulties of bringing the plot of adultery to a successful conclusion.

[30] We return to the question of Marie's posterity in Chapter 7.

"some running water" (une ewe curant, l. 45), where two richly dressed
attendants entreat him to visit the lady's sumptuous tent. Guingamor, in
contrast, goes to the forest to hunt and happens on a beautiful maiden
bathing naked in a spring. To prevent her from leaving while he hunts the
boar he has been pursuing, he moves her clothing to the branches of an
oak tree. She spots him and cries out:

> Guingamor, don't touch my clothes. May it please God, let it
> never be said among knights that you have committed such a
> misdeed as to steal a girl's clothes in the thick of the forest.

> Guingamor, lessiez ma despoille.
> Ja Deu ne place ne ne voile
> qu'entre chevaliers soit retret
> que vos faciez si grant mesfet
> d'embler les dras d'une meschine
> en l'espoisse de la gaudine. (*Guingamor*, ll. 447–52)

In casting its protagonist as a hunter and sexual predator, this variant
highlights, by contrast, the courtliness and stately propriety of Lanval's
first meeting with his mysterious lady. At the same time, it unexpectedly illuminates a pivotal moment in *Bisclavret* – identifying, as it were,
the conventional theme of "how to trap someone by stealing his or her
clothes."

Similarly, the anonymous *lais* offer variant takes on the so-called
"Potiphar's wife" motif found in the queen's attempted seduction of
Lanval. In *Guingamor*, the amorous queen sets upon the protagonist,
insisting that "you ought to really love me" (moi devez vos tres bien
amer, *Guingamor*, l. 89). Lanval's reaction, as we saw in Chapter 3, is
immediate and uncompromising:

> "Lady," he said, "leave me alone! *I am not interested in loving
> you.* I have long served the king and don't want to violate my
> fidelity. Never, for you or your love, will I wrong my lord.

> "Dame," fet il, "laisseiz m'ester!
> *Jeo n'ai cure de vus amer.*
> Lungement ai servi le rei,
> ne li vueil pas mentir ma fei.
> Ja pur vus ne pur vostre amur
> ne mesferai a mun seignur!" (*Lanval*, ll. 271–6)

Guingamor, on the other hand, responds, after a moment's reflection:

> Lady, well do I know that *I should love you*: you are the wife
> of my lord the king, and so I should honor you as the wife of
> my lord.

> Bien sai, dame, q'*amer vos doi*,
> fame estes mon seignor le roi,
> et si vos doi porter honnor
> comme a la fame mon seignor. (*Guingamor*, ll. 95–8)

The essence of the two reactions is the same: to take up sexually with
the queen would be a breach of the loyalty that the protagonist owes to
the king. For Lanval, the two are in direct contradiction. Guingamor, in
contrast, sees the larger semantic field surrounding the concept of "love."
Like Georges Duby, he recognizes courtly love of one's lady as an extension of the feudal love due to one's lord. This understanding – and the
acknowledgment that indeed he *should* love her – creates the conditions
for further dialogue. Where *Lanval*'s queen reacts to the knight's rebuff
by accusing him of sodomy – "you don't like women; you like well-
fashioned young men, taking your pleasure with them" (de femme n'avez
talent. / Vaslez amez bien afaitiez, / ensemble od els vus deduiez, *Lanval*,
ll. 282–4) – *Guingamor*'s embellishes her appeal:

> I'm not talking about that kind of *love*. I want to *love* you
> with *druerie* and to be your *lover*. You are handsome and I am
> noble: if you put your mind to *loving* me, together we could
> be very happy.

> Je ne di mie *amer* ainsi,
> *amer* vos voil de druerie
> et que je soie vostre *amie*.
> Vos estes biax et je sui gente,
> s'a moi *amer* metez entente,
> molt poons ester andui hetié. (*Guingamor*, ll. 100–5)

Like Equitan, the queen needs to resignify "love," effacing the sense of
feudal obligation in favor of the discourse of erotic-romantic passion. Yet
even as her phrase, "Vos estes biax et je sui gente" closely mimics the
syntax of the line we cited earlier, "You are beautiful, and she is beautiful!" (Vus estes bels, e ele est bele!, *Guigemar*, l. 453), meant to assert the
perfect commensurability of Guigemar and his lady, its *content* – beauty
on the one hand, nobility on the other – reaffirms the social distance
between them.

The *lai* of *Graelent* adds yet a third variation to the mix. This time,
when the amorous queen makes her move, the protagonist responds:

"Lady," he said, "may it please you, but this cannot be, for *I am in the king's pay*: I pledged him loyally and faithfully to look out for his life and honor when I put myself in his power *the other day*. Never will I dishonor that." Then he took his leave and went away.

"Dame," dist il, "vostre merci,
mais il ne peut pas estre ensi,
car *je sui saudoiers le roi*;
loiauté li promis e foi,
e de sa vie e de s'anor,
quant a lui remes *l'autre jor*;
ja par moi honte n'i ara."
Dont prist congié, si s'en ala. (*Graelent*, ll. 121–8)

Though the upshot is the same – Graelent refuses to violate the trust he owes the king – he is no longer the king's vassal but, like Eliduc, his mercenary. Questions of honor have been transferred from the realm of *féodalité* to the world of short-term, contractual, monetary relations. The consequences of incurring the queen's wrath are likewise directly expressed in economic terms; the king

held back his pay. He hadn't given him any of it: the queen dissuaded him. She spoke to the king, counseling him not to give him anything – only his equipment, so he wouldn't leave. The king kept him around in a state of impoverishment so he could not serve anyone else.

li detenoit ses saudees;
ne l'en avoit nules donees,
la roïne li destornoit.
Au roi disoit e conseilloit
ke nule rien ne li donast
fors le conroi, qu'il n'en alast;
povre le tenist entor lui,
qu'il ne peüst servir autrui. (*Graelent*, ll. 145–52)

As the king forcibly retains his military service by keeping him in dire poverty, Graelent suffers the full material and social consequences of losing the king's favor:

What will Graelent do now? It's no surprise if he is sad; he has nothing left to pawn other than a nag, which is hardly worth much. He can't leave town, since he has no mount.

> Que fera ore Graelens?
> N'est merville s'il est dolens;
> ne li remest que engagier
> fors un ronci, nest gaires cier.
> Il ne puet de la vile aler,
> car il n'avait sor quoi monter. (*Graelent*, ll. 153–8)

Even in his despondency at having been passed over in King Arthur's distribution of wives and land, Lanval could still mount "his warhorse" (*sun destrier, Lanval*, l. 41) and escape the court for an outing in the country.[31] Graelent, in contrast, is left only with a nag or packhorse – a telling humiliation in this self-consciously horse-based culture in which knights (*chevaliers*) are literally defined by their mounts. Even this he is forced to pawn – making him courtly literature's most oxymoronic figure, the horseless knight. *Graelent*'s vision of the dire poverty threatening those who lose the king's favor reveals the relative mildness of the trials first besetting Lanval and underscores the importance of the wealth his mysterious mistress provides him.

Examples of the interplay between Marie's *Lais* and the anonymous Breton *lais* could easily be multiplied. As in so much medieval literature, the line between intertextual variants, on the one hand, and reception and adaptation, on the other, is often difficult to draw. In Chapter 7 we will take up the question of the "posterity" of Marie's texts, looking at the way her *Lais* were taken up in romance-length works such as Gautier d'Arras's *Ille et Galeron* and Renaut's *Galeran de Bretagne*.

From short forms to long ones

So quintessentially courtly are Marie's *Lais*, so intertwined with the romance tradition of Chrétien de Troyes and the *Tristan* tales, that it is easy to overlook one of their most salient characteristics: their brevity. There, as (to a much greater extent) in the *Ysopë*, the juxtaposition of short self-contained narratives, each framed by its own prologue and epilogue, offers up a kaleidoscopic variation of visions on ways to negotiate questions of love, loyalty, and power in the context of feudal society. The lessons they convey or the moralities they implicitly or explicitly exemplify are multiple and situational, and liable to be contradictory: in the

---

[31] That he would ride his *destrier* for a nature outing might have struck a dissonant note for a medieval audience. Perhaps he had been forced to sell or pawn his palfrey?

Lais, adulterous love is neither "right" nor "wrong" *a priori* but depends on the circumstances of one's marriage and the way one conducts one's extra-marital affairs. In a way, their logic resembles that of the form destined to become increasingly prominent in late medieval Latin Europe: the frametale collection, in which individual tales may be mobilized in support of predetermined positions (as in the misogynist/anti-misogynist debates of *The Seven Sages of Rome*) or assembled to illustrate the varieties of philosophical and human experience (as in *The Decameron* or *The Canterbury Tales*).[32] In contrast, the *Lais* and the *Ysopë*, lacking explicit frames, leave readers largely to their own devices in adjudicating the apparently contrary lessons of juxtaposed tales – using their surplus of reason to decipher the situational wisdom conveyed by each tale individually and by the collection as a whole.

Not so in the *Espurgatoire seint Patriz*. There, as in the *Vie seinte Audree*, the significance of what is to be "remembered" is given in advance. In these two religious texts, the lessons purveyed are not subject to the vagaries of social differentiation. Instead, both experiential and generic variety are accommodated within long continuous narratives explicitly intended to bridge the gap between Latin and vernacular, religious and secular discourse, elite and "simple" readers. Sequences of accumulation or intensification – like the torments of Purgatory or the miracles of Saint Audrey – are embedded in extended narratives structured by Owein's biographical–geographical itinerary or Audrey's historiographical–hagiographical one. In the *Espurgatoire*, the generic and stylistic gaps between Owein's torments and his vision of the earthly and celestial paradise are naturalized by the progression of his exemplary spiritual journey. In the *Vie seinte Audree*, the discontinuities between different kinds of narrative segments are rougher, as the historical and genealogical contexts of Audrey's life pull against her desire to abandon that world, and the poverty and charity she embraced in her lifetime vie with the violence of the miracles enacted after her death.

Whatever the texts we attribute to her name, the author we call Marie de France is a figure of her times. From her turn to the vernacular and her grounding in feudal-courtly society to the artfulness of her play with repetition and variation, she shares techniques and interests with other writers of her day, both named and anonymous. The fascination of her proper name and the gender it implies have commanded the attention of genera-

---

[32] In the eastern and Mediterranean traditions from which many frametale collections derive, the organization of the text is frequently pedagogical: a dialogue between father and son or master and pupil as a means of moral and practical education.

tions of modern readers, eager to gloss the obscurities that have collected around that name. In the Middle Ages, other writers also preserved the memory of Marie's texts, but often in the mode of adaptations and appropriation, to which we turn in our final chapter.

7

Posterity: The Afterlives of Marie's Works

One of the only things Marie de France tells us about herself is that she does not want to be forgotten, and when she gives readers her name, it is so that they will remember it:

> Hear, lords, the stories of Marie, who is not forgotten in her own time.

> Oëz, seignur, que dit Marie,
> ki en sun tens pas ne s'oblie. (*Guigemar*, ll. 3–4)

> At the end of this composition that I have composed and put into French, I will name myself for remembrance: my name is Marie and I am from France.

> Al finement de cest escrit
> que en romanz ai treité e dit,
> me numerai pur remembrance:
> Marie ai nun, si sui de France. (*Ysopë*, epilogue, ll. 1–4)

This desire to be remembered as an author is also found in the *Vie seinte Audree* and it is one of the primary reasons for the attribution of the poem to Marie de France by some critics.[1] In the last lines of the *Audree*, in an oddly disjunctive ending, the author/translator writes:

> I have finished translating into French the book of the Life of Saint Audrey just as I found it in Latin, and recording the miracles I have heard. I do not wish for any of it to be forgotten. For this reason I pray to the glorious and precious Saint Audrey that she pity me and hear me and that in her mercy she aid my soul and those for whom I pray to her. The one who forgets

---

[1] June Hall McCash, "*La vie seinte Audree*: A Fourth Text by Marie de France?" *Speculum* 77 (2002): 744–77; Logan E. Whalen, *Marie de France and the Poetics of Memory* (Washington, DC: The Catholic University of America Press, 2008), pp. 163–73.

herself is foolish. Here I write my name "Marie" so that I will be remembered.

Issi ay ceo livre finé
En romanz dit et translaté
De la vie seintë Audree
Si com en latin l'ay trové,
Et les miracles ay öy,
Ne voil nul mettrë en obli.
Pur ce depri la glorïuse
Seinte Audree la precïeuse
Par sa pité k'a moy entende
Et ce servise a m'ame rende,
Et ceus pur ki ge la depri
K'el lur aït par sa merci.
Mut par est fol ki se oblie.
Ici escris mon non Marie
Pur ce ke soie remembree. (*La vie seinte Audree*, ll. 4611–25)

Whether or not this expression of a desire to be remembered lends support for the attribution of *La vie seinte Audree* to the author of the *Lais*, *Ysopë*, and *L'espurgatoire seint Patriz*, it is worth noting that the concern for posterity is not unique to Marie de France. Her near-contemporary Chrétien de Troyes expresses a similar sentiment in his *Erec et Enide*:

Now I begin a story that will be remembered as long as Christendom endures. Of this Chrétien boasts.

Des or comencerai l'estoire
Que toz jors mais iert en memoire
Tant con durra crestïentez.
De ce s'est Crestïens ventez.[2]

Like Chrétien, Marie de France does not insist only on her personal fame, but also claims posterity for the narratives she translates. She wants them to be remembered and she attributes the same motivation to the Bretons who originally composed the *lais*:

I, Marie, have put the book of the Purgatory into French, so that it will be remembered and so that lay people may understand and have access to it.

---

[2] Chrétien de Troyes, *Erec et Enide*, ed. Jean-Marie Fritz (Paris: Librairie Générale Française, 1992), ll. 23–6.

Jo, Marie, ai mis, en memoire,
le livre de l'Espurgatoire
en romanz, k'il seit entendables
a laie genz e covenables. (*Espurgatoire*, ll. 2297–300)

I thought of *lais* that I had heard. I knew well and did not
doubt that they had been composed by those who first heard
them and put them into circulation, to preserve the memory of
adventures they had heard. I had heard several of them and did
not want to let them be forgotten.

Des lais pensai qu'oïz aveie.
Ne dutai pas, bien le saveie,
que pur remembrance les firent
des aventures qu'il oïrent
cil ki primes les comencierent
e ki avant les enveierent.
Plusurs en ai oïz conter,
nes vueil laissier ne oblïer. (*Lais*, *Prologue*, ll. 33–40)

While other authors dramatize memory or the rhetorical techniques of
memory in their works, Marie may be unique in her persistent expression
of concern for the posterity of her works and of her own identity as their
author.

In this chapter we explore ways in which Marie de France and her
texts were actually remembered. First we look for evidence of Marie's
posterity in the manuscripts that contain her works. We have no extant
manuscripts from Marie's lifetime – only one of her works (*Ysopë*, ms.
Y) exists in a manuscript that appears to date from before the mid thirteenth century. As we shall discuss below, some of the manuscripts associate her works with an author named Marie, but in many her narratives
were copied as anonymous works. Secondly, we examine how Marie is
remembered by other authors. Taking inspiration from Sarah Kay's study
of Chrétien de Troyes as an author-function, we describe the historical
awareness of Marie in textual, rather than biographical terms.[3] Finally, we
turn to two thirteenth-century works apparently based on two of Marie's
lais, Renaut's *Galeran de Bretagne* and Gautier d'Arras's *Ille et Galeron*.
We argue that Marie's posterity in romance may tell us something about
the poetics of the shorter narratives of the *Lais*.

---

[3] Sarah Kay, "Who Was Chrétien de Troyes?" *Arthurian Literature* XV, ed. James P.
Carley and Felicity Riddy (Cambridge: D. S. Brewer, 1997), pp. 1–35.

The manuscripts of Marie's works

Although we speak of Marie's *Lais* as a collection, all twelve *lais* are compiled together with the *General Prologue* in only one manuscript: British Library Harley 978. This manuscript, dated to the mid thirteenth century, contains the only version of the *Guigemar* prologue in which Marie names herself: "Lords, hear the words of Marie who is not forgotten in her time" (Oëz, seignur, que dit Marie, / ki en sun tens pas ne s'oblie, *Guigemar*, ll. 3–4). The Harley manuscript is one of five compilations in which the *lais* associated with Marie are found. Of these, only three include more than one *lai*, while two manuscripts include only one (along with other texts). *L'aüstic*, *Chaitivel*, and *Eliduc* are found only in the Harley manuscript.[4] Apart from Harley 978, manuscript copies of Marie's *lais* include no authorial attribution and in three manuscripts they are compiled with other anonymous *lais*. As we have noted, because the Harley manuscript, where Marie is identified as the author of the *Lais*, is earlier than other manuscript versions of the *lais*, where there is no authorial attribution, Keith Busby has suggested that "it is quite possible that the genre became largely divorced from the name of its most celebrated practitioner in less than a century after her death." As he further suggests: "It is as if the anonymity of the *lais* originally composed by the Bretons, which Marie claims as her sources, re-emerges in the course of the thirteenth century, as the poems become absorbed into the general corpus of unattributed vernacular narrative."[5]

Although Marie's authorship of the *Lais* is not remembered in the manuscript tradition, her connection to the *Ysopë* is more firmly retained. There are even author portraits in four *Ysopë* manuscripts.[6] Unlike her *lais*,

---

[4]   *Equitan*, *Le Fraisne*, *Bisclavret*, *Les dous amanz*, *Milun*, and *Chievrefueil* are found in two manuscripts, *Guigemar* in three, and *Lanval* and *Yonec* in four manuscripts. On the manuscript tradition, see Jean Rychner, ed., *Les Lais de Marie de France* (Paris: Champion, 1978), pp. xxi–xxii. On Harley 978, see Rupert T. Pickens, "Reading Harley 978: Marie de France in Context," in *Courtly Arts and the Art of Courtliness*, ed. Keith Busby and Christopher Kleinhenz (Cambridge: Brewer, 2006): 527–42. For a provocative reading of the twins in *Le Fraisne* in relation to the two manuscript versions of the *lai*, see Laurence de Looze, "Marie de France et la textualisation. Arbre, enfant, oeuvre dans le *lai* de *Fresne*," *Romanic Review* 81.4 (1990): 396–408, esp. 405–8.

[5]   Keith Busby, *Codex and Context: Reading Old French Verse Narrative in Manuscript* (Amsterdam: Rodopi, 2002), 1: 473. Busby offers an extended discussion of the Marie manuscript tradition in "The Manuscripts of Marie de France," in *A Companion to Marie de France*, ed. Logan E. Whalen (Leiden: Brill, 2011), pp. 303–17.

[6]   Busby, *Codex and Context*, 1: 214–15; 473–8; Karl Ringger, "Prolégomènes à l'iconographie des oeuvres de Marie de France," in *Orbis Medievalis*, ed. George Günter, Marc-René Jung, and Kurt Ringger (Bern: Francke, 1978), pp. 329–42; Sandra L. Hindman, "Æsop's Cock and Marie's Hen: Gendered Authorship in Text and Image in

Marie's fables are recorded in collections that are more or less complete, however, the epilogue in which Marie gives her name is not included in sixteen of the twenty-five extant manuscripts. Since Marie's identification of her source and her patron appear only in the epilogue, it may be intended to establish a connection between a work written by a foreigner and a national literature of which King Alfred is the most prestigious figure, yet the large number of extant manuscripts of the *Ysopë* dating from the thirteenth to the fifteenth centuries suggests that the collection was very popular with or without the author's name. Indeed, the medieval diffusion and reception of Marie's *Ysopë* and *Lais* is the exact opposite of the modern appreciation for the *Lais* over the fables: the *Ysopë* was read and copied throughout the Middle Ages, while the *Lais* may have had a more restricted dissemination.[7] Harley 978, the manuscript that includes all the *lais*, is one of several manuscripts that include all 102 fables with the prologue and epilogue, and has been the basis for all recent editions of Marie's fables.[8]

The story of Saint Patrick's Purgatory was similarly popular in the Middle Ages, and there were many vernacular translations of the *Tractatus*, including seven surviving verse renditions in French.[9] Marie's, the earliest of the French translations, is preserved in a single manuscript, BN fr. 25407, from the end of the thirteenth or beginning of the fourteenth century.[10]

The inclusion of Marie's *Lais* and *Ysopë* in a single manuscript may suggest that a compiler associated both works with a common author.

Manuscripts of Marie de France's *Fables*," in *Women and the Book: Assessing the Visual Evidence*, ed. Lesley Smith and Jane H. M. Taylor (Toronto: University of Toronto Press, 1996), pp. 45–56; Susan L. Ward, "Fables for the Court: Illustrations of Marie's *Fables* in Paris, BNF, MS Arsenal 3142," in *Women and the Book*, pp. 190–203.

[7] Françoise Vielliard, "La tradition manuscrite des fables de Marie de France: essai de mise au point," *Bibliothèque de l'Ecole des Chartes* 147 (1989): 371–97 (at 374, 389).

[8] For a discussion of the choice of Harley 978, see Richard Trachsler, "Les Fables de Marie de France. Manuscrits et editions," *Cahiers de civilisation médiévale* 44 (2001): 45–63. For an indication of the order of the fables in each manuscript, see Karl Warnke, ed., *Die Fabeln der Marie de France* (Halle: Neimeyer, 1898), pp. xiv–xiv. Harriet Spiegel gives a table indicating which fables occur in each manuscript: Marie de France, *Fables* (Toronto: University of Toronto Press, 1994), pp. 279–82. Whalen also includes a table of extant manuscripts in *Marie de France and the Poetics of Memory*, pp. 184–5.

[9] Kurt Ringger, "Die altfranzösischen Verspurgatorien," *Zeitschrift für romanische Philologie* 88 (1972): 389–402. For a summary, see Michael J. Curley, trans., *Saint Patrick's Purgatory: A Poem by Marie de France* (Tempe: Medieval and Renaissance Texts and Studies, 1997), pp. 1–3.

[10] This manuscript description is taken from Yolande de Pontfarcy, ed. and trans., *L'espurgatoire seint Patriz* (Louvain and Paris: Peeters, 1995), pp. 19–38. She cites studies of the manuscript in the introduction to her edition, p. 19, n. 43.

Busby has pointed to the "gravitational effect" of the fables, by which Marie's authorship of the fables may have caused her other works to be grouped with them for at least two manuscripts, either during the production of the manuscript or in the later assembly of the codex.[11] But since not all manuscripts associate her name with her works, it remains difficult to establish how well Marie de France was known as an author based on manuscript evidence. We do, however, have other evidence that both she and her works were known to other authors, but it seems that her works were remembered more often than her name. This is not unusual, since borrowing and rewriting without attribution were common compositional techniques for medieval authors. The circulation of Marie de France's name and works may also reflect a recognition of "Marie" as what Sarah Kay has described as an "anonym." To paraphrase Kay's description of "Chrétien de Troyes": "a part of [Marie's] self-presentation as an author would be the assumption of a position bordering on anonymity." In other words, Marie's insistence on her own name would aim less at personal remembrance than at claiming an authority for her works. If that is true, then her medieval posterity shows that she was indeed remembered in the many translations and rewritings of her *Lais*.[12]

Marie's fame

Although Marie's authorship of the *Lais* is recorded in only one manuscript, she is named as their author in Denis de Piramus's *La vie seint Edmund*. Probably writing in the 1190s, Denis begins his narrative by explaining that up to this point he has spent his time foolishly, composing frivolous poetry at court, but now he repents of his youthful pursuits and sets himself to a higher goal.[13] Then he cites examples of the literature of falsehood that he now rejects: first the romance *Partoponeu de Blois* and then the works of "Dame Marie":

---

[11] Busby, *Codex and Context*, p. 478.

[12] Kay, "Who Was Chrétien de Troyes?" pp. 1–35 (at 32). For a view of Marie's anonymity that defines an authorial presence behind the name, see R. Howard Bloch, *The Anonymous Marie de France* (Chicago: University of Chicago Press, 2003).

[13] For discussion of the composition date, see Ian Short, "Denis Piramus and the Truth of Marie's *Lais*," *Cultura Neolatina* 67 (2007): 319–40 (at 326–8). Using the earlier date of c. 1170 proposed by the editor of *La vie seint Edmund*, Carla Rossi has situated Marie in a literary conversation with Denis Piramus and the authors of *Partonopeu de Blois* and *Ipomedon*. *Marie de France et les érudits de Cantorbéry* (Paris: Garnier, 2009), pp. 122–44. For the date of 1170, see *La vie seint Edmund le rei, poème anglo-normand du XIIe siècle par Denis Pyramus*, ed. Hilding Kjellman (Göteborg: Elanders, 1935), pp. cxxv–cxxix.

And Dame Marie, too, who put into rhyme and structured and composed verse *lais* that are not at all true. And she is much praised and her verses loved, for counts and barons and knights love her work greatly and hold it dear. And they love the text and have it read with much pleasure and have it copied often. The *lais* often please ladies who hear them willingly and with joy, for they are what they like.

> E dame Marie autresi,
> Ki en ryme fist e basti
> E compensa les vers de lays,
> Ke ne sunt pas de tut verais.
> E si en est ele mult loee
> E la ryme partut amee,
> Kar mult l'ayment si l'unt mult cher
> Cunte, barun e chivaler;
> E si en ayment mult l'escrit,
> E lire le funt si unt delit,
> E si les funt sovent retreire.
> Les lays soleient as dames pleire,
> De joye les oyent e de gré
> Qu'il sunt sulum lur volenté.[14]

Denis names "Dame Marie" not to critique her craft but to accuse her stories of untruth. They are not like the *Life of Saint Edmund* that Denis translates, a written, eyewitness document with several Latin sources. As Ian Short points out, "the most decisive argument that Denis can deploy in vaunting the superiority of his own composition over *Partonopeu* and the *lais* concerns a higher level of truth above and beyond questions of documentary veracity, namely that of the ultimate authority of God speaking directly through his saint's exemplary life and his miracle-working powers."[15] Denis's citation of Marie in his claim for the merits of his own translation over the frivolous pleasures of imaginative literature suggests that, in at least some circles, Marie's authorship of the *lais* was known.

Marie is also identified as the author of fables in a manuscript from the second half of the thirteenth century. In BN fr. 1446, a single copyist has recorded *Le couronnement Renard* and Marie's *Ysopë*. *Le couronnement* is linked to the fables by an epilogue in which the narrator cites Marie as a model:

---

14 Citation from the prologue re-edited by Short, "Denis Piramus," pp. 339–40.
15 Short, "Denis Piramus," pp. 333–4.

And so for count William who honored me with this charge, I
take my prologue like Marie, who translated the *Ysopë* for him.

Et pour çou du conte Guillaume,
Qui ceste honor eut encharcie,
Pris mon prologue com Marie,
Qui pour lui traita d'Izopet.[16]

This passage marks the transition from *Le couronnement de Renard* to
the *Ysopë* and it is followed by the rubric "Hereafter you will hear the
proverbs of Æsop" (Ici apriés porrés oïr les provierbes Yzopet) and a
portrait of Marie. Though Marie could not have written her fables for the
same Guillaume de Dampierre to whom the *Couronnement* is dedicated,
the clear desire to link the two texts through their common dedication
to a "cunte Willame" (epilogue, l. 9) seems to point to Marie's fame as
the author of a fable collection.[17] (The author may be playing on Marie's
dedication of the *Ysopë* or the author or scribe may be unwittingly con-
flating them.)

Critics have shown that several collections of fables were modeled on
Marie's *Ysopë*, and it has been posited that Marie's fables were the basis
for Berechiah b. Natronai ha-Naqdam's thirteenth-century fable collection in Hebrew.[18] Any influence of Marie's *Espurgatoire* on subsequent
versions of Owein's story has not been identified. But neither of these
texts provoked as many imitations and rewritings as the *Lais*, despite the
relatively small number of surviving manuscripts that contain them, and
none of the authors who rewrite the *Lais* identify Marie as their author.

Rewriting Marie's *Lais*

Marie's *lais* seem to have had a strong influence on the genre. Most
critics assume that surviving anonymous Breton *lais* were modeled on

[16] *Le couronnement Renard, poème du treizième siècle*, ed. Alfred Foulet (Princeton:
Princeton University Press, 1929), ll. 3360–3.
[17] See discussion in Busby, *Codex and Context*, pp. 478–9; Sylvia Huot, *From Song to
Book* (Ithaca: Cornell University Press, 1987), pp. 32–5; and Foulet, *Le couronnement*, pp.
xxxii–iii. Foulet also discusses similarities between *Le couronnement* and selected fables,
pp. xxxiii–vi. Rossi proposes a similar desire to link *Evangile aux femmes* to Marie's
fables in the reference to a "Marie de Compiegne" in the incipit to the *Evangile*, and she
notes that two manuscripts include both texts. *Marie de France et les érudits*, pp. 146–9.
For Marie and Count William, see above, p. 43.
[18] Charles Bruckner, ed. and trans., *Les fables* (Louvain: Peeters, 1991), pp. 9–11;
Warnke, *Die Fabeln*, pp. lx–lxxx; Vielliard, "La tradition manuscrite," p. 389; Michael
Chernick, "Marie de France in the Synagogue," *Exemplaria* 19.1 (2007): 183–205.

Marie's *lais*, and many of them are collected together with Marie's *lais* in manuscripts. The only surviving complete manuscript of her *Lais* was composed in Britain, and some critics believe that the many fourteenth-century versions of Breton *lais* in Middle English revived interest in a genre that was already out of fashion in France. However, rather than a revival, the fourteenth-century written record may suggest that French *lais* continued to circulate in England up to that time and that there could well have been more translations than are currently extant.[19] *Sir Landeval*, an English translation of *Lanval*, was composed in the fourteenth century and Thomas Chester used this translation, along with two other sources, in his *Sir Launfal*, from the late fourteenth century.[20] Chester's audience is thought to have been more popular than the presumably noble audience for Marie's *Lais*. *Le Fraisne* was translated and rewritten in Middle English as *Lay le Freine*, and all of Marie's *lais* except Eliduc were translated into Old Norse prose in the thirteenth century.[21] There may also have been a Middle Dutch translation of *Lanval*, now lost.[22]

Two extant Old French romances are based on Marie's *lais*. Gautier d'Arras's *Ille et Galeron*, apparently inspired by *Eliduc*, was composed very soon after Marie's *Lais*. *Galeran de Bretagne*, composed in the thirteenth century by an otherwise unknown author called "Renaut," clearly takes its story from Marie's *Le Fraisne*.[23] These romance narratives build on Marie's *lais* and change them in ways that suggest that even if Marie was not remembered as the author of the *Lais*, her texts continued to circulate and to inspire rewritings and translations into new forms.

---

[19] For discussion see Elizabeth Archibald, "The Breton Lay in Middle English: Genre, Transmission and the Franklin's Tale," *Medieval Insular Romance: Translation and Innovation*, ed. Judith Weiss, Jennifer Fellows, and Morgan Dickson (Cambridge: Brewer, 2000), pp. 55–70 (at 66).

[20] A. J. Bliss, ed., *Sir Launfal* (London: Nelson, 1960).

[21] *Strengleikar. An Old Norse Translation of Twenty-one Old French Lais*, ed. Robert Cook and Matthias Tveitane (Oslo: Norsk Historisk Kjeldskrift-Institutt, 1979). For discussion see Sif Rikhardsdottir, "The Imperial Implications of Medieval Translations: Old Norse and Middle English Versions of Marie de France's *Lais*," *Studies in Philology* 105.2 (2008): 144–64.

[22] Wilhelm Hertz, *Spielmannsbuch. Novellen in Versen aus dem zwölften und dreizehnten Jahrhundert* (Stuttgart: Cotta, 1900), p. 369.

[23] The author was once identified as Jean Renart, based on similarities between *Galeran de Bretagne* and Jean's *Escoufle*, but this identification is no longer credited, and apart from his name, "Renaut" (much like Marie de France, in fact) is otherwise unknown. For a summary of the authorship debate, see Marion Vuagnoux-Uhlig, *Le couple en herbe: Galeran de Bretagne et l'Escoufle à la lumière du roman idyllique médiéval* (Geneva: Droz, 2009), pp. 187–8.

Composed between 1167 and 1178, *Ille et Galeron* could have been based on the same source Marie used for *Eliduc*, though it is likely that Gautier d'Arras learned the story from Marie's *lai* rather than from an oral Breton *lai* or other written source.[24] *Ille et Galeron* projects the dilemma of Eliduc, the man with two lovers, into the subsequent generation. The romance recounts the story of Eliduc's son, Ille, whose mother is not identified. Ille loves and marries Galeron. He is wounded in a tournament and fears that she will no longer love him because of his disfigurement, so he leaves Brittany, ending up in Rome where he helps the emperor end a war and wins his daughter, Ganor. Ille declines to marry Ganor because he is already married, and the pope declares that if Galeron can be found the marriage will not take place. Since Galeron has left Brittany to search for Ille and in fact has lived in Rome for four years, earning her keep by sewing, the pope's messengers come back from Brittany with the news that she has disappeared. The pope decides that the marriage will take place. Ille, in Rome, hears of it, and confronts Galeron in the church. She confirms that she loves him, and they return together to Brittany where Galeron gives birth to two sons. Before the birth of her third child, she vows to enter a convent if the birth goes smoothly. A daughter is born, and Galeron takes the veil. Ille returns to Rome, where the emperor has died, and marries Ganor, with whom he has three sons and a daughter who, curiously, bears the same name as Ille and Galeron's daughter, Ydoine.

Gautier reworks the plot of a man with two lovers, inserting it into a more realistic frame that includes many references to historical or contemporary characters and events, and he includes characters from Breton history in the story. Everyday life is described in detail, as are battle scenes. Gautier also brings the story into a moralistic frame, since it is a story about serial monogamy rather than a man's adulterous liaison. In this respect, *Ille et Galeron* resembles *Le Fraisne* more than *Eliduc*.[25]

Gautier seems to have known *Eliduc* in some form. No other extant *lai* includes a character called "Eliduc" or recounts the story of a man who marries a second wife after his first retires to a convent. Gautier does not

[24] Frederick A. G. Cowper supports the identification of Marie's *lai* as one of Gautier's sources, "The Sources of *Ille et Galeron*," *Modern Philology* 20.1 (1922): 35–44, as does Per Nykrog in "Two Creators of Narrative Form in Twelfth-Century France: Gautier d'Arras – Chrétien de Troyes," *Speculum* 48.2 (1973): 258–76. John E. Matzke disputes the source, but recognizes resemblances to *Eliduc* in the final sections of *Ille et Galeron* in "The Source and Composition of *Ille et Galeron*," *Modern Philology* 4.3 (1907): 471–88 (at 479).

[25] Sharon Kinoshita, "Two For the Price of One: Courtly Love and Serial Polygamy in the *Lais* of Marie de France," *Arthuriana* 8.2 (1998): 33–55.

mention Marie de France, but he does refer to *lais*, taking his distance
from what he sees as their oneiric quality (in this he echoes Denis Piramus's critique of Marie's *lais* as untrue):

> The great quality of *Ille et Galeron* is that it contains no make-
> believe or digressions, and you will find no lies in it. Some *lais*
> give those who hear them the impression that they have slept
> and dreamed.

> Grant cose est d'Ille et Galeron:
> n'i a fantome ne alonge
> ne ja n'i troverés mençonge.
> Tex lais i a, qui les entent,
> se li sanlent tot ensement
> com s'eüst dormi e songié. (*Ille et Galeron*, ll. 931–6)[26]

Gautier rejects marvelous "lies" and the unrealistic developments that
characterize *lais*. Although he does not mention Marie de France by
name, his disparagement of *lais* suggests that he knew *Eliduc*. Moreover,
the opening lines of *Ille et Galeron* suggest that he may also have known
her *Prologue* to the *Lais*. Gautier dedicates his romance to Beatrix of
Burgundy, second wife of Frederick Barbarossa, and, using a vocabulary
that resembles Marie's, he claims that she is worthy of praise, although,
he notes, praise may be turned to those who are not worthy:

> This is the truth [the letter = the honor of the empress], but one
> can turn praise [the gloss] to whomever one wishes; but it will
> all come out in the wash.

> Çou est la letre, mes la glose
> puet on atorner faussement
> sor cui c'on veut; mes longement
> ne se tient nule doreüre
> a envers d'une laveüre. (*Ille et Galeron*, ll. 10–14)

Not only does Gautier here seem to echo Marie's *Prologue* to the *Lais*,
where she claims that ancient authors wrote obscurely so that those who
came after them could gloss their works and add the surplus of their own
understanding (gloser la letre / e de lur sen le surplus metre, ll. 15–16),
but he also disputes the value of the gloss which can turn to falsehood

---

[26] Gautier d'Arras, *Ille et Galéron*, ed. Yves Lefèvre, Classiques Français du Moyen
Age 109 (Paris: Champion, 1988).

(atorner faussement, l. 14). Gautier thus seems to take his distance from Marie's definition of literary craft. Read alongside his criticism of the false-hoods recounted in *lais*, Gautier's definition of his own literary project insists on its truth and on its difference from the *lais* of Marie de France.

Gautier engages most fully with Marie's *Eliduc* when he thematizes a rejection of his source in descriptions of Ille's departure from Rome and from Ganor after his reunion with Galeron. Taking leave of Ganor, Ille points out that she is an emperor's daughter while he is the son, not of a count or a duke, but of Eliduc of Brittany. Ille's suggestion that Ganor might find a more worthy husband launches a long response in which Ganor repeatedly denies the significance of Ille's ancestry:

> She heard these words and said, "By God, king of heaven, what do I care about your ancestor?... What has your father got to do with me?... I never thought of him when I conceived the desire to love you. I never cared to hear anything about your father.... When I fell in love with you, I never thought of your ancestor."

> Cele a le parole entendue
> et dist: "Por Diu, le roi celestre,
> que monte a moi de vostre ancestre?...
> De vostre pere a moi que taint?...
> Onques de lui *ne me sovint*
> quant ceste volentés me vint
> de vos amer, de vos joïr.
> Il ne me tint nul jor d'oïr
> de vostre pere nule rien....
> Onques qant j'acointai vostre estre
> *ne me sovint* de vostre ancestre." (*Ille et Galeron*, ll. 4710–44)

Ille's suggestion that Ganor should not love him because he is not noble enough may comment on Marie's *Eliduc*, where the question of the suitability of a mercenary knight's marriage with a king's daughter is never addressed. Ganor adamantly rejects Ille's suggestion that he is un-worthy of her, and she explicitly rejects his father's story. She did not think of his father when she fell in love with him, Ganor repeats; in a more literal translation of her words, she did not *remember* Eliduc (ne me sovint, l. 4735). It is tempting to see her words as an extension of Gautier d'Arras's rejection of *lais* that recount untruths, especially since this is one point where Gautier follows the script of *Eliduc*. Recall that in Marie's *lai*, when Guilliadun learns that Eliduc already has a wife, she falls into a faint:

She falls forward on her face in a faint, all white and pale. She stays in the faint and she does not revive or breathe.

Desur sun vis cheï pasmee,
tute pale, desculuree.
En la pasmeisun demura,
qu'el ne revint ne suspira. (*Eliduc*, ll. 853–6)

In *Ille et Galeron* when Ganor finishes her angry speech about the irrelevance of Ille's father, Eliduc, to their situation, she too faints into the arms of the seneschal who catches her: "A tant se pasme entre les bras / le senescal qui le reqeut, / qui mout tres durement s'en deut" (ll. 4774–6). Ganor's faint is temporary; unlike Guilliadun, she revives quickly. Although Gautier does not represent the apparent death of the lover found in *Eliduc*, he does repeat the faint, and even comes back to it as a sign of Ganor's love for Ille. When Galeron withdraws into a convent, Ille remembers Ganor, who fainted (qui se pasma, l. 5361) from love when he left her, and he wonders if he might yet win her.

Gautier d'Arras rejects the dream-like events recounted in *lais* and composes a romance based on *Eliduc*, but one in which unexplained developments are omitted or rationalized, and the adulterous desire of the married protagonist for a king's daughter is rewritten as Ille's fidelity to his first love and his subsequent marriage to the second only when his wife enters a convent after a difficult childbirth. Yet Gautier's rejection of the model of the *lai* is not complete. The end of the romance repeats the resolution of the *lai* in the sequential marriages of the protagonist made possible by the first wife's withdrawal to a convent, and the story seems to debate its own relationship to Marie's *lai* in Ganor's extended speech about the irrelevance of Ille's father Eliduc to his claim that he cannot marry a king's daughter. Gautier remembers Marie even as he rejects her.

A similar engagement with Marie's *lais* is found in *Galeran de Bretagne*, a romance clearly based on the story of Marie's *Le Fraisne*. The name of the *lai* and its hero, like the references to Breton history and historical characters in *Ille et Galeron*, emphasizes the association with Brittany more insistently than Marie does in the corresponding *lai*. The heroine is named "Fresne" (though her name has lost the article that is attached to it in Marie's *lai*, where she is known as "le Fraisne"), and the situation that gives rise to the story repeats that found in the *lai*. A noblewoman sees a mother of twins and says that she must have taken a lover, since, in her view, two infants indicate two lovers. She herself subsequently gives birth to twin daughters and sends one of them away to avoid the charge of adultery. This exiled daughter, found in an ash tree and named

"Fresne," is raised in a convent. In *Galeran de Bretagne* the girl is raised along with the abbess's nephew, Galeran; they fall in love, then they are separated when Galeran's parents die and he returns to his lands. After a long separation from Fresne and after he receives false news of her death, Galeran is poised to marry her sister, Fleurie, when Fresne appears at his court. Her mother identifies her by the dress she has made out of the rich cloth that was placed in her cradle as a pillow when she was abandoned, and the lovers are reunited.

Galeran de Bretagne elaborates the basic plot of the *lai* and transforms the knight's seduction of the young woman into the love of two children raised together. The author invents their separation and individual quests for each other, and their reunion at the end of the romance. *Galeran de Bretagne* includes multiple intertextual references and is dominated by the theme of the idyllic romance, but it retains many elements not just of Marie's *Le Fraisne*, but also of other *lais* in her collection.[27] (In Chapter 6 we discussed the many ways that repetition and variation are at play in Marie's own collection.) The baby sent away with rich bedding and identifying signs is found in *Milun*, and identifying apparel is also represented in *Guigemar*. The tree become protagonist is found in *Le Fraisne*, but also perhaps in *Chievrefueil*, and the insistence on semblance and resemblance is certainly at play in *Yonec*.[28] The story of the man who must choose between two women is also recounted in *Eliduc*. These resemblances highlight the common themes among Marie's *lais*, but also point to their elaboration in *Galeran de Bretagne*.[29] The romance form may invite new interpretations of the story, but we insist here on the extent to which *Galeran de Bretagne* remains tied to Marie de France's *Lais*. In other words, the economy of Marie's narration in the *Lais* is expanded in

---

[27] In her reading of *Galeran de Bretagne* in terms of feminine filiation and heroism, Vuagnoux-Uhlig insists on the transformation of Marie's Fraisne into an independent and active heroine. *Le couple en herbe*, pp. 185–281, esp. 252–3.

[28] Ernst Hoepffner notes *Galeran*'s resemblance to *Milun* in "Des *Lais* de Marie de France dans *Galeran de Bretagne* et *Guillaume de Dole*," *Romania* 56 (1930): 212–35 (at 217–18). On the tree become *lai* and the protagonist become text in *Le Fraisne*, see de Looze, "Marie de France et la textualisation." For the insistance on resemblance, see Romaine Wolf-Bonvin, "Du *lai* du *Freisne* à *Galeran de Bretagne*: La fabrique des filles-fleurs," in *Ce est li fruis selonc la lettre: Mélanges offerts à Charles Méla*, ed. Olivier Collet, Yasmina Foehr-Janssens, and Sylviane Messerli (Paris: Champion, 2002), pp. 571–89 (at 576).

[29] For Milena Mikhaïlova, the rewriting of *Le Fraisne* as a romance narrative liberates the story from its source in Marie's *lai* and allows for the introduction of a notion of the tragic into the play of resemblance in the story. "De la différance aux ressemblances: du *lai* de *Fresne* au roman de *Galeran*," PRIS-MA 13.2 (1997): 199–207.

a romance narrative that remains attached to the structures of the *lai* in several crucial ways. This is particularly evident in the story's resolution.

In Marie's *Le Fraisne*, any resemblance between the twin sisters remains unnoted in the story – Gudrun's barons urge him to marry Codre, and he agrees to follow their advice. In *Galeran*, the twin sister Fleurie's resemblance to Fresne motivates Galeran's decision to marry her, but this decision is qualified in language that echoes Marie de France's description of her own literary project:

> But he takes only the semblance of Fresne that the maiden Fleurie bears. He comforts himself with this, that he loves only the appearance, but the rest (the surplus) continues to bother him.

> Mais cil n'y prent que la semblance
> Fresnein que la pucelle porte,
> Flourie; de tant se conforte,
> Qu'il n'y ayme que le semblant,
> Mais li sourplus l'i va troublant.
>
> (*Galeran de Bretagne*, ll. 6442–6)

Whereas in the *Prologue* to her *Lais*, Marie describes glossing as "adding a surplus of meaning" (de lur sen le surplus metre, *Prologue*, l. 16), *Galeran* uses "sourplus" to name what escapes likeness.[30] It marks a rupture rather than similarity; it suggests difference from Marie's *lai* rather than continuity. When read alongside the multiple and ambiguous meanings of *semblance* in Marie's *lais* (discussed in Chapter 5), *Galeran de Bretagne*'s notion of resemblance appears much reduced, and individuality is recorded as *sourplus.* In its plot but also in its reworking of notions of resemblance and what escapes resemblance, Renaut's romance implicitly references its source and engages with *Le Fraisne* and with the project of rewriting Marie's *Lais*.[31]

As in Marie's *Le Fraisne*, in *Galeran de Bretagne* the cloth sent along with the baby is key to the resolution of the story in the recognition of the exiled twin and her marriage to her lover. But in *Galeran*, Fresne cuts the richly embroidered cloth made by her mother and reworks it into a beautiful dress:

---

[30] Paul Vincent Rockwell, "Twin Mysteries: Ceci n'est pas un Fresne. Rewriting Resemblance in *Galeran de Bretagne*," in *Conjunctures: Medieval Studies in Honor of Douglas Kelly*, ed. Keith Busby and Norris J. Lacy (Amsterdam: Rodopi, 1994), pp. 487–504 (at 500–1).

[31] For a study of resemblance in the two texts, see ibid.

Fresne goes to cut and tear her cloth. She takes it and tears and cuts it. Never did a seamstress cut a dress like this one with so few cuts. She thinks that she will wear it and so she cuts a mantle and a shift....With thread of silk and gold they sewed the dress so beautifully that it seemed as if it had been woven in its shape, for the designs in the fabric were displayed just as they had been before, and the four sections appeared with the images portrayed on them as if they had just been made, there was no scrap or remainder.

> ... [Fresne] va son drap tailler et fendre;
> Prent le, sel fent et si le taille;
> Oncques ouvriers a mains de taille
> Ne taille robe comme ceste.
> En pencee a qu'elle s'en veste;
> S'en a taillé mantel et cote....
> De fil d'or et de soie ensemble
> Ont la robe si bel cousue
> Com s'elle fust ainsi tissue,
> Car l'euvre com davant y pert;
> Si sont li quartier si apert,
> Ou les ymages sont pourtraictes,
> Com s'elles fussent arsoir faictes:
> N'y a ne piece ne chantel.
>
> (*Galeran de Bretagne*, ll. 6746–61)

The narrator stresses the cutting apart of the cloth, the skill of the seamstress, and the apparently seamless product in which the representations so laboriously embroidered on the cloth by Fresne's mother appear in integral form, with no fragmentation or loss. The narrator describes Fresne's act of creation as a deliberate re-presentation of her mother's cloth. On another level, the cloth may represent Marie's *Lais*, cut apart and reinvented by Renaut.[32]

The dress, like the bed cover in Marie's *lai*, allows Fresne's mother to recognize her, but in *Galeran* voice rather than cloth reveals Fresne's identity to her lover, and here we may see another example of Renaut's engagement with his source. Fresne goes to Galeran's wedding celebration, the narrator tells us, and when she sees him, she approaches, singing:

---

[32] For Dragonetti, the "matière" that Renaut reworks is not just *Le Fraisne* but the entire collection of Marie's *Lais*. Renaut's romance, like Marie's *Lais*, constantly reflects its own musical poetics through the recall of the lost musicality of the Breton lay. Roger Dragonetti, *Le mirage des sources: L'art du faux dans le roman médiéval* (Paris: Seuil, 1987), pp. 231–6.

With a sweet *lai* she disturbs him. She leaves aside the other
lais and chooses the one that Galeran taught her. She does not
mistake the words or the tune, she sings about Galeran the
Breton.

Par un doulx lay le desconforte;
Les autres laiz, celuy a pris
Que Galeren li a apris.
El dit ne mesprent n'en la note:
De Galeren le Breton note.

(Galeran de Bretagne, ll. 6996–7000)

Galeran recognizes his lover when she sings a *lai* called "Galeran the
Breton" that he taught her when they first fell in love (ll. 1972–82; 2278–
327). This is not Marie's *lai* – it is a song about the capricious nature of
love – but the song is consistently called a *lai*, and suggests not just the in-
tertextuality of *Galeran de Bretagne* and Marie's *Le Fraisne*, but also the
reflexivity of composition found in *lais* like *Chaitivel* and *Chievrefueil*.

Galeran expands Marie's *Le Fraisne* but never leaves it behind. It
refers back to the *lai* in its plot and structure, and in its definitions of its
own origins. Renaut never names Marie de France, and we don't know
whether he knew that she was the author of the *lai* of *Le Fraisne*. His
reference to "sourplus" suggests that he might have known her prologue
and the echoes of Marie's other *lais* in the narrative suggest that he
might have known her collection. Whether he knew the entire collection
or a single *lai*, Renaut defines his literary project in relation to Marie's,
claiming to rework it even as he follows its poetic logic in the structure of
his romance and in the place that the "*lai* de Galeran de Bretagne" holds
in the story's development and resolution.

Marie's posterity

If "Marie de France" as an author figure is somewhat lost to view by the
medieval authors who recorded, read, and rewrote her works, she has
certainly found her "*remembrance*" in the twentieth and twenty-first centuries. Marie de France has become a canonical writer, with a scholarly
society and journal dedicated to scholarship on her works, a presence in
the major anthologies and companions to medieval literature, and even a
revived interest in her historical identity. And she has become a canonical *woman* writer. If her historical identity remains disputed, her gender
does not, and as the first woman known to have written in French, she is

regularly studied by feminist critics and by scholars interested in gender studies.

Marie has increasingly been recognized as a British writer as well, particularly as the acknowledgment of the importance of the French of England in medieval British literary production has grown. The inclusion of an entry on Marie in *The Feminist Companion to Literature in English* confirms her status in both feminist and British studies.[33]

As we have suggested above, the afterlives of Marie's works – in their manuscript contexts, in their fame among her contemporaries, and in their imitations – suggest their influence and readership, even though they may have circulated without the name of their author. Marie's claim not to be forgotten in her own time (ki en sun tens pas ne s'oblie, *Prologue*, l. 4) is difficult to verify; however, in our time she is remembered as one of the most important authors of the Middle Ages.

---

[33] Virginia Blain, "Marie de France," *The Feminist Companion to Literature in English*, ed. Virginia Blain, Patricia Clements, and Isobel Grundy (New Haven: Yale University Press, 1990), p. 714.

FURTHER READING

The annotated bibliographies of scholarship on Marie de France published by Glyn S. Burgess are essential tools for scholars of Marie de France:

Burgess, Glyn S. *Marie de France: An Analytical Bibliography*. London: Grant and Cutler, 1977.
——. *Marie de France: An Analytical Bibliography, Supplement No. 1*. London: Grant and Cutler, 1986.
——. *Marie de France: An Analytical Bibliography, Supplement No. 2*. London: Grant and Cutler, 1997.
—— and Giovanna Angeli. *Marie de France: An Analytical Bibliography. Supplement No. 3*. Research Bibliographies and Checklists, n.s. 8. Woodbridge, Suffolk: Tamesis, 2007.

Editions and translations of works by Marie de France
[* = editions used in this volume]

Das Buch vom Espurgatoire S. Patrice der Marie de France und seine Quelle. Ed. Karl Warnke. Halle: Max Niemeyer, 1938.
**L'espurgatoire Seint Patriz*. Ed. and trans. Yolande de Pontfarcy. Louvain and Paris: Peeters, 1995.
Die Fabeln der Marie de France. Ed. Karl Warnke. Halle: Niemeyer, 1898.
**Les fables*. Ed. and trans. Charles Bruckner. Louvain: Peeters, 1991.
Fables. Ed. and trans. Harriet Spiegel. Toronto: University of Toronto Press, 1987.
Les Lais de Marie de France. Ed. Jean Rychner. Classiques Français du Moyen Age 93. Paris: Champion, 1966.
**Lais de Marie de France*. Ed. Karl Warnke, trans. Laurence Harf-Lancner. Paris: Librairie Générale Française, 1990.
Lais. Ed. Alfred Ewert, intro. Glyn S. Burgess. London: Bristol Classical Press, 1995.
**The Life of Saint Audrey, A Text by Marie de France*. Ed. and trans. June Hall McCash and Judith Clark Barban. Jefferson: McFarland, 2006.
Saint Patrick's Purgatory: A Poem by Marie de France. Trans. Michael J. Curley. Tempe: Medieval and Renaissance Texts and Studies, 1997.

La vie seinte Audree, poème anglo-normand du XIIe siècle. Ed. Östen Södergård. Ippsala: Lundaquistska, 1955.

Authorship

Baum, Richard. *Recherches sur les oeuvres attribuées à Marie de France.* Heidelberg: C. Winter, 1968.

Hindman, Sandra L. "Æsop's Cock and Marie's Hen: Gendered Authorship in Text and Image in Manuscripts of Marie de France's *Fables.*" In *Women and the Book: Assessing the Visual Evidence,* ed. Lesley Smith and Jane H. M. Taylor. Toronto: University of Toronto Press, 1996. Pp. 45–56.

McCash, June Hall. "La vie seinte Audree: A Fourth Text by Marie de France?" *Speculum* 77.3 (2002): 744–77.

Pontfarcy, Yolande de. "Si Marie de France était Marie de Meulan." *Cahiers de Civilisation Médiévale* 38.4 (1995): 353–61.

Rossi, Carla. *"La vie seinte Audrée,* un nuovo tassello per ricostruire l'identità di Maria di Francia?" *Atti del Convegno Romania Romana, Roma, giugno 2006, Critica del testo* 9:3 (2006). Pp. 871–886.

———. *Marie de France et les érudits de Cantorbéry.* Recherches Littéraires Médiévales 1. Paris: Classiques Garnier, 2009.

Wogan-Browne, Jocelyn. "Re-routing the Dower: The Anglo-Norman Life of St. Audrey." In *Power of the Weak: Studies on Medieval Women,* ed. Jennifer Carpenter and Sally Beth MacLean. Urbana: University of Illinois Press, 1995. Pp. 25–56.

Manuscripts

Busby, Keith. *Codex and Context; Reading Old French Verse Narrative in Manuscript.* 2 vols. Amsterdam and New York: Rodopi, 2002.

Trachsler, Richard. "Les Fables de Marie de France. Manuscrits et éditions." *Cahiers de Civilisation Médiévale* 44 (2001): 45–63.

Vielliard, Françoise. "La tradition manuscrite des fables de Marie de France: essai de mise au point." *Bibliothèque de l'Ecole des Chartes* 147 (1989): 371–97.

Complete works of Marie de France

Bloch, R. Howard. *The Anonymous Marie de France.* Chicago: University of Chicago Press, 2003.

Mickel, Emmanuel. *Marie de France.* New York: Twayne, 1974.

Whalen, Logan E. *Marie de France and the Poetics of Memory.* Washington, D.C.: Catholic University of America Press, 2008.

———, ed. *A Companion to Marie de France.* Brill's Companions to the Christian Tradition, vol. 27. Leiden: Brill, 2011.

Lais

Bloch, R. Howard. "The Dead Nightingale: Orality in the Tomb of Old French Literature." *Culture and History* 3 (1988): 63–78.

——. "The Lay and the Law: Sexual/Textual Transgression in the *Lais* of Marie de France." *Stanford French Review* (1990): 181–210.

Bruckner, Matilda. "Textual Identity and the Name of a Collection." In her *Shaping Romance: Interpretation, Truth, and Closure in Twelfth-Century Romance.* Philadelphia: University of Pennsylvania Press, 1993. Pp. 157–206.

——. "*Le Fresne*'s Model for Twinning in the *Lais* of Marie de France." *MLN* 121.4 (2006): 946–60.

Burgess, Glyn S. *The Lais of Marie de France: Text and Context.* Athens: University of Georgia Press, 1987.

Burgwinkle, William. "Queering the Celtic: Marie de France and the Men Who Don't Marry." In his *Sodomy, Masculinity, and the Law in Medieval Literature: France and England, 1050–1230.* Cambridge: Cambridge University Press, 2004. Pp. 138–69.

Cowell, Andrew. "Deadly Letters: *Deus Amanz*, Marie's *Prologue* to the *Lais*, and the Dangerous Nature of the Gloss." *Romanic Review* 88 (1997): 337–56.

Dragonetti, Roger. "Le lai narratif de Marie de France." In his *La musique et les lettres.* Geneva: Droz, 1986. Pp. 99–123.

Freeman, Michelle A. "Marie de France's Poetics of Silence: The Implications for a Feminine *Translatio*." *PMLA* 99.5 (1984): 860–83.

Gaunt, Simon. "Fictions of Orality in Marie de France's *Lais*." In his *Retelling the Tale: An Introduction to Medieval French Literature.* London: Duckworth, 2001. Pp. 49–70.

Griffin, Miranda. "Gender and Authority in the Medieval French Lai." *Forum for Modern Language Studies* 35 (1999): 42–56.

Huchet, Jean-Charles. "Nom de femme et écriture féminine au Moyen Age: Les *Lais* de Marie de France." *Poétique* 48 (1981): 407–30.

Jambeck, Karen K. "'Femme et tere': Marie de France and the Discourses of *Lanval*." In *Discourses on Love, Marriage, and Transgression in Medieval and Early Modern Literature*, ed. Albrecht Classen. Medieval and Renaissance Texts and Studies, 278. Tempe: Arizona Center for Medieval and Renaissance Studies, 2004. Pp. 109–45.

Kay, Sarah. "The Virgin and the Lady: The Abject and the Object in Adgar's *Gracial* and the *Lais*." In her *Courtly Contradictions: The Emergence of the Literary Object in the Twelfth Century.* Stanford: Stanford University Press, 2001. Pp. 179–215.

Kinoshita, Sharon. "Cherchez la femme: Feminist Criticism and Marie de France's *Lai de Lanval*." *Romance Notes* 34.3 (1994): 263–73.

——. "Two for the Price of One: Courtly Love and Serial Polygamy in the *Lais* of Marie de France." *Arthuriana* 8.2 (1998): 33–55.

————. "Colonial Possessions: Wales and the Anglo-Norman Imaginary in the *Lais* of Marie de France." In her *Medieval Boundaries: Rethinking Difference in Old French Literature*. Philadelphia, 2006. Pp. 105–32.

Krueger, Roberta. "Marie de France." In *The Cambridge Companion to Medieval Women's Writing*, ed. Carolyn Dinshaw and David Wallace. Cambridge: Cambridge University Press, 2003. Pp. 172–83.

Leicester, Marshall. "The Voice of the Hind: The Emergence of Feminine Discontent in the *Lais* of Marie de France." In *Reading Medieval Culture: Essays in Honor of Robert W. Hanning*, ed. Robert M. Stein and Sandra Pierson Prior. Notre Dame: University of Notre Dame Press, 2005. Pp. 132–61.

Leupin, Alexandre. "The Impossible Task of Manifesting 'Literature': On Marie de France's Obscurity." *Exemplaria* 3 (1991): 221–42.

Maddox, Donald. "Triadic Structure in the Lais of Marie de France." *Assays* 3 (1985): 19–40.

McCracken, Peggy. "Women and Medicine in Medieval French Narrative." *Exemplaria* 5.2 (1993): 239–62.

————. "Animals and Translation in the *Lais* of Marie de France." *Australian Journal of French Studies* 46.3 (2009): 238–49.

Mikhaïlova, Milena. *Le présent de Marie*. Paris: Diderot, 1996.

Nichols, Stephen G. "Working Late: Marie de France and the Value of Poetry." In *Women in French Literature: A Collection of Essays*, ed. M. Guggenheim. Stanford French and Italian Studies 58. Saratoga: Anma Libri, 1988. Pp. 7–16.

Fables

Amer, Sahar. "Marie de France Rewrites Genesis: The Image of Woman in Marie de France's *Fables*." *Neophilologus* 81 (1997): 489–99.

————. *Ésope au féminin: Marie de France et la politique de l'interculturalité*. Amsterdam and Atlanta: Rodopi, 1999.

Batany, Jean. "Le rat des villes et le rat des champs: traditions littéraires et conjonctures sociales." *Bien dire et bien aprandre: Bulletin du Centre d'Etudes médiévales et dialectales de l'Université de Lille III* 5 (1987): 27–41.

Bloch, Howard R. "Altérité et animalité dans les *Fables* de Marie de France." *Littérature* 130 (2003): 26–38.

Jambeck, Karen K. "The *Fables* of Marie de France: A Mirror of Princes." In *In Quest of Marie de France: A Twelfth-Century Poet*, ed. Chantal A. Maréchal. Lewiston: Edwin Mellen Press, 1992. Pp. 59–106.

————. "Truth and Deception in the Fables of Marie de France." In *Literary Aspects of Courtly Culture*, ed. Donald Maddox and Sara Sturm-Maddox. Cambridge: D. S. Brewer, 1994. Pp. 221–30.

Mann, Jill. "Marie de France: the Courtly Fable." In her *From Aesop to*

Reynard: Beast Literature in Medieval Britain. Oxford: Oxford University Press, 2009. Pp. 53–97.

Spiegel, Harriet. "The Male Animal in the Fables of Marie de France." In *Medieval Masculinities*, ed. Clare A. Lees, Thelma Fenster, and Jo Ann MacNamara. Minneapolis: University of Minnesota Press, 1994. Pp. 111–28.

Espurgatoire seint Patriz

Curley, Michael J., trans. *Saint Patrick's Purgatory: A Poem by Marie de France*. Tempe: Medieval and Renaissance Texts and Studies, 1997.

Foulet, Lucien. "Marie de France et la légende du purgatoire de S. Patrice." *Romanische Forschungen* 22 (1908): 599–627.

Le Goff, Jacques. *The Birth of Purgatory*. Trans. Arthur Goldhammer. Chicago: University of Chicago Press, 1984.

Pike, Donald L. "Le dreit enfer vus mosterruns: Marie de France's *Espurgatoire seint Patriz*." *Viator* 32 (2001): 43–57.

INDEX

Already Published

CPSIA information can be obtained at www.ICGtesting.com
Printed in the USA
BVOW11s2305160314

347711BV00003B/98/P